THE NATION IN THE VILLAGE

THE NATION IN THE VILLAGE

The Genesis of Peasant National Identity
in Austrian Poland, 1848–1914

KEELY STAUTER-HALSTED

CORNELL UNIVERSITY PRESS

Ithaca and London

First published 2001 by Cornell University Press
First printing, Cornell paperbacks, 2004

Printed in the United States of America

Library of Congress Cataloging-in-Publication Data

Stauter-Halsted, Keely, 1960–
  The nation in the village : the genesis of peasant national identity in Austrian Poland, 1848–1914 / Keely Stauter-Halsted.
    p. cm.
  Includes bibliographical references and index.
  ISBN 0-8014-3844-6 (cloth: alk. paper)
  ISBN 0-8014-8996-2 (pbk.: alk. paper)
  1. Peasantry—Galicia (Poland and Ukraine)—Political activity. 2. Peasantry—Galicia (Poland and Ukraine)—History—19th century. 3. Peasantry—Galicia (Poland and Ukraine)—History—20th century. I. Title.
HD1536.P7S7 2001
943.8'6032—dc21

Cornell University Press strives to use environmentally responsible suppliers and materials to the fullest extent possible in the publishing of its books. Such materials include vegetable-based, low-VOC inks and acid-free papers that are recycled, totally chlorine-free, or partly composed of nonwood fibers. Books that bear the logo of the FSC (Forest Stewardship Council) use paper taken from forests that have been inspected and certified as meeting the highest standards for environmental and social responsibility. For further information, visit our website at www.cornellpress.cornell.edu.

Cloth printing   10 9 8 7 6 5 4 3 2 1

Paperback printing   10 9 8 7 6 5 4 3 2 1

Contents

Illustrations

Acknowledgments

I am deeply indebted to a number of individuals and institutions for supporting this project both intellectually and materially. I began my inquiry into East European nation forming, social history, and cultural theory at the University of Michigan, working with Roman Szporluk, Raymond Grew, and Geoff Eley. While at Michigan, my work was supported by the Rackham Graduate School, Foreign Language Area Studies grants, and the International Research and Exchanges Board, with funds provided by the U.S. Department of State (Title VIII program), the National Endowment for the Humanities, and the American Council of Learned Societies. None of these organizations is responsible for the views expressed.

The project was further transformed during faculty appointments first at the University of Northern Iowa, and later at Michigan State University. While at UNI, I was the recipient of a summer research grant, as well as friendship and support from colleagues in the History Department, including Tim O'Connor, Greg Bruess, and Charlotte Wells. A fellowship from the American Council of Teachers of Russian helped me to gain access to the Central State Historical Archives in L'viv and the papers of the Galician Viceroy's office.

While at MSU, I have benefited from an All University Research Grant (AURIG), short-term funding from IREX for return trips to Poland, as well as the generous support of the Department of History. Lewis Siegelbaum and Harold Marcus read and commented on the entire manuscript, as did Robert Blobaum and John-Paul Himka, the reviewers for Cornell University Press. Arista Cirtautas, of the University of Virginia, talked me through theoretical quandaries as the manuscript proceeded. Bartek Plichta proofread the Polish, and Ellen White provided maps. John Ackerman,

Susan Tarcov, Karen Hwa, and others at the Press were consistently both kind and professional as they shepherded the manuscript through the various stages of publication.

During research trips to Poland, I had the privilege of working in the Jagiellonian University Library in Cracow, the State Archives for the Cracow District, the Institute for the History of the Peasant Movement in Warsaw, the Ossolineum in Wrocław, and the Ethnographic Museum in Cracow. The staff of each of these collections was friendly and helpful, perhaps most exceptionally the Ukrainian-speaking staff at the Central State Historical Archives in L'viv, who cheerfully worked with me to access long unused Polish material. Alicja Małeta at Cracow's Ethnographic Museum and Pawel Popieł of the Iconographic Collection at the Zakład Historii Ruchu Ludowego in Warsaw were enormously helpful in locating and reproducing illustrations to accompany the text. Professor Antoni Podraza at the Jagiellonian University served as advisor and advocate during my initial research stay in Poland. Jerzy and Halina Groch, and their daughter Magda, have been my generous hosts and friends in Cracow through numerous return trips to that glorious city. Jerzy succumbed to cancer during the final preparation of the manuscript, depriving the world of an outstanding geographer of Galicia and a loyal friend.

This book has encompassed the entire lifetimes of my two children, Christopher and Caroline. Their toddler and preschool years have been all-consuming and have sometimes made writing a challenge, but the joyful distraction they provide has made these hectic times enormously gratifying. As Christopher enters his early grade school years and begins asking how Mommy's "story" is coming, repeatedly offering his "help" in finishing it, and proclaims Poland is the most important country in Europe, I realize what an impact it has had on his young life. The task of tending two small children and making progress on a book manuscript was made easier by the children's supportive grandmothers, Marilyn Stauter and Judy Halsted, who managed to drop things in their own busy lives long enough to insert themselves gracefully in ours so I could leave for short research stints or make deadlines, and by a series of trusted babysitters, including most especially Cassandra Schell, who helped get Caroline through her first year of life while I wrote in the basement. Most of all, my husband, David Halsted, who was with me at the project's inception, who shaped his own work and learned Polish to be with me in Poland, who edited and proofread, advised and extolled, even as his own career experienced shifts and bumps, who spent long days and longer weeks alone with small kids, is really the strongest force behind this project, and it is to him that the book is dedicated.

THE NATION IN THE VILLAGE

Introduction: The Roots of Nationalism in the Polish Village

On a snowy Shrove Tuesday night in February 1846, Polish-speaking serfs from the district of Tarnów huddled in the forests in the foothills of the Carpathian Mountains. Afraid to remain in their cottages lest they fall into the hands of marauding bands of aristocrats, the peasants had fled in order "to hide from the Poles." An ill-fated gentry rising had begun in Cracow, and armed bands of "Polish" rebels were rumored to be roaming the Galician countryside searching for those who opposed their efforts to resurrect the old noble-led Polish state.[1] Trembling in fear of their Polish lords, the Tarnów serfs sought to keep as great a distance as possible from the national insurrection sweeping the countryside.[2]

The peasants' behavior during the 1846 rising, in which they ultimately slaughtered some 1,100 noblemen, contrasted sharply with the enthusiasm for Polish symbols they expressed a half century later. During the summer of 1894, farmers from throughout Austrian Poland gathered to celebrate the centennial of Tadeusz Kościuszko's insurrection in defense of Polish independence. Villagers marched in parades honoring the fallen

---

[1] Historians have not fully explored the links between peasant attacks on gentry rebels and the conclusion of carnival week. For an overview of the historiography of the 1846 revolt, see Thomas W. Simons Jr., "The Peasant Revolt of 1846 in Galicia: Recent Polish Historiography," *Slavic Review* 30, no. 4 (December 1971): 795–817. The classic work on the Galician jacquerie is still Stefan Kieniewicz, *Ruch chłopski w Galicji w 1846 roku* (Wrocław, 1951).

[2] The one exception to the often-violent opposition among peasants to the national uprising of 1846 was in the highland village of Chochołów. See Władysław Łyś, *Powstanie chochołowskie: w 110 rocznicę, 1846–1956* (Warsaw, 1956), and Rafał Gerber, ed., *Powstanie chochołowskie 1846 roku: Dokumenty i materiały* (Wrocław, 1960).

1

Austrian Officers Buying the Heads of Polish Gentry in 1846. Czartoryski Museum, Cracow. Sketch 7377. Courtesy of the Ethnographic Museum, Cracow. Inventory number III/15008/F. Reproduction by Jacek Kubiena.

general and staged elaborate reenactments of the great Battle of Racławice, competing among themselves to play Polish pikemen rather than the despised Russian soldiers. Two generations after their emancipation from serfdom, Polish-speaking peasants could cheer "Long live Poland" while celebrating a symbolic moment in the old noble republic.[3] But what did Polish peasants *mean* when they referred at the end of the nineteenth century to an entity called "Poland" and how did this conception differ from their understanding of Poland or Polishness in 1846? What accounts for the peasants' transformed vision of the "nation" and their place within it?

This study situates the rise of peasant nationalism in the context of the precarious position emancipated peasants occupied within "modern" political institutions and ideas. In one sense, Polish villagers in the Austrian Empire had access to and experience in a wide range of progressive public institutions. They were able to take advantage of Habsburg politi-

---

[3] Village commemorations of the Kościuszko Rising are reported in *Przyjaciel Ludu*, April–July 1894, and *Związek Chłopski*, April–May 1894. For the reconstruction of General Kościuszko into a peasant hero, see Keely Stauter-Halsted, "Peasant Patriotic Celebrations in Austrian Poland: The Centennial of the Kościuszko Uprising and the Rise of the Kościuszko Cult in Galician Villages," *Austrian History Yearbook* 25 (1994): 79–95.

cal reforms and administrative decentralization that swept newly freed peasants into civic life in large numbers during the 1860s and 1870s. The political mobilization of Galician smallholders would help shape a distinct leadership cadre in peasant communities, consisting of village mayors, secretaries, council members, and parliamentary deputies. These local leaders gradually established working relationships with intellectuals and gentry landowners in order to accomplish shared goals of economic reform and cultural regeneration. The public agenda devised by this peasant elite and their upper-class allies was increasingly articulated in terms of the welfare of the nation. Such a conjunction of social forces helps explain the process by which the Polish political nation expanded to include larger sections of the population and wider cultural content.

The book explores the transition from serf to citizen in the Polish lands by examining the formation of a peasant national identity (or identities) between emancipation in 1848 and the outbreak of the Great War. Although national consciousness would evolve among many villagers only after the reemergence of the Polish state in 1918, the postemancipation years were critical to shaping new public attachments in the countryside.[4] During the half century following the end of serfdom, upper-class notions of the nation and its future came into direct and sustained contact with the attitudes of Polish-speaking peasants, prompting a complex process of negotiation between the bearers of the patriotic "message" and their peasant audience.[5]

Yet even as Galician peasants were experiencing the benefits of modern civic life, their cultural outlook remained rooted in the rituals, customs, and beliefs of "premodern" agricultural communities.[6] They contributed some of these notions to the national idea, helping to expand the patriotic message beyond a small group of upper-class patriots.[7] The result was a

---

[4] On the development of peasant national consciousness during World War I and the early years of the Second Republic, see Jan Molenda, "The Formation of National Consciousness of the Polish Peasants and the Part They Played in the Regaining of Independence by Poland," *Acta Poloniae Historica*, nos. 63–64 (1991): 121–48.

[5] The links between national and local politics have been studied by Maurice Agulhon, *The Republic in the Village: The People of the Var from the French Revolution to the Second Republic* (Cambridge, 1982), and Tony Judt, *Socialism in Provence, 1871–1914: A Study in the Origins of the Modern French Left* (Cambridge, 1979). Also helpful is Peter McPhee, "Popular Culture, Symbolism, and Rural Radicalism in Nineteenth-Century France," *Journal of Peasant Studies* 5, no. 2 (January 1978): 238–50.

[6] Florencia Mallon discusses many of the theoretical problems associated with the rise of peasant national consciousness in *Peasant and Nation: The Making of Postcolonial Mexico and Peru* (Berkeley, 1995).

[7] Miroslav Hroch characterizes the penetration of the national message to the broad masses as stage C in a three-step process beginning with a small group of patriotic intellectuals (stage

polyphony of voices that eventually emerged to contest national meaning. By focusing on peasant activism, this study thus complements theoretical work on the sources of nationalist ideology among intellectual and bourgeois activists,[8] revealing the ongoing tension between the national images of the political and cultural center (in this case the Polish gentry) and those of marginalized groups, including the Polish peasantry.[9]

Movements for national unification and independence that seek to unite disparate social groups behind a single political cause frequently camouflage the heterogeneous nature of national identity.[10] National heterogeneity can be made to appear homogeneous through the deployment of ambiguous national imagery and the reinterpretation of cultural icons to make them more accessible to marginal groups.[11] Polish villagers remembered Tadeusz Kościuszko as a peasant liberator, for example, while the gentry regarded him as a symbol of the old noble democracy. Similarly, the annual commemoration of the Polish Constitution of May 3 (1791) was the occasion for the expression of opposition to foreign rule among the upper classes and, at the same time, for staging agrarian rituals around maypoles in the countryside. By suffusing older, upper-class national icons with meanings rooted in village traditions, Polish peasants were able to coopt national imagery for themselves and establish a basis on which they could participate in national rituals; upper-class Poles would perform a

---

A) and progressing to the urban bourgeoisie (stage B). See Miroslav Hroch, *Social Preconditions of National Revival in Europe: A Comparative Analysis of the Social Composition of Patriotic Groups among the Smaller European Nations* (Cambridge, 1985), 14–30. Anthony D. Smith has stressed the importance of premodern cultural elements, including myths, memories, symbols, and values in defining modern nations, in *The Ethnic Origins of Nations* (Oxford, 1986).

[8] The prototypical work on capitalist transition and the spread of nationalist movements is Hroch, *Social Preconditions*. See also Ernest Gellner, *Nations and Nationalism* (Ithaca, 1983); Karl Deutsch, *Nationalism and Social Communication: An Inquiry into the Foundations of Nationality* (Cambridge, Mass., 1953); Benedict Anderson, *Imagined Communities: Reflections on the Origins and Spread of Nationalism* (London, 1991); and Eugen Weber, *Peasants into Frenchmen: The Modernization of Rural France, 1870–1914* (Stanford, 1976).

[9] On multiple discourses within the village and alternative nationalisms, see Mallon, *Peasant and Nation*, esp. 11–12. On discursive polyphony in defining the peasantry, see Cathy A. Frierson, *Peasant Icons: Representations of Rural People in Late Nineteenth Century Russia* (New York, 1993), 3–6.

[10] Jürgen Habermas has argued that societies employing democratic institutions often seek to create the appearance of a shared political culture in order to mobilize the population behind common goals. See "The European Nation-State—Its Achievements and Its Limits," in *Mapping the Nation*, ed. Gopal Balakrishnan (London, 1996), 284–93.

[11] On the cultural ambivalence of modern nations, see Homi K. Bhabha, "Introduction: Narrating the Nation," in *Nation and Narration*, ed. Bhabha (London, 1994), 1–7.

similar discursive sleight of hand with symbols from folk culture.[12] Hidden behind the amalgam, then, are competing subcultures vying for representation in the dominant discourse.[13] In this submerged heterogeneity I believe the peasant national agenda can be found.

Civil Society and the Creation of a Rural Public Sphere

To peel back the layers of meaning beneath the dominant symbols of modern nations, I have examined the public discussions within which many of these symbols evolved. National icons took on particular meanings for peasants, and consensus was reached on their significance via interactions within rural political life. "Politics" in the peasant context consisted of public debate in a wide variety of contexts, from casual meetings on the village green to sessions of official associations, political institutions, and, perhaps most important, interactions within popular culture. Village society witnessed the open exchange of ideas via informal gatherings at the local tavern and chats during winter flax-spinning sessions. These regular and remarkably ritualized discussions formed part of an expanding rural civil society.[14] As clubs, reading circles, and, eventually, election committees arose in the countryside, opportunities for public debate, compromise, and consensus formation widened further. Participation in the institutions of rural civil society helped peasants develop strategies and goals for use in more formal political bodies such as the Viennese Reichstag and Reichsrat, the Galician provincial diet (Sejm), and the organs of the Peasant Party (Stronnictwo Ludowe).[15] Each forum provided an important

[12] This two-way transformation of national cultures is discussed in Dirk Hoerder and Inge Blank, "Ethnic and National Consciousness from the Enlightenment to the 1880s," in *Roots of the Transplanted*, vol. 1: *Late Nineteenth-Century East Central and Southeastern Europe*, ed. Hoerder and Blank (Boulder, 1994), 43–46.

[13] On the ways in which opposing interests can make conflicting claims through cultural practices, see E. P. Thompson, *Customs in Common: Studies in Traditional Popular Culture* (New York, 1993), 1–6; and Suzanne Desan, "Crowds, Community, and Ritual in the Work of E. P. Thompson and Natalie Davis," in *The New Cultural History*, ed. Lynn Hunt (Berkeley, 1989), 47–71.

[14] On the concept of civil society, see John Keane, *Democracy and Civil Society: On the Predicaments of European Socialism, the Prospects for Democracy, and the Problem of Controlling Social and Political Power* (London, 1988); Keane, ed., *Civil Society and the State: New European Perspectives* (London, 1988); Jean L. Cohen and Andrew Arato, *Civil Society and Political Theory* (Cambridge, Mass., 1992); and Arato, *Civil Society, Constitution, and Legitimacy* (Lanham, Md., 2000).

[15] Works on Polish populism and the rise of the Peasant Party include Stefan Kieniewicz, *The Emancipation of the Polish Peasantry* (Chicago, 1969); Olga Narkiewicz, *The Green Flag:*

arena of contested meaning, a locus of conflict and debate, in which different and opposing publics maneuvered for space.

Participation in these civil institutions helped create the preconditions
for the formation of a rural public sphere. Voluntary association in clubs,
societies, and cultural organizations in the countryside allowed for the
open exchange of opinions and the formation of consensus within village
communities. Jürgen Habermas has argued that these opinion-forming
bodies, existing outside of formal politics, are crucial to the functioning of
democracies since they bring pressure to bear on the political process as an
alternative to electoral participation.[16] I expand the notion of public
sphere beyond the urban and bourgeois roots Habermas envisions to take
account of rural interactions and peasant actors, including those denied
suffrage rights.[17] The open discussions that grew out of the burgeoning
associational life in the Polish countryside, including a lively peasant press
and an extensive agricultural circle movement, helped to create local public spheres that would eventually be brought in closer interaction with the
national, Polish-speaking cultural and political arena. At the same time,
negotiation of national agendas took place in the realm of popular culture.
Public entertainment, including festivals and parades, the performance of
songs, ballads, and folktales, and the presentation of plays and popular
spectacles, provided regular opportunities for villagers to articulate and
debate symbols of group identity.

One of the outcomes of this public debate was the formation of a leadership cadre in the village consisting of peasants who perceived themselves
to be harder working, better educated, more pious, and ultimately more
patriotic than their fellows. The moral hierarchy this demarcation created
established the lines along which much public contestation would occur in
the village. Those who were "in" the elite camp struggled constantly to define themselves against the masses in the "out" group. Nationalist language
was increasingly substituted in this negotiation as a code for a whole bas-
ket of rural priorities. The "nation" for the subset of "elite" villagers came
to represent "progressive" values, while for the vast majority of illiterate,

---

Polish Populist Politics, 1867–1970 (London, 1976); and Krzysztof Dunin-Wąsowicz, *Dzieje
Stronnictwa Ludowego w Galicji* (Warsaw, 1956).

[16] Jürgen Habermas, *Structural Transformation of the Public Sphere: An Inquiry into a Category of Bourgeois Society* (Cambridge, Mass., 1990).

[17] Geoff Eley has argued persuasively for expanding the contexts in which Habermas's idea
of public sphere can be embodied. See his "Nations, Publics, and Political Cultures: Placing
Habermas in the Nineteenth Century," in *Culture/Power/History: A Reader in Contemporary Social Theory*, ed. Nicholas B. Dirks, Geoff Eley, and Sherry B. Ortner (Princeton,
1994), 297–335.

"superstitious" peasants, images of the nation remained closely tied to folk legends and a set of premodern beliefs. These multiple meanings of the Polish nation colored the peasantry's understanding of public interactions as they began to take part in modern political processes at the turn of the twentieth century.

Village life was joined to outside communities by linkages that helped encourage broader associations in the countryside.[18] Even before emancipation, peasants enjoyed ties to cultural and economic life beyond the parish. Patterns of influence, from trade networks to kinship associations and larger religious communities, extended beyond the individual village. This study begins with the abolition of serfdom in 1848, not because the integration of Polish peasants into larger communities began with their emancipation, but because this new status changed the nature of that integrative process.[19] Emancipation altered the power relations separating lord from peasant, creating the possibility of alliances across social classes. Villagers became the focus of "Polonization" efforts by the Polish upper classes who set out to attract their support for national liberation movements. The half century following emancipation in Poland saw the "mobilization" of Polish peasants behind a national agenda, but the nature and content of that national project were to a great extent the work of peasants themselves, based on networks and agendas established within the village.

Studies of peasant movements have tended to focus on flashpoints in village society where relationships between the village and the state break down.[20] Yet change in village society comes in small increments as well as in convulsions. Even when not faced with destabilizing changes, peasant

---

[18] The classic study on the interdependency between "great" and "little" traditions is Robert Redfield, *Peasant Society and Culture: An Anthropological Approach to Civilization* (Chicago, 1956). See also P. M. Jones, *Politics and Rural Society: The Southern Massif Central, c. 1750–1880* (London, 1985), 313–27; Mallon, *Peasant and Nation*, 89–90; and Prasenjit Duara, *Culture, Power, and the State: Rural North China, 1900–1942* (Stanford, 1988), 194–216.

[19] Sociologists William Thomas and Florian Znaniecki have argued for a sharper break between the preemancipation village social structure and relations among emancipated peasants, stressing the increase in information flow after liberation that they believe sharpened conflict within the Polish countryside. See their seminal study, *The Polish Peasant in Europe and America*, 2 vols. (Chicago, 1919).

[20] Classics in this very rich genre include Eric Hobsbawm, *Primitive Rebels: Studies in Archaic Forms of Social Movement in the Nineteenth and Twentieth Centuries* (New York, 1959); James Scott, *The Moral Economy of the Peasant: Rebellion and Subsistence in Southeast Asia* (New Haven, 1976); Teodor Shanin, *The Roots of Otherness: Russia's Turn of Century*, 2 vols. (New Haven, 1986); and Eric R. Wolf, *Peasant Wars of the Twentieth Century* (New York, 1969).

societies experienced a process of dynamic social and political change, and villagers engaged in active debate about their common futures.[21] Much of the work of nation forming occurred during this process of organizing civil life and negotiating issues of concern to the village community. While revolutions and uprisings provide momentary consensus and serve to mobilize large numbers of relatively inactive individuals behind national goals, the analysis of day-to-day interactions *between* moments of tumult offers us a more nuanced appreciation of peasant politics.

Nested Identities

Nationalism was by no means the only identity available to newly emancipated peasants in the former Polish territories, nor was a psychological attachment to "Poland" preordained. Identification with the Austrian state, the Catholic Church, the native region, and with "peasantness" itself remained strong, even as a sense of national consciousness was honed in the village. The Austrian crown had long attracted the loyalty of its rural subjects by promulgating laws designed to protect them from the worst abuses of their gentry landlords.[22] Peasant attacks on gentry insurgents during the 1846 revolt were but one violent reminder of long-standing village support for Vienna. The abolition of serfdom by the Austrian emperor rather than at the initiative of Polish landholders helped strengthen this peasant attachment to the crown. Polish-speaking villagers remained faithful to the memory of royal protection long after the end of serfdom, sending petitions and delegations to Vienna to appeal to the emperor and referring to themselves as the "emperor's people" even in the early years of the twentieth century.[23]

The close affinity Polish peasants felt for the Austrian crown was reinforced by their attachment to the Catholic Church. Religious practice clearly differentiated Polish speakers from the Uniate (Greek Catholic) Ruthenians and Jews with whom they shared the villages of central and eastern Galicia. The church would become a site of contestation during the battle for peasant mobilization, pitting the Austrian state against Pol-

---

[21] For access to the literature on peasant mobilization, including the debate between breakdown theories of peasant engagement and mobilization or solidarity theory, see Samuel Clark and James S. Donnelly Jr., eds., *Irish Peasants: Violence and Political Unrest, 1780–1914* (Madison, 1983), 12–16.

[22] Regarding the reforms of serfdom under Empress Maria Teresa and Emperor Joseph II, see Stefan Inglot, ed., *Historia chłopów polskich*, 3 vols. (Warsaw, 1972), 161–65, 181–99.

[23] Sociologist Franciszek Bujak was surprised to receive this response to his inquiry "Who are you?" (*Kim jesteś?*) when conducting surveys among the peasants of Żmiąca, a village in the Carpathian foothills, in 1901 and 1902. Franciszek Bujak, *Żmiąca: Wieś powiatu Limanowskiego. Stosunki gospodarcze i społeczne* (Cracow, 1903), 131.

ish agitators in a struggle over the symbolic meaning of church association. Battle lines were not cleanly drawn in this conflict over identities, however, as parish priests found themselves caught between their rural constituency and the more conservative, pro-Austrian church hierarchy.

Less formal but no less compelling were associations villagers continued to feel as rural producers. The legacy of serfdom eroded only very slowly, and the social distance peasants felt from their former landlords remained wide. Even as late as 1907, Jakub Bojko could write about the "two souls" of the Polish peasant—the soul of the serf and the soul of the free man—which competed for attention in almost every field of peasant endeavor.[24] Until the electoral reform of 1907, villagers continued to vote in a separate curia, and their social status had to be recorded on every official document from school matriculation records to imperial petitions.

Finally, local and regional identities continued to play a role in peasant attitudes and behavior even as they were integrated into larger networks of influence. The Carpathian *górale* (mountaineers), for example, enjoyed a long tradition of organized violence and rebellion against their lords, while the "crakowian" peasants from the district around the old capital perceived themselves as more "civilized" and sophisticated than their more "provincial" cousins. These regional, extraregional, and social attachments helped nuance the ways in which peasants filtered the possibility of national affiliation, creating a pattern of nested identities.[25] The development of a Polish national consciousness was thus neither natural nor automatic. Indeed, extraregional associations such as loyalty to empire, church, or nation appear to have ebbed and flowed depending on the circumstances of the moment and the utility of a particular attachment.

Peasantness as a Historical Category

There has been a great deal of debate among anthropologists and social historians about the nature of peasant society and the definition of "peasant."[26] The self-identity of Polish smallholders in the nineteenth century was a question less of objective definition than of the specific social and cultural realities of postemancipation Poland. Prior to emancipation and

[24] Jakub Bojko, *Dwie dusze* (Warsaw, 1949).

[25] Prasenjit Duara discusses the connection between such overlapping identities and the evolution of a polyphonous nationalism in *Rescuing History from the Nation: Questioning Narratives of Modern China* (Chicago, 1995). The influence of local attachments and particular historical memories among peasants on modern electoral alignments is discussed in Jones, *Politics and Rural Society*, 107, 145–77.

[26] The range of definitions of peasantness can be accessed through Teodor Shanin, *Russia as a Developing Society* (New Haven, 1985), 66–92; Scott, *Moral Economy*, 2–6; Wolf, *Peasant Wars*, xiii–xv; and Redfield, *Peasant Society*, 25–34.

to a great extent thereafter, the term peasant (*chłop* in Polish) coincided with the legal status of the serf or *pańszczyzniak*. Nonpeasant agricultural producers enjoyed the legal standing (if not always the external trappings) of the gentry, or *szlachta*,[27] and "intellectuals" such as village priests and country schoolteachers were clearly marked by their educational level and professional activities.

The term "peasant" specifically designated those who worked the landlord's estate in exchange for the right to farm their own small plots. Even after the cessation of the landlord's legal rights over his serfs, a deep cultural chasm separated small farmers from large landholders. The mentality of generations of subjugation helped to separate Polish social strata, while distinctions in legal rights, landholding patterns, and public responsibilities reinforced this historic divide. During the half century following emancipation, Polish society continued to view former serfs and their descendants as "peasants" despite the fracturing of this social group into landless laborers and middling farmers. To be a *chłop* in nineteenth-century Poland was to share certain elements of a subculture, including attitudes and customary practices inherited from serfdom.[28] This status and this self-concept were not easily eroded. Neither the acquisition of large amounts of land, learning a trade, nor even migration to the city led to the complete effacing of peasant identities.[29]

A "peasant" in this study is thus anyone who is actively involved in working the soil as a primary occupation, or whose family and hence cultural identity are attached to work on the land and to interactions within the village community.[30] Obviously, the Polish "peasantry" as I have described it was not a homogenous social entity. It was also not a social "class" in the Marxian sense since its members did not share the same relationship to the means of production.[31] In order to highlight this het-

---

[27] On the symbolic importance attached to clothing styles, architecture, and furniture by impoverished members of the lower gentry, see Teodora Ruppertowa, "O szlachcie drobnej (inaczej cząstkowej)," *Wisła* 2 (1888): 754–61.

[28] Jan Słomka, *From Serfdom to Self-Government: Memoirs of a Village Mayor*, trans. William John Rose (London, 1941), 148–73.

[29] The interplay between village roots and urban environments long after peasants migrated to large cities has been examined by David L. Hoffmann in *Peasant Metropolis: Social Identities in Moscow, 1929–1941* (Ithaca, 1994).

[30] This definition follows that of P. M. Jones, who has argued that economic distinctions are less important than the shared forms of cultural behavior in defining peasants. *Politics and Rural Society*, 87–89.

[31] For an argument supporting the emergence of a coherent peasant "class" after emancipation, see Jerome Blum, *The End of the Old Order in Rural Europe* (Princeton, 1978), 432–41.

erogeneity, I have consciously sought to flesh out divisions within peasant communities. One of my goals is to nuance our understanding of social diversity among agricultural producers, while at the same time drawing general conclusions about peasant nationalism as a whole.

Galicia as Metaphor

The setting for this study is the crownland of Galicia and Lodomeria, located in the northeastern portion of the Habsburg lands.[32] This southernmost section of the old Polish Republic (the western part of which was known as Małopolska or Little Poland, while the eastern section mostly comprised the Ruthenian Palatinate) was annexed to the Austrian monarchy in the partitions of 1772 and 1795; the city of Cracow itself was transferred to Austrian jurisdiction after the failed gentry revolt of 1846. As the home of the ancient capital of Cracow with its historic monuments, churches, and royal castle, Galicia held a vital place in Poles' collective memories of prepartition times. The crownland was composed of some 46 percent Polish speakers (mostly in the west with large landlords scattered throughout the east), 42 percent Ruthenians (in central and eastern Galicia), 10 percent Jews (concentrated in the larger towns and rural *shtetlach* throughout the province), and 2–3 percent German speakers.[33] The social composition of the Polish portion of the crownland was similar to that of the Prussian and Russian partitions, with some 2–3 percent wealthy aristocrats, many with loyalties to the Austrian crown, 8–10 percent gentry landholders, an active and growing intelligentsia, and an overwhelming majority (80–85 percent) of small peasant farmers.

Throughout the Polish lands, intellectuals and gentry farmers spent the postemancipation period attempting to mobilize workers and peasants surreptitiously behind competing political programs. Only in Galicia, however, was this competition for lower-class support open and legal. The

[32] For an overview on the role of Galicia within the Habsburg monarchy, see Piotr Wandycz, "The Poles in the Habsburg Monarchy," in *Nation-Building and the Politics of Nationalism: Essays on Austrian Galicia*, ed. Andrei S. Markovitz and Frank E. Sysyn (Cambridge, Mass., 1982). For the role Galician Poles played in relations with the empire, see Peter F. Sugar, "The Nature of the Non-Germanic Societies under Habsburg Rule," *Slavic Review* 22, no. 1 (March 1963): 1–30. Also of interest is Samuel Koenig, "Geographic and Ethnic Characteristics of Galicia," *Journal of Central European Affairs* 1, no. 1 (April 1941): 55–65.

[33] For controversies surrounding figures on the ethnic makeup of Galicia, see John-Paul Himka, *Galician Villagers and the Ukrainian National Movement in the Nineteenth Century* (New York, 1988), xxii–xxiii; and Paul Robert Magocsi, *Galicia: A Historical Survey and Bibliographic Guide* (Toronto, 1983), 121–23. An invaluable resource for information on Jewish population distribution is Bohdan Wasiutyński, *Ludność żydowska w Polsce w wiekach XIX i XX: studjum statystyczne* (Warsaw, 1930), esp. 90–158.

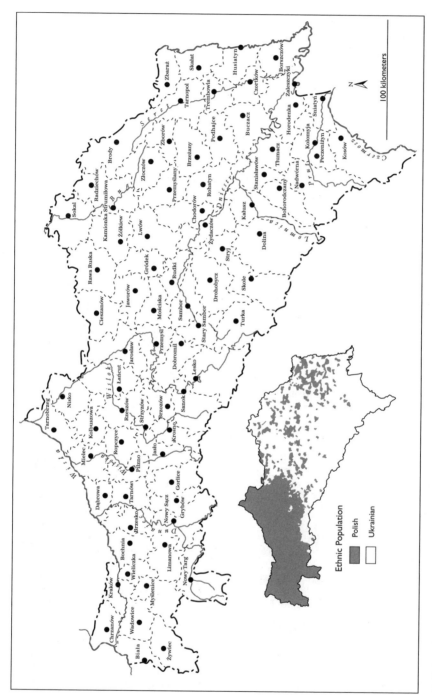

Galician districts, 1910. Courtesy of Ellen White, based on information from Krzysztof Groniowski and Jerzy Skowronek, *Historia Polski 1795–1914* (Warsaw, 1971).

number and range of civil institutions available to peasants expanded dramatically in postemancipation Austrian Poland, making peasant participation in public life far greater here than in the Russian or Prussian partitions. In contrast to the much more repressive political climate imposed by the tsar following the failed January Rising (1863–64), and the Germanization efforts in post-unification German Poland, the Habsburg monarchy experienced a period of decentralization in the last third of the nineteenth century. Experimentation with federalism brought the introduction of village self-government in 1866 and autonomous rule by Polish administrators after 1867, transferring the center of Polish nationalist agitation from the Russian partition to Galicia.

At the same historical moment that Poles in the Austrian Empire were experiencing unprecedented political and cultural freedoms, their compatriots in Russia and Germany were struggling for much more fundamental rights. The bulk of Polish attention in the Congress Kingdom (Russian Poland), for example, was devoted to extraparliamentary efforts to attain basic rights for the province and to protect and preserve the Polish language and religion. Polish residents of the Congress Kingdom were so preoccupied with these larger concerns that a specifically rural agenda remained a lower public priority.[34] Similarly, the conservative Polish aristocrats who served in the Polish Circle of the Prussian Landtag and the German Reichstag had largely abandoned their parliamentary tactics by the 1880s in order to fight linguistic and territorial colonization by the newly united German Empire. Extraparliamentary efforts such as the school strikes of 1906–7 engaged many small farmers in pro-Polish activism, yet such passive resistance did not prompt the construction of a political program such as the one Galician peasants eventually devised.[35]

---

[34] On post-January political conditions in Russian Poland (known as the Congress Kingdom), see Robert Blobaum, *Rewolucja: Russian Poland, 1904–1907* (Ithaca, 1995); Helena Brodowska, *Ruch chłopski po uwłaszczeniu w Królestwie Polskim, 1864–1904* (Warsaw, 1967); Richard D. Lewis, "The Revolution in the Countryside: Russian Poland, 1905–1906," *Carl Beck Papers in Russian and East European Studies* 506 (Pittsburgh, 1986); and Theodore R. Weeks, *Nation and State in Late Imperial Russia: Nationalism and Russification on the Western Frontier, 1863–1914* (DeKalb, Ill., 1996).

[35] On the shifting position of the Poles in the Prussian and German Empires, see Richard Blanke, *Prussian Poland in the German Empire, 1871–1900* (Boulder, 1981); William W. Hagen, *Germans, Poles, and Jews: The Nationality Conflict in the Prussian East, 1771–1914* (Chicago, 1980); John J. Kulczycki, *School Strikes in Prussian Poland, 1901–1907: The Struggle over Bilingual Education* (Boulder, 1981); Lech Trzeciakowski, *Kulturkampf w zaborze pruskim* (Poznań, 1970); and Trzeciakowski, *Pod pruskim zaborem, 1850–1918* (Warsaw, 1973).

The Austrian crown and the Galician administration, by contrast, permitted and even encouraged associational life in the countryside. Austrian officials themselves established many of the institutions that would later play a vital role in the political and cultural integration of Galician Poles. The erection of commune councils reporting to district offices, the reopening of the Galician diet with peasant membership, the expansion of the network of primary schools to meet mandatory imperial education requirements were all initiated from Vienna. With the advent of Galician autonomy came permission to create regional political parties and hold local elections. All of this was accomplished with only minimal intervention by the censor (though self-censorship was clearly applied), who was more sensitive to explicit attacks on the imperial family or criticism of the established church than to peasant activism.

It was in Galicia that newspapers intended for the peasantry, such as the long-running *Wieniec i Pszczółka* (The Wreath and The Bee) circulated relatively freely throughout the countryside. Galician peasants were regularly elected to the provincial diet after 1861, and the first Peasant Party on Polish soil (the Stronnictwo Ludowe) was founded in Galicia in 1895. The public discussions and debates surrounding these elections, the platforms of the early years of the Peasant Party, the negotiations on public issues within the diet reveal the shifting positions Polish-speaking peasants held on national affairs. These institutions created a rural public sphere that linked its participants to wider publics beyond the village. Opinion-forming bodies in the countryside came into contact with regional and national organizations in which membership was voluntary and debate was relatively open.

In the Galician case, each of the institutions in which peasants participated also left a paper trail of invaluable documentation. Rare for the study of largely illiterate societies, we have the views of villagers themselves preserved in hundreds of letters published in rural periodicals, in the speeches transcribed by parliamentary stenographers, and in the archival records of the Peasant Party. The perceptions of rural leaders are recorded in the large number of peasant memoirs produced during a series of memoir-writing competitions held under the interwar Polish Republic. Moreover, an army of ethnographers combed the Polish countryside beginning in the mid-nineteenth century, collecting peasant songs, folktales, and poems. The role played by gentry organizers in mobilizing Polish villagers can be gleaned from editorials, parliamentary transcripts, election speeches, and the extensive reports of associations such as agricultural circles and reading clubs. Even the Polish intellectuals' shifting understanding of the role and notion of the "folk" can be thoroughly charted through the trail left by academics and civil servants including sociologists, economists, dieticians, and novelists.

Galicia, then, was the only partition in which extraparliamentary debate was open and unfettered, and associational life provided ample opportunities for participation. Therefore, it constitutes an ideal testing ground in Eastern Europe for the interaction between the broadening membership in national movements and the expansion of the public sphere. A similar process occurred during the broadening of national membership in the German lands as *Bauern* reached an accommodation with *Junker* farmers over tariffs in the late nineteenth century.[36] French *paysans* considered themselves increasingly "French" as they drew closer to Parisian culture before World War I.[37] National identity was fostered in postcolonial Mexico, as peasants were encouraged to participate in political life beyond the village.[38] And in early-twentieth-century China, the rural elite drew village society closer to the state as common interests developed through institutional ties.[39] As peasants came to think of themselves as Poles (or Frenchmen or Mexicans or Chinese), those who formerly served as the sole representatives of the nation had to consider the implications of a socially expanded national clientele.

The book is divided into two main sections, the first dealing with the evolution of "politics" in the Galician village and the second with the rise of peasant national consciousness. Chapter 1 outlines the tumultuous changes the emancipation decree brought to village society, suggesting some of the sources for the peasantry's public agenda later in the century. Chapter 2 examines peasant interactions in civil institutions and the formation of a rural public sphere after emancipation. This chapter pays particular attention to local divisions and animosities, which splintered peasant communities everywhere into factions and rivalries. Unified against outsiders, however, peasant representatives took on larger battles when they were elected to serve in the 1848 Reichstag and the 1861 Galician

---

[36] For an introduction to the German case, see Geoff Eley, *Reshaping the German Right: Radical Nationalism and Political Change after Bismarck* (Ann Arbor, 1991), and David Blackbourn, *Class, Religion, and Local Politics in Wilhelmine Germany* (New Haven, 1980). Also demonstrating shared economic interests between large landholders and the peasantry are Robert Moeller, "Peasants and Tariffs in the *Kaiserreich*: How Backward Were the *Bauern*?" *Agricultural History* 55, no. 4 (October 1981): 370–84; and Stephen B. Webb, "Agricultural Protection in Wilhelmine Germany: Forging an Empire with Pork and Rye," *Journal of Economic History* 42, no. 2 (June 1982): 309–26.

[37] Weber, *Peasants into Frenchmen.*

[38] Mallon, *Peasant and Nation.*

[39] Duara, *Culture, Power, and the State.*

Sejm, the subject of chapter 3. The great gulf dividing elements of "Polish" society from one another was made strikingly clear to peasant and lord alike as a paradigmatic conflict raged in these institutions between village customary law and the formal practices of the state. Retreating once again to their homes in the aftermath of their failed attempts at political dialogue with their former lords, Galician peasants sought to make government work at the local level by taking an active part in the machinery of the self-governing commune. It was here in the organs of village self-government, examined in chapter 4, that Polish peasants engaged in an ongoing political dialogue, which would allow them to articulate the beginnings of a public agenda for themselves and to devise strategies for pursuing their village-based political ends.

Part II looks at the construction of a Polish peasant from several different angles, assessing the contested nature of national imagery as peasants entered public life on a wider scale. Chapter 5 examines the shifting uses of "folk" symbols among Polish intellectuals as idealism blended into realism, romanticism into positivism. Peasant images (of costumes, songs, and celebrations) were contested first among the intelligentsia and later within the village as local actors strove to model the upper-class vision of a "good Pole." Chapter 6, in turn, outlines the Polish gentry's efforts to mobilize peasants behind *their* "national" agenda. National expectations were communicated to villagers through institutions such as agricultural circles, prompting peasants themselves to take an active role in shaping organizational activities. Civil society institutions introduced by gentry activists provided a medium for negotiation across social and cultural boundaries on agendas for rural reform. This system of supraclass alliances, representing a key component in the evolving dialogue between upper-class and peasant societies in Poland, was also reflected in the interaction of elites in the village, discussed in chapter 7. Partly as a result of the stratification of village society, some members of the peasant "elite" set about establishing working relationships with local notables such as priests and schoolteachers, cementing bonds of cooperation on social reform projects. Still, the schoolhouse, the church, the community center, and the tavern all remained contested sites as peasant and intellectual, priest and gentry competed to mobilize villagers behind divergent social programs.

Chapters 8 and 9 complete the assessment of national political integration in partitioned Poland. Chapter 8 examines images of the nation in village cultural practices, tracing the ways in which upper-class and urban national symbols merged with village rituals. Finally, chapter 9 considers the implications for national politics of a distinct set of peasant public demands. Villagers grew more politically sophisticated and sought concessions on their rural agendas in exchange for their support of national programs. By the eve of the First World War and the reunification of the Polish lands, several versions of national sentiment and political self-consciousness had emerged in the countryside. Villagers had developed a greater awareness of their contribution to political life and a rudimentary understanding of the significance a united Polish "nation" might have for them. The effectiveness of this emerging rural civic spirit was sharply reduced, however, by the splintering of peasant political alliances in the early years of the twentieth century.

PART I

Politics in the Postemancipation Galician Village

Chapter One

Emancipation and Its Discontents

Emancipation gave peasants their freedom, but took away their shoes.

Count Kazimierz Badeni,
discussing the 1806 emancipation of peasants
in the Duchy of Warsaw

Public debate in the early postemancipation village was driven by a violated sense of justice regarding the emancipation settlement, which kept peasants mired in poverty while providing civic institutions through which to appeal for reform. The imperial patent of April 17, 1848, granting Galician peasants personal freedom and ownership of their land, was little celebrated in the villages of Austrian Poland.[1] For most of the impoverished peasants of this remote crownland, the emancipation decree merely represented a shift in economic burdens and the onset of new sources of financial exploitation. After 1848, indemnity payments took the place of corvée labor and in-kind deliveries to the manor.[2] Villagers' access to common lands where they had historically grazed their cattle and collected firewood (so-called *serwituty* or servitudes) was restricted, putting their subsistence at risk.[3] Enfranchisement brought new responsibilities as citizens, including the need to pay imperial and crownland taxes. Unable to fulfill

---

[1] The Austrian emperor ended serfdom in Galicia several months before emancipating serfs elsewhere in the Habsburg lands in the hopes of preventing a recurrence of the violent attacks by Polish peasants on their lords in 1846. See Robert A. Kann, *A History of the Habsburg Empire, 1526–1918* (Berkeley, 1974), 303.

[2] Indemnities were paid out of the imperial treasury until 1857, when crownland governments assumed half the cost of reimbursing landlords. The Galician government, in turn, passed this debt onto smallholders. See Stefan Kieniewicz, *Galicja w dobie autonomicznej* (Wrocław, 1952), vii–xi; and Inglot, *Historia chłopów*, 164–65, 244–45.

[3] Although the original emancipation document awarded these lands to the peasants, the Servitude Patent of 1853 liquidated servitude rights and established a crownland commission to regulate conflicts over jurisdiction. Between 1858 and 1890, the commission examined some 32,000 servitudes cases and decided for the peasants in only a few hundred. Inglot, *Historia chłopów*, 245–48; Kieniewicz, *Galicja*, x–xi; and Stanisław Kowalczyk et al., *Zarys historii polskiego ruchu ludowego* (Warsaw, 1965), 10–11.

21

their obligations as taxpayers, many peasants were forced in the months and years following emancipation to seek employment on manorial estates, where they were often promised the use of forests and pastures in exchange for their labor.[4] They thus returned to their previous servile relations.

Of greater immediate impact on peasant farmers than the dawning of a changed legal status at mid-century were the harsh continuities in their lives. Among these were the constant pressure of land shortages, a growing rural population, primitive farming techniques, persistent hunger and preharvest famine, intermittent epidemics, and an almost complete absence of correctives available to help the peasants out of their immiserated situation. Since Galician peasants at mid-century lived very close to the margins of survival, among the immediate concerns that would form the core of their political agenda were issues related to subsistence.[5] In particular, issues surrounding their ability to farm as successful smallholders would engage them politically.[6]

Historic landholding patterns and a perennial shortage of arable land were among the leading sources of discontent among Galician peasants. Despite an Austrian law explicitly forbidding the partition of peasant land, plot sizes diminished throughout the nineteenth century in relation to the steadily rising rural population and inheritance traditions that mandated equal division of lands among all adult children.[7] In the years following emancipation, the average peasant plot dropped by about one-third, from 15.5 acres (11.4 morgs) in 1848 to 11.8 acres (8.7 morgs) a decade later.[8] By 1899, 80 percent of peasant farms had less than 5 acres

---

[4] Regarding the tax structure in Galicia and assessments for newly enfranchised peasants, see *Wieniec*, October 2, 1879, 154–55; *Przyjaciel Ludu*, March 1, 1891, 72; Inglot, *Historia chłopów*, 250–56; Stanisław Szczepanowski, *Nędza Galicyi w cyfrach i program energicznego rozwoju gospodarstwa* (Lwów, 1888), 109–11.

[5] Regarding the "subsistence ethic" that discouraged impoverished small farmers from risk taking, see Scott, *Moral Economy*. Scott's theory has been challenged by, among others, John Young, *Peasant Revolution in Ethiopia: The Tigray People's Liberation Front, 1975–1991* (Cambridge, 1997).

[6] For a contrasting view of the degree of socioeconomic hardship Galician peasants suffered, see Stella Hryniuk, *Peasants with Promise: Ukrainians in Southeastern Galicia, 1880–1900* (Edmonton, Alberta, 1991).

[7] In a carefully documented study of twenty Galician villages, Wincenty Styś argues that land divisions and land shortages drove peasants to community activism and radical politics during the interwar period. Wincenty Styś, *Rozdrabnianie gruntów chłopskich w byłym zaborze austrjackim od roku 1787 do 1931* (Lwów, 1934).

[8] Stefan Kieniewicz, *Pomiędzy Stadionem a Goslarem: Sprawa włościańska w galicji w 1848 r.* (Wrocław, 1980), 10; Franciszek Bujak, "Wieś zachodnio-galicyjska u schyłku XIX wieku," in *Wybór pism*, vol. 2: *z dziejów społecznych i gospodarczych Polski X–XX w.*, ed. Helena Madurowicz-Urbańska (Warsaw, 1976), 281–83.

of land, and the number of so-called dwarf plots (0–1 acre), whose owners could not support themselves solely through farming, had increased to 17 percent of the total peasant holdings.[9]

Land hunger and the repeated partition of peasant plots were easily the most pressing concern among Galician smallholders in the generation following emancipation. Respondents to a mid-1870s survey complained about the "shrinking plot sizes . . . [which] occurred in all areas of the crownland."[10] In some districts, plot averages diminished to as little as one-fifth of their 1848 size.[11] Peasant memoirists describe village farms in terms of plots of 2 and 3 morgs, while those "over 10 morgs (14 acres) can be counted on one's fingers."[12] These tiny plots stood in marked contrast to the average size of manorial farms, which was estimated to be about one hundred times that of peasant holdings.[13]

Nor was it easy for peasants to consolidate or purchase enough land to build a profitable farm. As a result of inheritance traditions and dowry acquisitions, peasant holdings tended to be scattered among several fields or strips far from one another and from the farmhouse, making efficient farming difficult. Thus, an average peasant farmed twenty separate lots in 1859, and within a generation this number had doubled.[14] Moreover, land prices on so-called rustical (peasant) land, which was priced significantly higher than manorial land, shot up during the decades following emancipation in response to pressure from those wishing to enlarge their holdings.[15]

The rising demand for peasant land was the result less of population growth than of the almost complete absence of alternative occupations available to small farmers. By the 1880s, the additional cash introduced into the Galician economy by peasant migrants working abroad would stimulate still greater demand for scarce farmland. Of the five million inhabitants of the Galician crownland, over four million of them (some 80 percent) were actively engaged in farming, a number that could scarcely be

[9] Narkiewicz, *Green Flag*, 22; Inglot, *Historia chłopów*, 248–56.

[10] Tadeusz Pilat, *Wiadomości statystyczne o stosunkach krajowych* (Lwów, 1881), 6–7.

[11] Ibid., 6–7.

[12] See, for example, Stanisław Pigoń, *Z Komborni w świat. Wspomnienia młodości* (Cracow, 1957), 67–68.

[13] At emancipation, some 3,000 manorial lords possessed about 42 percent of the total farmland of Galicia; roughly 500,000 peasant farmers had less than 58 percent. Inglot, *Historia chłopów*, 248–50; Kowalczyk et al., *Zarys historii*, 10.

[14] On shifts in landholding patterns in the Polish lands with the parcelization of large estates before World War I, see Kieniewicz, *Emancipation*, 203–14; Inglot, *Historia chłopów*, 254–57.

[15] *Wieniec*, December 7, 1890, 357; Inglot, *Historia chłopów*, 254–57; Pilat, *Wiadomości statystyczne*, 10, 37–39.

sustained in a province consisting of poor agricultural land.[16] Industrial development, which might otherwise have drawn on the overpopulated countryside, lagged behind in comparison with other Habsburg provinces. Neither of the crownland's two key cities, Cracow or Lwów, was a significant center of trade or industry.

Galicia had been cut off from many of its natural markets with the partitions of Poland in the late eighteenth century and had since served primarily as a supplier of raw materials to Austria's more industrialized regions.[17] Galician farmers, unable to send their sons to work in cities or in the professions (the priesthood being the one exception), thus "knew no occupation other than farming." The early postemancipation years thus saw the continuation of inheritance traditions dictating that "plots must be divided [among all sons] with each succeeding generation."[18] By the 1860s, population growth had resumed, increasing the pressure on land prices still more.[19]

The demand for land was further exacerbated by a low level of agricultural productivity on Galician farms, where primitive agricultural techniques continued to be employed long after emancipation. Economic historian Franciszek Bujak has described the implements Galician farmers employed in 1850 as "exactly the same as those used in the thirteenth century," including inefficient wooden plows, wagons made entirely of wood, and carving knives for chopping straw. Moreover, farmers reportedly still relied on the wind to winnow grain.[20] During the 1860s, most Galician farmers made the switch to iron plows—the "most significant shift" in agricultural technology after emancipation, according to contemporary specialists.[21] Yet the three-field system (one fallow field and two planted) continued to be the norm for the first generation of emancipated peasants, neither manure nor artificial fertilizers were employed, and increases in

---

[16] Galicia's population density of 80 inhabitants per square kilometer was comparable to that of much more urban and industrialized regions such as the German lands (87 people per kilometer) and Italy (99 per kilometer). Other East European countries were far less densely populated—Congress Kingdom (63), Hungary (50), Romania (42). Szczepanowski, *Nędza Galicyi*, 1–3; Narkiewicz, *Green Flag*, 22.

[17] For an analysis of how Galicia faired economically under Austrian rule, see Wandycz, "Poles in the Habsburg Monarchy," 71–74.

[18] Pilat, *Wiadomości statystyczne*, 6–7.

[19] At 27 years for men and 28½ years for women, Galicia had one of the lowest life expectancy rates in all of Europe. Szczepanowski, *Nędza Galicyi*, 29.

[20] Bujak, "Weiś zachodnio-galicyjska," 288–90; Pigoń, *Z Komborni*, 22–23; Pilat, *Wiadomości statystyczne*, 25–26.

[21] Pilat, *Wiadomości statystyczne*, 25–26.

Departure for the harvest, Stare Bystre, Nowy Targ district. Photo by Władysław Eliasz-Radzikowski. Courtesy of the Ethnographic Museum, Cracow. Inventory number III/1942/F. Reproduction by Jacek Kubiena.

farming output were gained almost exclusively through expanding cultivated land by putting pasture and forest land under the plow.[22]

Small wonder, therefore, that Galicia was estimated to have one of the lowest rates of agricultural productivity in Europe in the quarter century after emancipation.[23] Grain yields were especially low, forcing the predominantly agricultural province to import cereal from elsewhere in the empire.[24] Moreover, Galician farmers were unwilling to take the economic risk required to diversify their agricultural production. In the first two decades after emancipation, peasant cultivation remained limited to grain (mainly rye). Only gradually in the 1860s and 1870s were cattle breeding and dairy farming added, and bee keeping and fruit growing came still later.[25]

---

[22] Bujak, "Wieś zachodnio-galicyjska," 288–290; Pigoń, *Z Komborni*, 22–23.

[23] Szczepanowski argues that "measured in terms of total milk, potatoes, or grain," Galicia produced "less than almost any other country in Europe." *Nędza Galicyi*, 6–7, 14.

[24] Kowalczyk et al., *Zarys historii*, 13; Franciszek Magryś, *Żywot chłopa działacza* (Warsaw, 1987), 4–5.

[25] Bujak, *"Wieś zachodnio-galicyjska,"* 288–90; Inglot, *Historia chłopów*, 169–79; Pilat, *Wiadomości statystyczne*, 34–35; Magryś, *Żywot chłopa*, 22.

Low productivity made for chronic malnourishment. Galician peasants spent much of their lives on the edge of starvation especially during the preharvest period when peasants were often forced to eat "different types of weeds," grass, or leaves of beech trees.[26] Their meager diet of potatoes, cabbage, turnips and other vegetables was further reduced during the forty-day fast preceding Easter, further undermining the health of the rural population after long winters. "It is not surprising," concluded one memoirist, "that on such a diet people were thin, and as spring approached, after the great fast, were frail like straw."[27]

Many former serfs remembered the 1840s as a time of unrelenting hunger, starvation, and disease. Severe rains and flooding destroyed most Galician grain and potato crops in 1844, resulting in "horrible misery" and epidemics that year and the next. A cholera epidemic followed the massacre of 1846 and recurred again in 1854–55; and a severe famine attended the potato blight of 1850.[28] Famine was often responsible for emptying entire villages as people left to search for food.[29] A crownland-wide famine in 1847, due partly to the destruction of crops during the 1846 rising, is estimated to have affected 90 percent of the population, killing some 227,000 people.[30] This and other famines were so severe as to have reportedly prompted resort to cannibalism—contemporary authors report at least two cases of adults murdering and eating children.[31] The frequent outbreaks of cholera and "hunger typhus" that decimated the population every few years, in combination with persistent food shortages, caught the Galician farmer in a cycle of working "lethargically because he is inadequately nourished and [not living] better because he works too little."[32]

The periodic famines and epidemics that visited the countryside appear

---

[26] During the period 1813–57, in particular, heavy rains spoiled the crops, making hunger an annual phenomenon. Józef Burszta, *Społeczeństwo i karczma: Propinacja, karczma i sprawa alkoholizmu w społeczeństwie polskim XIX wieku* (Warsaw, 1951), 162–64. Szczepanowski estimated that some fifty thousand annual deaths could be attributed to starvation in Galicia. *Nędza Galicyi*, 26–27. See also Magryś, *Żywot chłopa*, 4–5, 38–39; Józef Putek, *Pierwsze występy polityczne włościaństwa polskiego, 1848–1861* (Cracow, 1948), 22–23.

[27] Pigoń, *Z Komborni*, 26–27; Bujak, *Żmiąca*, 120–21.

[28] Janina Leskiewiczowa, ed., *Zarys historii gospodarstwa wiejskiego w Polsce*, vol. 2 (Warsaw, 1964), 362; Bujak, "Wieś zachodnio-galicyjska," 284–85; and Inglot, *Historia chłopów*, 248–56, 200–204.

[29] Kurczak, *Pamiętnik*, Zakład Historii Ruchu Ludowego (hereafter ZHRL), P-56a, 22.

[30] Kieniewicz, *Pomiędzy Stadionem a Goslarem*, 19.

[31] Józef Plechta, "Rada Narodowa obwodu sądeckiego i pierwsze wystąpienie posłów chłopskich," *Rocznik Sądecki* 8 (1967): 48–49.

[32] Bujak, "Wieś zachodnio-galicyjska," 284–285; Szczepanowski, *Nędza Galicyi*, 26–27.

to have left more lasting impressions on Galician villagers than the legal changes involved in their emancipation from serfdom. The ravages of cholera, typhus, smallpox, and syphilis regularly made their mark on peasant consciousness.[33] The cholera epidemic that swept through Galicia in 1855 remained vivid in many peasant memories partly because in its wake appeared a "wave of orphans . . . wandering without any memory of whence they came or what they were named."[34] Peasant memoirists frequently refer to disease and death as their earliest memories.[35] Contemporary observers described Galician farmers as "stunted and emaciated from various breeds of illness," and the crownland as a whole was said to possess "the highest number of people not fit for military duty" in the entire empire.[36]

A Violated Sense of Justice

Beyond the villagers' vital interest in health and longevity lay a range of issues impinging on ethics and public justice. These concerned the division of rights and burdens between landlords and peasants arising out of the emancipation settlement. Gentry landholders continued to have jurisdiction over common lands and maintained a monopoly over the production and sale of alcohol (*propinacja*) until 1910. They contributed less than the peasants for local road and bridge repair, and maintained hunting and fishing rights on peasant land. Because these issues were often experienced as violations of the peasantry's shared understanding of justice, politics in the early postemancipation years tended to unite newly enfranchised peasants in public struggles against their former lords. Class or estate solidarity remained stronger than ethnic affiliation in these early years, a situation that would begin to erode only when individual villagers formed mutually beneficial links with nonpeasants.

While the actual conditions of emancipation in Galicia contrasted sharply with the indemnification process in the other two partitions of the former Polish Republic, relations between peasants and landlords

[33] Regarding the incidence of smallpox and syphilis and their distribution throughout the crownland, see Pilat, *Wiadomości statystyczne*, 85–86.

[34] Pigoń notes that this was the second wave of wandering orphans in the Galician countryside within a decade. The first was the result of the deaths and arrests after the massacre of 1846. Pigoń, *Z Komborni*, 21.

[35] Franciszek Magryś (b. 1846), for example, recounts his difficult start in life. His mother contracted typhus soon after he was born and was unable to nurse him. Once his mother recovered, his father became sick and died. Magryś, *Żywot chłopa*, 23.

[36] Szczepanowski, *Nędza Galicyi*, 28. Szczepanowski's assessment has since been challenged by, among others, Hryniuk in *Peasants with Promise*.

remained equally strained in the Polish lands outside of Galicia during the years following the end of serfdom. The piecemeal nature and inordinate complexities of the indemnification process in the Polish provinces of the Prussian Kingdom, for example, meant a protracted struggle over property rights, rent payments, and ownership of common lands lasting from 1811 to 1850. Moreover, a long tradition of peasant resistance in Silesia and the granting of the peasantry's personal freedom by the Emperor Napoleon (rather than the Polish *szlachta* or the Prussian crown) in parts of Poznania helped fuel tensions between villagers and estate owners during the early postemancipation period. It was not until Bismarck initiated his colonization campaign beginning in the 1870s that lord and peasant established alliances to drive German settlers from their land.[37]

Similarly, the tsar's effort to punish the gentry for the nationalist rising of 1863 meant that Polish peasants in the Congress Kingdom were endowed with relatively large landholdings at the expense of their former lords. Here too a tradition of independent peasant activism meant the continuation of strained relations in the countryside in the aftermath of emancipation. The period immediately preceding the January Rising saw particularly deep tensions as Russian Polish serfs abandoned their lands in large numbers and refused to pay dues or work on large estates, believing that their freedom would come soon. In the longer run, however, the emancipation settlement in Russian Poland helped produce a stronger, more self-sufficient peasantry, less economically distanced from gentry landholders than in the Galician countryside. Holdings of former serfs in the Congress Kingdom increased by 5–8 percent as a result of the emancipation *ukaz*, while some 140,000 landless peasants were granted holdings. Over time, smallholders in Russian Poland even managed to increase their arable land through favorable servitude settlements and purchases of estate holdings. These modest improvements in their living standards would help encourage gentry-peasant accommodation and even alliances by the latter years of the nineteenth century.[38]

In Austrian Galicia, the debate over the use of forest and pasture lands held in common under serfdom was to rage in the countryside for almost a half century, helping to drive an ongoing wedge between emancipated peasants and their gentry neighbors. The servitudes issue was most heat-

---

[37] Kieniewicz, *Emancipation*, 58–71; Norman Davies, *God's Playground: A History of Poland*, vol. 2: *1795 to the Present* (New York, 1982), 185–88; Blum, *End of the Old Order*, 407–8.
[38] Lewis, "Revolution in the Countryside," 1–3; Helena Brodowska, *Chłopi o sobie i Polsce: rozwój wsiadomości społeczno-narodowej* (Warsaw, 1984), 51; Brodowska, *Ruch chłopski*, 311.

edly contested between the early 1850s and about 1870, slowing briefly after the appointment of the servitude commission in 1853 and during the 1861 Sejm (see chapter 3).[39] The constantly disputed status of these lands confused Galician villagers about their land rights. "This thing which yesterday was mine, has become yours today, but the day after tomorrow it may become mine again," complained one peasant to the Galician Sejm.[40] The conflict pitted traditional usage rights against written law in a series of clashes that invariably resulted in the peasant's loss of land.

A combination of economic desperation and a violation of village perceptions of justice prompted peasants to defend their customary rights first by occupying the forests, then in courts of law, and later with force. Requiring peasants to invest their limited resources in lengthy legal suits, the servitudes issue contributed to "the impotence of the farmstead, disorder in the forests, and the impossibility of improving the existence of smallholders," as one nobleman put it. More important for future social relations, however, was the "mental irritation of the entire population" caused by the constant tension between peasant and lord over the issue of common lands.[41]

An equally contentious issue dividing peasant and lord was that of legal control over the production and sale of alcohol (*propinacja*). Under serfdom, alcohol had been the monopoly of the landlord, who typically operated a brewery or distillery on his estate and commissioned one of his manorial administrators (or later a local Jew) to sell spirits in the village tavern. The revenues from these exclusive rights led to some of the most egregious abuses under serfdom, including the *przymus konsumpcji*, which required each peasant family to purchase a minimum quota of drinks per year in the lord's tavern regardless of whether they were consumed.[42]

Although quotas for peasant alcohol consumption were officially eliminated throughout Austria in 1775, a number of cases of serfs forced to pay for alcohol minimums appeared in later years, and in 1849 this compulsory drinking requirement was eliminated again in Galicia. Villagers often blamed the gentry's alcohol monopoly for inflated prices and the dominance of purportedly dishonest Jewish tavern keepers in village commerce (see below regarding the social role of taverns and tavern keepers). A crownland committee assigned to recommend adjustments to the *propinacja* law

---

[39] Himka, *Galician Villagers*, 48–53. Himka notes that more than three-fourths of the village communes in eastern Galicia were involved in legal disputes with the manor over servitudes during the second half of the nineteenth century.

[40] *Stenograficzne sprawozdania Sejmu Krajowego*, hereafter *SsSK* (Lwów, 1861), 353.

[41] Deputy Count Wodzicki to Sejm, *SsSK* (1861), 324.

[42] Burszta, *Społeczeństwo i karczma*, 8–10, 28–29.

following emancipation did not report its findings to the Sejm until 1875, when the Sejm voted to extend the gentry's monopoly until 1910.[43]

After emancipation, the mechanization of distilleries led to the rapid growth of vodka production and a dramatic increase in the number of rural taverns. As one Sejm deputy complained in 1865, "even the smallest settlements of a few cottages now possess at least one tavern."[44] The roads were cluttered with taverns,[45] and landlords continued to pressure villagers to purchase large quantities of vodka so they could earn profits to pay their laborers, whom they compensated by providing coupons to the tavern.[46] Often the innkeeper served as the lord's cashier, and "the worker [was] sent to the tavern for his pay." As Deputy Father Kaczala complained during a debate on these practices in the 1865 Sejm, "What happens there? The Jew . . . always says that he has no money . . . [and so] they take spirits instead."[47] The *propinacja* issue helped to perpetuate a cycle of mistrust and economic abuse in the countryside, little changed from the days of serfdom.

Beyond the key issues of servitudes and *propinacja,* a whole range of other legal inequalities helped prevent the development of common ground between peasants and nonpeasants in the immediate postemancipation period. The Game Law permitted lords to hunt wherever they wished, including peasant lands, yet villagers were forbidden to possess arms or to hunt—even to protect their farms from wild animals. The Road Law placed the burden of rural road and bridge repair (including those on the lord's land) primarily on the peasants' shoulders. The village was responsible for maintaining rural schools and for the upkeep of the church and the parsonage, and yet the *szlachta* retained control over the appointment of priests (who, in turn, served also as educators; see chapter 5).[48]

---

[43] On the role of alcohol and the tavern in village life, see Burszta, *Społeczeństwo i karczma*; Józef Kleczyński, *Propinacja i szynkarstwo* (Cracow, 1888); Inglot, *Historia chłopów,* 245–48; Kowalczyk et al., *Zarys historii,* 10–11; Jan Madejczyk, *Wspomnienia* (Warsaw, 1965), 53; Franciszek Kącki *Ks. Stanisław Stojałowski i jego działalność społeczno-polityczna* (Lwów, 1937), 19.

[44] Sejm deputy Father Kaczala to 1865 Sejm, as quoted in Burszta, *Społeczeństwo i karczma,* 43.

[45] One memoirist noted that a single eighteen-kilometer stretch of high road in central Galicia passed some twelve taverns by the 1880s and a similar seven kilometers of road in another village had no fewer than four. Franciszek Magryś as cited in Burszta, *Społeczeństwo i karczma,* 43.

[46] The issue of workers paid in tavern coupons was also discussed in an 1858 session of the Galician Agricultural Society. Burszta, *Społeczeństwo i karczma,* 44.

[47] Father Kaczala to 1865 Sejm, in ibid., 43.

[48] Formally, the bishop nominated village priests. Yet he could choose only the one put forward by the magnate because the latter served as the bishop's patron in a given village. Kowalczyk et al., *Zarys historii,* 10–11.

Legal differences such as these, privileging gentry landholders over peasant farmers in the division of public responsibilities, would form the core of the peasant agenda as villagers began to take part in formal politics. The gentry's persistent (and often inadvertent) violations of the ethical code that underlay village interactions helped prevent the formation of alliances across the Polish social spectrum for many years after the bonds of serfdom had been legally severed.

The shift in civic status that accompanied the enfranchisement of Galician peasants had little immediate impact on villagers' political activism or on the strength of their various public identities. The early postemancipation period was one in which public concern continued to be voiced on a familiar range of economic and ethical issues and village culture continued to reflect long-standing perceptions of outsiders. Alongside these important cultural and economic continuities, however, emancipation also introduced a series of shifts in the peasantry's legal status and economic opportunities.

Emancipation brought a crucial change in relations between peasants and their former lords as Austrian officials took over the administrative functions of the landlord in the village. No longer dependent exclusively on the will of the estate owner, peasants were now governed directly by regional administrators responsible to the imperial government. Government authorities—at first Austrian officials and later members of the Polish provincial government—supervised the elections and activities of village councils, ratified the actions of village mayors, and judged legal issues for peasant litigants. Whereas under serfdom manorial authorities retained control over most of the peasantry's legal and administrative affairs, the postemancipation power structure ensured checks on gentry authority and allowed peasants a channel for pursuing their legal rights. Emancipation thus liberated Galician peasants from many of the subject conditions that underlay their relationships with the gentry and established the conditions under which villagers might eventually pursue a new basis for interaction with their former lords.

Chapter Two

The Roots of Peasant Civil Society: Premodern Politics in the Galician Village

The inhabitants of Rudawa insist that it is very rare for one of their own people to cast spells. [However,] it is generally maintained that in the neighboring village of Radwanowice, there is a nest of witches.

Wisła (1891)

To the extent that the idea of the nation seized the imagination of the masses during the course of the nineteenth century, it borrowed to some degree from the pre-political concept of generating stereotypes.

Jürgen Habermas,
"The European Nation-State—Its Achievement and Its Limits"

The contribution Polish peasants would eventually make to national politics and patriotic sentiment was very closely tied to the rhythms of life in the village. Patterns of public interaction established under serfdom conditioned peasant behavior in crownland, imperial, and national political struggles. Before emancipation and during the first generation thereafter, Galician villages were largely cut off from the sustained influence of estate or imperial administrators. Instead, rural communities devised methods for regulating their own affairs, many of which continued to function even after formal governmental bodies and official organizations came to the countryside in the 1860s and 1870s. A mutable set of customary practices and rituals helped to guide peasants in resolving local conflicts, in processing information from outside the village, and in dealing with "outsiders" of various types.

These village-level systems of interaction can be characterized as "premodern" in several important respects. First, membership in the "traditional" bodies governing village society was rarely open or voluntary, as was the case for "modern" civil institutions. Rather, social standing, gender, confessional affiliation, and other factors determined participation in (or exclusion from) many local organizations. Second, early intravillage

32

civic groups typically functioned on the basis of orally transmitted tradition rather than written codes of conduct. Although customary law could be and often was perceived as just, peasants had little opportunity to participate formally in its promulgation or challenge the ways in which it was executed. Finally, and perhaps most significantly for the evolution of national ideology, the opinions and behaviors guiding rural public life often grew out of assumptions of otherworldly causality and supernatural sources of power. These elements of pre-Christian and prerational systems of thought had a profound impact on the way villagers perceived outsiders—both those within the rural community and the unseen "other" beyond the village. Stereotypes, such as the association of outsiders with witches among the residents of Rudawa (see epigraph),[1] provided a crucial link between prepolitical perceptions and the "modern" idea of the nation, conditioning the peasantry's understanding of the meaning of the nation itself.

One of the fundamental conditions guiding interactions within rural civil society—both before and after emancipation—was the existence of semipermanent factions and interest groups within village communities. Even before the introduction of formal civic institutions to the countryside, patterns of contestation grew out of occupational, generational, gender, and socially based interest groups. Rudimentary mechanisms helped Galician villagers deal with disagreement and conflict and encouraged them to articulate consensus views. As Florencia Mallon has observed in the case of Latin American villagers, "communal consensus, when arrived at, was the product of complex articulations of interests, discourses, and perspective within village society."[2] Just as in Peru or Mexico, village society in nineteenth-century Poland was both heterogeneous and dynamic in its articulation of a constantly shifting range of opinions. In the politically "premodern" village, the tavern, the council of elders, and religious celebrations provided multiple contexts for working out these divergent views, forming the institutional beginnings of a rural public sphere.

Intravillage fissures and antagonisms were ignored, however, once the village was faced with threatening influences from outside the local community. As villagers closed ranks in opposition to outsiders—whether in the next village or in a foreign land—they often employed premodern stereotypes to characterize the boundary separating the local "us" from the alien "them." Perceptions from the preemancipation era continued to

---

[1] Stanisław Połączek, "Z podań i wierzeń ludowych, zapisanych we wsi Rudawie pod Krakowem," *Wisła* 5 (1891): 629, 633.
[2] Mallon, *Peasant and Nation*, 65.

shape villagers' opinions of outsiders through the end of the nineteenth century and beyond. The eventual expansion of the boundaries of the peasantry's imagined communities came about in terms of cultural references familiar to rural society. Clearly, the transformation of the peasantry's legal status after 1848 was not accompanied by an immediate shift in attitudes and patterns of negotiation in the village. Rather, the package of beliefs, expectations, and behaviors that had evolved in the comparative isolation of serfdom continued to operate as a powerful influence on Galician peasants as they took on extravillage identities.

Peasant Identity and the Formation of Village Interest Groups

Galician peasants were not mobilized uniformly to participate in political life outside the village, nor did they construct public identities as "Poles" in a monolithic fashion. Rather, even though cultural institutions in the preemancipation village tended to unite peasants against the upper classes, the nineteenth-century village was characterized by clear social demarcations.[3] A pattern of dissension within village society helped account for the ways in which certain subgroups would be propelled into crownland political organizations.[4] Fissures in village social unity arose already under serfdom since each family's commitment to the landlord depended on the size of its holdings and the number of draft animals it possessed. Key aspects of village public life were also organized in hierarchical fashion based on differences in economic status among residents. Social rank was displayed and reinforced via obligatory rituals, the degree of ostentation displayed at weddings and christenings, and the quality of one's cart or sled and domestic furnishings.[5] High social standing earned a family the right to front-row seats in the church, leading positions in ceremonial processions, and a place at the main table in the tavern where "the farmers sat in order of age and property."[6]

---

[3] William Thomas and Florian Znaniecki emphasize the role of increased information flow to Polish villages in eroding public consensus during the early years of the twentieth century. See their *The Polish Peasant in Europe and America*, especially vol. 1, 146ff.
[4] For the ways in which local rivalries and personalities can affect national political choices, see Judt, *Socialism in Provence*, esp. 201ff.
[5] Recognition of personal possessions as a reflection of social difference was perhaps most pronounced among small farmers who were actually members of the lower gentry. See Teodora Ruppertowa, "O szlachcie drobnej (inaczej cząstkowej)," *Wisła* 2 (1888): 754–61; and Stanisław Michalski, ed., *Dzieje szkolnictwa i oświaty na wsi polskiej*, vol. 1: *do 1918* (Warsaw, 1982), 96–101.
[6] Walery Łoziński, *Zaklęty dwór* (1926), 3–14, as cited in Burszta, *Społeczeństwo i karczma*, 175. Regarding the various sources of peasant status, see Michalski, *Dzieje szkolnictwa*, 99–101.

Map of the village of Bienkówka, Cracow district, illustrating the small parcels into which peasant farmland was divided. Courtesy of the Ethnographic Museum, Cracow. Inventory number X/94/M. Reproduction by Jacek Kubiena.

Social divisions often resulted from the physical location of a family's cottage in the layout of the village. Since much of Galician territory lies either in the rugged Carpathian mountains or in the rambling foothills to their north (including those surrounding Cracow), villages were built on undulating terrain, with rows of cottages and community buildings on higher or lower ground, which had the effect "of seeming to divide the village into segments."[7] On one segment of a typical mountain village, for example, was the manor building, above which was often a row of community buildings such as the church, the rectory, the communal house, the school, and the cemetery. Peasant homes were lined up on either side of the main street leading upward and downward from the center, with cultivated fields spreading to the left and the right. The farther from the village center, the less prestigious was the position of the peasant family. At one end or the other of the village, on the road leading out of town, was the local tavern, forming the outermost edge of the hamlet and a sort of second town center.

[7] Pigoń, *Z Komborni*, 51.

In a settlement of several hundred homesteads, social stratification stemmed partly from proximity to the church or the tavern. Stanisław Pigoń describes the rigid social structure that was associated with such a geographical layout in his native village:

> The oldest, "star" section of Kombornia was located, of course, down below, between the estate and the church. From there the settlement expanded upward, toward the north, toward inferior land and in the direction of the forest. . . . The conviction lingers on among the original families "from below" that they are the cream of the village, and they continue to view as inferior those from near the forest. The village girls especially give themselves airs in competition with one another, not sparing the use of scornful nicknames. . . . For a longtime farmwife from "below" to receive as a daughter-in-law—even if she were well off—a [resident from the village periphery] would be seen as a bitter fate.[8]

Professional and income differentials among peasants further exacerbated structural divisions within the village. Even before emancipation brought shifts in the economic structure of Galician villages, the countryside of southern Poland was characterized by great occupational diversity. Relatively few Galician peasants, both before and after emancipation, were self-sufficient, subsistence farmers. Instead, almost one-half of all Galician "peasants" before emancipation and in the early post-emancipation years were tenant farmers (5–15 percent), farmhands (25–30 percent), or craftsmen.[9] The different ways in which "peasants" earned their livings contributed to the stratification of rural interests even before the peasant movement was formally launched. After emancipation, a narrow stratum of "middling" peasant farmers arose, who possessed some 20–50 morgs (15–37 acres) of land, hired agricultural laborers, and did not need to engage in cottage industries for survival. The interests of this socioeconomic group diverged sharply from those of the growing population of rural wage laborers. This kind of economic diversity contributed to an eventual fracturing of the peasant movement, in which middling farmers and village craftsmen were disproportionately represented.

On a higher rung than the stratum of landless agricultural wage earners but below the middling farmers was the handful of craftsmen inhabiting

---

[8] Ibid., 9–15.

[9] Although a fraction of Galician "farmers" were landless already in the Middle Ages, a much higher percentage of the rural population lacked sustainable farms by the last years of serfdom and relied partly on cottage industries, predominantly cloth making. See Bujak, *Żmiąca*, 99–100.

Galician villages. Home weaving, in particular, began as a means of supplementing income earned from the family farm in the early postemancipation period and grew to become the primary means of support for many peasant families as plot sizes shrunk beneath the subsistence level.[10] Every village had its share of blacksmiths, shoemakers, tailors, weavers, potters, and tanners—many of whom served several local communities. Because of their high literacy rates, village craftsmen tended to play an influential role in the early peasant movement.[11] Each village also contained several representatives of the rural intelligentsia—priests, organists, and teachers—who were often of peasant background. These rural professionals operated as liaisons between groups outside the village and the peasants themselves (see chapter 7).

Deeper than the social divisions engendered by occupational and economic differences among rural families were the splits brought about by the ethnic and religious diversity that characterized Galician villages. Most rural communities were home to a combination of Polish Roman Catholics, Ukrainian Greek Catholics, Germans (either Lutheran or Roman Catholic), and Jews. The existence of numerous ethnic groups clustered together within a single village boundary yet sharing few cultural institutions, encouraged the formation of group identity among co-religionists. The Polish speakers created ethnic stereotypes that later would sharpen into nascent national perceptions. Especially in central Galicia, where villages were often divided equally among Polish and Ukrainian speakers, linguistic and religious differences (including variant church calendars) served to reinforce the separate ethnic identities of the two groups.[12]

Scattered throughout the western Galician countryside were settlements of German-speaking colonists whose larger than average landholdings and higher social status (many of them were urban administrators and officials) helped create rifts with the Polish-speaking rural population.[13] Gypsies also lived in relatively small numbers throughout central and western Galicia.[14] Village culture reflected a recognition of and even fascination with the cultural differences separating ethnic and religious groups in the countryside. Folk songs satired the laziness of the "Lutheran" farm boy,

[10] Magryś, *Żywot chłopa*, 28–41, provides details on cloth weaving and its role in the Galician economy.
[11] Inglot, *Historia chłopów*, 205–7; Pilat, *Wiadomości statystyczne*, 18.
[12] Pigoń, *Z Komborni*, 88–92; Magryś, *Żywot chłopa*, 53–55.
[13] *Pszczółka*, July 25, 1878, 2; Pilat, *Wiadomości statystyczne*, 18–19; and Magryś, *Żywot chłopa*, 55–56.
[14] Gypsy settlements existed predominantly in the districts of Łańcut, Sanok, and Stare Miasto. Pilat, *Wiadomości statystyczne*, 18–19.

calling him a "dirty rascal." The "Jewish God," was depicted as like a devil in "long red trousers . . . sitting on a chimney smoking a pipe."[15] Gypsies appeared regularly in Christmas plays (*szopki*) in the role of petty thieves or swindlers.[16]

The Jewish presence in Galician villages was probably the strongest single source of ethnic tension. Jews made up 10 to 12 percent of the total population of late-nineteenth-century Galicia, with concentrations of up to 60 percent in major towns and close to 100 percent in many small rural settlements (*shtetlach*).[17] Statistically, only about 3 percent lived within village communes, yet some 25 percent resided in *shtetl* communities of between a few hundred and a few thousand inhabitants.[18] Although emigration to urban areas and abroad reduced the number of Jews in Galician villages during the last quarter of the century,[19] peasant resentment toward this "foreign" element appears to have strengthened in this period.

Preemancipation sources reflect an attitude of limited trust and interde-

---

[15] Jan Bystroń, *Pieśni ludu krakowskiego* (Cracow, 1924), 129–30.

[16] The role of petty crook or swindler in Polish *szopki* (Christmas plays) was played interchangeably by a villager dressed as a Gypsy or as a Jew. See Jańczuk, "Szopka w Kornicy," *Wisła* 2 (1888): 736–37, 746–47.

[17] Jewish communities in Galicia swelled with immigrants from the Russian partition after the late-eighteenth-century partition of the Polish Republic. By 1869 Jews made up 10.6 percent of the total Galician population of 5.4 million, and by 1890 they composed 11.6 percent. Beginning in 1900, the Jewish portion of the total population dropped, though their raw numbers continued to climb. The last prewar census lists Jews as 10.9 percent of the total Galician population. The distribution of this population also varied, with some 7.7 percent of the west Galician population being Jewish in 1900 and 12.9 percent in eastern Galicia.

Of the 686,000 Jews living in Galicia in the 1880s, Szczepanowski estimates that some 150,000 managed taverns (in either a rural or an urban area); 2,000 were landowners; and 92,000 were characterized as "farmers or of undesignated profession." In addition, 188,000 were described as being occupied with trade, presumably including the management of country stores over which Jews had a monopoly until the 1880s. William O. McCagg Jr., *A History of Habsburg Jews, 1670–1918* (Bloomington, 1989), 118–19; Wasiutyński, *Ludność żydowska*, 90–92; Kieniewicz, *Galicja*, vii–x; Himka, *Galician Villagers*, xxiii; Szczepanowski, *Nędza Galicyi*, 130–33; Piotr Wrobel, "The Jews under Austrian-Polish Rule, 1869–1918," *Austrian History Yearbook* 25 (1994): 97–138; John-Paul Himka, "Ukrainian-Jewish Antagonism in the Galician Countryside during the Late Nineteenth Century," in *Ukrainian-Jewish Relations in Historical Perspective*, ed. Peter J. Potichnyj and Howard Aster (Edmonton, 1988), 111–58.

[18] Wasiutyński, *Ludność żydowska*, 90–92. For an overview of relations between *shtetl* Jews and Catholic peasants, see Saul Miller, *Dobromil: Life in a Galician Shtetl, 1890–1907* (New York, 1980).

[19] On causes of the declining Jewish presence in late-nineteenth-century villages, see Magdalena Opalski, *The Jewish Tavern-Keeper and His Tavern in Nineteenth-Century Polish Literature* (Jerusalem, 1986), 31–35. An excellent overview of Jewish conditions in Galicia is Israel Bartal and Antony Polonsky, eds., *Polin: Studies in Polish Jewry*, vol. 12: *Focusing on Galicia: Jews, Poles, and Ukrainians, 1772–1918* (London, 1999).

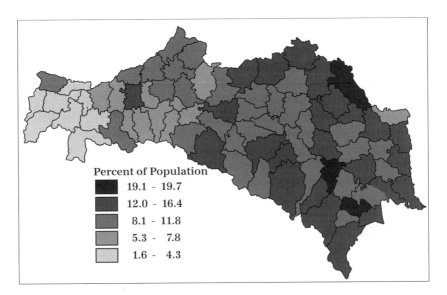

Percent of Population
- 19.1 - 19.7
- 12.0 - 16.4
- 8.1 - 11.8
- 5.3 - 7.8
- 1.6 - 4.3

Jewish minority, 1900. Courtesy of Ellen White, based on information from Bohdan Wasiutyński, *Ludność żydowska w Polsce w wiekach XIX i XX. Studjum statystyczne* (Warsaw, 1930).

pendency between Christian and Jewish villagers, a relationship that began to erode in the aftermath of emancipation and the onset of peasant capitalism. In the eighteenth and early nineteenth centuries, the Jewish tavern keeper was reportedly a respected figure. Sources comment that "the peasant spoke with him openly, listened to his advice, sought his help, escaped to his protection . . . such an important role did the Jew play in the peasant's life."[20] Serfs often perceived Jewish tavern keepers as more trustworthy than the lord in the hierarchy of village power relations. Jewish innkeepers listened "patiently to the peasant's complaints, often wrote down prescriptions, or bled him. The very same villager who looked with suspicion on the lord found a trust in his relations with the Jew."[21]

Tensions and misunderstandings between the two religious communities increased in the years following emancipation owing partly to the cultural isolation of many rural Jews. As one contemporary Jewish scholar commented, "European culture made no inroads . . . and the spirit of the enemies of education reigned" among *shtetl* Jews who were largely "governed

[20] Schnur-Popławski, *Cudzoziemcy w Galicyi, 1787–1841* (1893), 50–51, as cited in Burszta, *Społeczeństwo i karczma*, 174.
[21] Ibid., 174; Himka also discusses Jewish tavern keepers who gave advice to Catholic officers holding commune council meetings in the bar after 1866. *Galician Villagers*, 180.

Shtetl Jew from Podole. Photograph by M. Grim. Courtesy of the Ethnographic Museum, Cracow. Inventory number III/109/F. Reproduction by Jacek Kubiena.

by the miracle-worker Hasids."[22] Moreover, Jews themselves risked being ostracized by their *shtetl* neighbors if they made gestures of accommodation toward Catholics. "Anyone who used a 'foreign' language was excluded from his own [group]!" writes one Jewish contemporary. "Even taking part in political matters was perceived as an act against the religion, not to mention attending public schools!"[23]

Emancipation reduced the Jews' middleman position between peasant and landlord, forcing many rural Jews to emphasize moneylending. At a time of increasing land hunger, the hitherto solidly based reciprocal relationship began to disintegrate. As the Jews' role in rural society became a primarily economic one, Catholic farmers increasingly perceived them as outsiders. Beginning in the 1870s, Christian peasants sought to organize their own credit institutions and village stores in order to undercut the interest rates and prices Jewish merchants demanded. Peasant leaders portrayed village Jews as economic exploiters who were doubly harmful to Polish Catholics because they were "foreign" and followed an alien religion. Respondents to a mid-1870s rural survey characterized the main occupations of rural Jews as "usury, litigation, exploitation of the peasants, purchasing stolen goods, accomplices to theft, smuggling, swindling, and clandestine alcohol sales" and judged them as having an "overall harmful effect on rural life."[24]

This perception of village Jews as exploiters of the Catholic population was reflected in the ideology of many early peasant leaders. Peasant activist Wincenty Witos, longtime Sejm deputy and interwar prime minister, depicted rural Jews in his memoirs as possessing clear economic advantages over Catholic peasants. In his native village of Wierzchosławice, Witos noted, Jewish tavern keepers managed "not only to survive, but to thrive" despite the "general level of poverty" in the community. Because of the purportedly exorbitant prices peasants were willing to pay for drinks in the tavern, Witos argued, "it is not surprising . . . that the peasants lived like the worst wretches, while the Jews were well off and almost always managed substantial estates."[25] Such proclamations were clearly based on an assessment of relative economic well-being, since Jewish historians characterized the lot of Galician Jews in much starker terms. Simon Dubnov described these same rural Jewish communities in the

---

[22] Naftali Schipper, *Dzieje Żydów w Polsce oraz przegląd ich kultury duchowej (z uwzględnieniem krajów ościennych)*, 2 vols. (Lwów, 1927), 2: 94.
[23] Ibid.
[24] Pilat, *Wiadomości statystyczne*, 19–20.
[25] Wincenty Witos, *Moje wspomnienia* (Warsaw, 1978), 100–102.

1890s as "reduced to a state of poverty that was unknown anywhere else in Europe."[26]

These divergent views of the economic status of Jews within Polish society grew partially out of the ongoing cultural differences separating the two communities and a growing position of "otherness" Jews held in the minds of many peasants. The increasingly rigid boundaries dividing Poles from Jews were confirmed in the comments made by Stanisław Potoczek, leader of the first, short-lived peasant party (Związek Stronnictwa Chłopskiego), in 1891. Potoczek proclaimed to a peasant audience, "What are the Jews to us? I view them as they view us, that is as foreigners, and . . . as an element that is not only foreign to us, but harmful to us and against which we must defend ourselves."[27] Attacks against Jews as purported economic leeches on the peasant livelihood may have helped the peasant party mobilize budding peasant capitalists intent on taking control over local commerce. For those with a more ambiguous relationship to the market economy, cultural references to the Jews as foreigners may have served a similar purpose. Economic concerns underscored and reemphasized ethnic markers, helping to strengthen national identity among Polish farmers and to demonize elements within the village against whom the "Poles" sought to defend themselves.

Rifts based on generational and gender status also made their mark on public life in the countryside. Generational tensions arose, for example, between fathers and sons over issues of education, land usage, and public responsibilities. (See chapter 3 regarding generational conflicts in the Galician Sejm.) Because of the importance of the rural educational establishment and the circulation of village newspapers in the development of a national sentiment among Polish peasants, the first wave of peasant supporters for the Polish national cause consisted primarily of a literate younger generation. (On the role of the schools in shaping peasant nationalism, see chapter 7.) Differences in educational level following emancipation played into long-standing conflicts between generations within the household over inheritance, dowries, and familial authority. Political

[26] Dubnov depicts the 1890s as a time when the Jews of Galicia were driven from most trades and crafts, when pauperism mounted from year to year, and "emigration came to be the only alternative for the hungry masses," tens of thousands of whom left home annually for America. Although Jews composed only about 12 percent of the Galician population, Dubnov argues they made up 90 percent of the crownland's poor. *History of the Jews: From the Congress of Vienna to the Emergence of Hitler* (New York, 1973), 5: 491–93.

[27] *Wieniec Polski*, December 31, 1891, 139–40. The Jesuit priest Father Stanisław Stojałowski, founder of the Peasant Party (Stronnictwo Ludowe), has also been accused of inciting a pogrom through his inflammatory remarks during the Reichstag election of 1898. See Dubnov, *History of the Jews*, 5: 492–93.

activism and ideological commitment often exacerbated preexisting tensions among the village population.

The gendered nature of farm labor also brought about differing political agendas in the countryside.[28] Women and men had separate and well-defined areas of influence in Polish farm life. Responsibility for tending the farmyard animals and kitchen gardens belonged to the female sphere of labor. Women tended to have decisive influence over their children's education, a responsibility that placed farmwives squarely in the path of occupational authorities elsewhere in Poland, where governments sought to Russify or Germanize their Polish subjects through the schools.[29] The work of planting and harvesting and fulfilling public labor obligations usually fell to men, although whole families typically turned out for the final days of the harvest. These separate domestic roles contributed to distinct sets of priorities for public action and conflicting political agendas. The early civic institutions (discussed in chapter 6) that grew up in the Polish countryside failed to consider the particular interests of rural women, especially in the areas of temperance, health care, and education.[30]

Folk songs and plays reveal the barely veiled frustration village women felt with masculine public activities. The predominantly male bastion of the tavern came in for particular criticism. Ethnographer Oskar Kolberg described farmwives who, during pilgrimages to religious festivals, "sit on wagons cursing the men who are not able to make their way from the tavern." Folk songs ask "why . . . the peasant woman [*chłopka*] works so

[28] The study of women's political activism in nineteenth-century Poland is still in its infancy. Among the most promising studies are Rudolf Jaworski and Bianka Pietrów-Ennker, eds., *Women in Polish Society* (Boulder, 1992), and Anna Żarnowska and Andrzej Szwarc, eds., *Kobieta i społeczeństwo na ziemiach polskich w XIX w.* (Warsaw, 1990). For a somewhat different angle, see Sławomira Walczewska, *Damy, rycerze i feministki: Kobiecy dyskurs emancypacyjny w Polsce* (Cracow, 1999).

[29] Women played a prominent role in resistance to German-language education in Prussian Poland, for example, where Polish mothers and schoolgirls led many of the strikes against German schools in 1901–5 and 1906–7. Kulczycki, *School Strikes*, 160–61. In the Congress Kingdom, women became involved in founding secret schools as an alternative to government-funded Russian schools and also helped disseminate secret educational materials to adults. Edmund Staszyński, *Polityka oświatowa caratu w Królestwie Polskim od Powstania Styczniowego do I Wojny Światowej* (Warsaw, 1968), 193–204; Ryszard Wroczyński, *Dzieje oświaty polskiej, 1795–1945* (Warsaw, 1980), 148–51; and Helena Brodowska, "Koła Oświaty Ludowej. Przyczynek do badań nad rozwojem świadomości chłopów," *Stowarzyszenie społeczne jako środowisko wychowawcze*, ed. Irena Lepalczyk (Warsaw, 1974), 113–46.

[30] Several journals devoted to women's issues and encouraging female civic activity began publication in the Polish lands during the 1890s and early twentieth century. These efforts were for the most part short-lived and, until the early twentieth century, comparatively ineffectual. Periodicals included *Ster*, *Przodownica*, and *Zorza*.

hard, / Only to turn her money over to him. / He had taler . . . and groschen, but he gave it all up for three rounds of schnaps." Courting songs also frequently involve young women rejecting an eligible village lad, arguing "I don't want you because you drink spirits . . . and play cards and you will be poor."[31] The emigration of men in search of work also became a subject of folk lamentations. Musical complaints bemoaned the long absences from Galician villages of males working on rafts transporting goods down the Vistula river. "The raftsman's wife," one song laments, "Sits alone at home / While the poor beggar raftsman / Works for bread."[32] Although peasant letters inform us of extensive female power within the family, this authority was rarely felt in the public sphere until the early twentieth century, leading to tensions directed at male involvement in organizations that excluded females.[33]

Women who did not conform to public expectations limiting their activities to the private sphere—or who refused to marry or remarry—were frequently ostracized for their behavior. Belief in the supernatural and in witchery was widespread in the nineteenth-century Polish countryside. Village women who were socially isolated, friendless, or who wandered about the village by themselves often were assumed to be in the service of the devil.[34] Widows were accused of being witches if they cut themselves off from village society, were "the source of quarrels, curses, beatings, and public boasting," or had "no friends because of [their] evilness."[35] Interestingly, in village popular culture, only accused witches (and later some

---

[31] Oskar Kolberg, *Lud: Kujawy*, vol. 3 (Wrocław, 1961) 52–53; Kolberg, *Lud: W Ks. Poznańskie*, vol. 12, no. 4 (Cracow, 1879), 270. Józef Konopka, *Pieśni ludu krakowskiego* (Cracow, 1840), 38.

[32] Konopka, *Pieśni ludu*, 143.

[33] Letters to early-twentieth-century newspapers devoted to female readership in the countryside emphasized the "great influence [women had] in private and social matters" and encouraged social and national activism among farmwives. See Eli Zaretsky, ed., *The Polish Peasant in Europe and America: A Classic Work in Immigration History* (Urbana, 1996), esp. 16–21.

[34] Toppen, *Aberglauben aus Masuren* (Gdańsk, 1867), 36–41, as cited in Jan Karłowicz, "Czary i czarownice w Polsce," *Wisła* 1 (1887): 17–19; Karol Matyas, "Chłop czarownik, Sylwetka etnograficzna," *Świat* (1888): 3–7. Oskar Kolberg's *Dzieła wszystkie* also includes several studies of witches and witchcraft, including "Czarownice," *Mazowsze*, vol. 42, no. 7 (Wrocław, 1961), 378; "Czary i czarownicy," *Góry i Podgórze*, vol. 45, no. 2 (Wrocław, 1961), 515; "Czarownice," *Mazowsze, Tarnowskie-Rzeszowskie*, vol. 48 (Wrocław, 1961), 272–76; and "Czary i czarownice," *Sanockie-Krośnienskie*, vol. 51, no. 3 (Wrocław, 1961), 41–52.

[35] See the fascinating series of case studies summarized in Karłowicz, "Czary," 14–20, 56–62.

female teachers) were able to carve out a consistently active social role outside the constraints of the family.

In traditional rural theater, female figures abound, but only the witch (who is typically paired onstage with the devil) had a speaking role.[36] The special powers that the *baby* (old women) possessed could bring about a variety of evils such as drying up cows' milk, making farmers ill, infesting barns with rodents, and causing drought.[37] Only on festival days, when village culture specifically mandated a reversal of customary practices, did rural society encourage an active role for women, and then only in taverns where they helped capture and constrain men. Even in this ritualized version of female activism, however, only married women were permitted to participate. Clearly women had to occupy a socially acceptable position in the village structure before they could be permitted to break out of that role even for a single night.

Female villagers' resentment and the tensions that grew up between the sexes in the Polish countryside were reflected in the structure of early civic organizations in Galicia. Gentry males established the first rural social institutions for peasant males; women of all social classes were largely excluded from public life. In response to the exclusivity of male-dominated institutions, Polish women began to extend their influence beyond the private sphere and establish their own parallel associations, many of them with a patriotic agenda.[38] Gendered agendas and the social divisions that sparked them became important forces for social activism, bringing increasing numbers of Galician villagers into public life in the years preceding Poland's reemergence as an independent state.

Social Networks and the Growth of Village Politics

The divisions within Galician village society at mid-century did not prohibit peasants from devising systems of governance and social networks to administer local affairs. Both the village *gromada* (council) and the tavern

---

[36] Jańczuk, "Szopka w Kornicy," *Wisła* 2 (1888): 729–53.

[37] Karłowicz, "Czary."

[38] These activities were sporadic and limited in the countryside until the early years of the twentieth century. Beginning in 1886, Polish women's activism was coordinated by the Women's Circle of the Crown and Lithuania (Koło Kobiet Korony i Litwy), which organized patriotic cultural and educational activities in all three partitions. Delegates from the circle attended international women's conferences throughout Europe and in 1907 helped found the Union for Women's Equality (Związek Równouprawnienia Kobiet). Staszyński, *Polityka oświatowa caratu*, 193–204; Jaworski and Pietrów-Ennker, *Women in Polish Society*, 22–25.

were sites where village residents could air grievances and resolve dis-
agreements. A growing clash between the church and the village inn as
centers of social life helped establish the beginnings of semipermanent
interest groups and prepolitical factions within rural communities. These
patterns of conflict and consensus formation would later be transferred to
interactions in formal political organs including regional councils, the
Galician Sejm, and the Viennese Reichsrat.

Within the village community itself, the *gromada* or council of elders
helped resolve conflicts among villagers and divide public burdens until
the introduction of the self-governing commune system in 1866. Membership in the council of elders was the privilege of an elite group within the
village, since participation was restricted to the leading male landholders.
In this crude system of representation, a handful of males was responsible
for the collective interests of the community. Members met regularly
"under the open skies" to deal with land disputes, the care of the handi-
capped and foundlings, the problems of wandering beggars, and other
issues of communal concern. This gathering constituted an informal court
of first instance for the serfs, who brought unresolved conflicts to the
manorial court. The *gromada* stressed compromise and consensus, taking
account of the financial status of each family in its deliberations. It divided
the care of village dependents among households in proportion to their
resources.[39] Similarly, the *gromada* devised quotas of contributions for
wandering beggars (sometimes as little as a few spoonfuls of food from
each household).[40]

Occasionally, bodies outside of these informal customary institutions
heard village grievances. The Austrian legal system, which held jurisdiction over Galician peasants after 1772, established a juridical process
encouraging peasants to take their grievances first to the manorial court
and then to crownland and imperial authorities if disputes were not
resolved to the petitioner's satisfaction.[41] Residents of the "royal villages"—administered by representatives of the crown rather than by private landlords—and of villages within the district of the Free City of Cracow (1815–48) frequently possessed their own courts, permitting them to
take an active approach to conflict resolution.[42]

---

[39] Pigoń, *Z Komborni*, 20–21; Bujak, *Żmiąca*, 127–28; Magryś, *Żywot chłopa*, 39.
[40] Pigoń, *Z Komborni*, 20–21.
[41] Tadeusz Pilat, *Pogląd historyczny na urządzenie gminne w Galicyi* (Lwów, 1878), 8–10.
Roman Rozdolski, *Die grosse Steuer- und Agrarreform Jozefs II* (Warsaw, 1961), as cited in
Inglot, *Historia chłopów*, 191–92; Brodowska, *Chłopi o sobie*, 6, 40–41.
[42] Pigoń, *Z Komborni*, 14, 68. Regarding the effects of the right to petition the lord on peasant attitudes, see also Antoni Podraza, "Ruch Ludowy w Polsce południowej na przełomie

At the opposite end of the representative spectrum from the *gromada,* membership in the parish church and participation in church-sponsored festivals and religious services involved the village majority. Shaping the peasants' identity from the earliest moments of their existence, church rituals and public celebrations helped reinforce commonalties among Roman Catholic villagers while excluding nonbelievers from the dominant village culture. The parish church, be it Roman Catholic or Greek Orthodox (the church attended by most Ukrainians), constituted the center of organized social life in most Galician villages. Besides regular and obligatory attendance at mass, villagers also met for baptisms, weddings, and funeral rites; to celebrate saints' days and feasts; and to take part in holy pilgrimages.[43]

Participation in these events was virtually mandatory for Catholic villagers and thus formed the core of rural social interactions throughout the nineteenth century. The church declared the many religious holidays—up to two hundred per year—free from work.[44] On these days, the entire village attended mass together, participated in special group meals, and often met for an evening in the village tavern. Peer pressure to participate in church-sponsored activities was enormous. Failure to participate annually in a religious pilgrimage was "viewed by public opinion as a sin."[45] The church also influenced cultural life through the village catechism school, which in the early postemancipation period typically was run by the organist in his house or in the rectory. (See chapter 7 on the shifting role of priest and organist in village society.) The priest or his organist assistant typically organized the few formal choirs or orchestras that existed in the countryside.[46]

The relative homogeneity of mass participation in church-sponsored events belies a much more complex set of social interactions. On the one hand, the extent to which church activities structured village public life helped to demarcate Polish Catholics from Greek Catholic Ukrainians, German Lutherans, or Jewish residents of a village. Yet memoirists tell of rising tensions between literate peasants and priests who forbade them to read certain village newspapers or who sought to dictate the peasants'

XIX i XX wieku," *Republika Tarnobrzeska w świetle faktów i dokumentów* (Tarnobrzeg, 1982), 23–24.

[43] Michalski, *Dzieje szkolnictwa,* 101–2.

[44] In central and eastern Galicia, both Roman and Greek Catholic holy days were celebrated, leading to between one hundred and two hundred days free from work. Inglot, *Historia chłopów,* 254–57.

[45] Bujak, *Żmiąca,* 140.

[46] See, for example, ibid., 139–42.

choice of electors for public office (see chapter 7). More important, already in the preemancipation period, the expanding network of village taverns represented a serious challenge to the church's authority and an ongoing source of competition for the peasant's leisure time.

The local tavern was one of the key institutions and sources of authority governing the peasant's daily life. Ethnographers refer to the tavern as "the most important building in the village" with the "greatest number of connections to life" in the countryside.[47] Just as the church organized activities for the dozens of holidays in the peasant calendar, so too was the tavern involved in parallel public rituals on days free from work. After the landlord's authority over peasants diminished following emancipation, social life in the village involved a delicate balance between church and tavern, leading some contemporary memoirists to complain that "today's peasant knows only two roads: one to the church and the other to the tavern."[48] Indeed, ethnographers describe the rhythm of the peasant's Sunday as encompassed by the two opposing spectacles of "the morning Sunday mass in the church before the bells of the organ, the smell of incense and the sight of the candles [which] brought to the peasant a strange sort of inebriation [and] afternoon and evening visits to the tavern with its obligatory music, dancing, singing, in the fumes of alcohol [which] gave him another type of intoxication."[49]

Religious rites, from baptisms and weddings to funerals and saint's day celebrations, were mirrored by equally obligatory tavern festivities. Many of these tavern-based ceremonies included elements of magic or supernatural beliefs that the church strongly discouraged. Soon after a village woman gave birth, for example, the tavern keeper traditionally sent a bottle of vodka, which mother and grandmother drank in the presence of the godparents and others, rubbing some into the crown of the small child's head in order to "baptize" the baby in a prechristening ceremony. Following the child's christening in the church, the entire group formed a procession to the tavern for three days of "drinking and gaiety." These festivities were interrupted only by obligatory feasts put on first by the godfather, next by the godmother, and finally culminated in the tavern itself with a feast sponsored by the parents of the newborn child, in which the guests "ate and drank until they fell down." Opponents of the centrality of village taverns to rural society complained that these activities both threat-

---

[47] Wincenty Pol as cited in Kolberg, *Lud: Krakowskie*, vol. 5 (Cracow, 1871), 139.
[48] Ibid., 167.
[49] Ibid.

ened the purity of Christian rituals and absorbed the financial resources of the farmers involved.[50]

Wedding rites involved a similar pattern of church and tavern activities. "Almost the entire village" turned out for four-day receptions, trooping directly to the tavern from the religious services.[51] Wakes organized around the tavern often violated church-imposed sanctions on dancing and other frivolities during the mourning period, especially in the case of young widows.[52] On Sundays, inns rivaled the church for attendance as many villagers remained in the tavern throughout the mass and thereafter.[53] Above all, peasants visited taverns on the dozens of so-called free days—days of fairs and religious festivals. Inns typically stood on each of the main roads leading out of villages and were placed at regular intervals on the routes to and from market towns so that peasant travelers could stop along the way.[54]

The role of tavern society in religious festivals was of particular concern to the parish clergy since "on every road leading to . . . a holy place one sees wagons and small carts full of drunken people in scenes that are at once funny and tragic."[55] The beginning and end of the Easter fast were particularly marked by tavern festivities such as the Ash Wednesday ritual empowering farmwives symbolically to capture fellow villagers with a rope and ransom them for bottles of vodka. In this annual "day of drunkenness with a feminine tenor" and other religiously inspired drinking bouts, such as the frenzied and drunken three-day celebration of Lent, the constraints of the fast period were regularly broken by playing music, dancing, and drinking alcohol.[56] Despite concerted efforts in the generations after emancipation, "the appeals of the law and the church" appeared to be powerless in the face of the expanding role village taverns played in rural social life.[57]

Public celebrations in rural inns represented a clear challenge to the

---

[50] Burszta, *Społeczeństwo i karczma*, 178–79.

[51] Magryś, *Żywot chłopa*, 41–42; Bujak, *Żmiąca*, 125–26.

[52] Typically, the widow's neighbors invited her to a meal in the tavern two days after the funeral (these festivities were also often referred to as a *pogrzeb* or funeral), where a fiddler was playing and the widow would be invited and prodded to dance after the meal. Kolberg, *Lud: Kujawy*, 52–53.

[53] Burszta, *Społeczeństwo i karczma*, 185–86; Bujak, *Żmiąca*, 122.

[54] Józef Ryszard Szaflik, *O rząd chłopskich dusz* (Warsaw, 1976), 10–11; Burszta, *Społeczeństwo i karczma*, 186–87.

[55] Kolberg, *Lud: Kujawy*, 52–53.

[56] Burszta, *Społeczeństwo i karczma*, 188; Szaflik, *O rząd chłopskich dusz*, 10.

[57] Magryś to *Związek chłopski* (1895): 236–37.

monopoly of the Catholic Church over the peasantry's free time. For this reason, parish priests often stood at the head of the antialcoholism campaigns that began in the 1870s. Using every means at their disposal, from the pulpit to the confessional, rural clerics sought to stem the tide of tavern socializing and drunkenness—a campaign that pitted their authority directly against that of the landlords, whose profits from tavern sales they threatened.[58] The clergy-led temperance movement also highlighted the role of the Jewish tavern keeper, who was beyond the control of the church, and was consequently blamed for drunkenness among the peasantry.[59]

The vital role Jewish tavern keepers played in village economic life compounded the influence tavern society had on emancipated peasants. Village taverns were doubly important as country stores, selling tobacco, tea, salt, and other farmhouse staples to communities isolated from the market. As one mid-century observer commented, "without them one can neither eat nor drink, nor clothe oneself. Even pens for writing are supplied by the Jews."[60]

The economic function served by the village tavern was furthered by the role its Jewish innkeeper played as a moneylender. The increased demand for cash in the aftermath of emancipation, coupled with the virtual absence of formal credit facilities in the countryside, meant that small farmers turned increasingly to moneylenders to meet their credit needs. Although imperial law technically prohibited usurious interest rates, the high demand for credit drove up the cost of borrowing money to as high as 250 percent, calculated weekly.[61] Since at these rates peasants had difficulty repaying even small debts, the countryside had high levels of indebtedness that led to the forced sale of farmland. The number of "liquidations," or forced auctions of peasant farms, increased dramatically over the half century following emancipation. Barely one hundred auctions took place in 1868, whereas by the end of the century over three thousand farms were sold annually to satisfy debts.[62] Even after the promulgation of

[58] Burszta, *Społeczeństwo i karczma* 194ff.; Szaflik, *O rząd chłopskich dusz*, 12–13; Leskiewiczowa, *Zarys historii*, 2: 519–20.

[59] Opalski, *Jewish Tavern-Keeper.*

[60] From S. Schnuer-Pepłowski, *Cudzoziemcy w Galicji, 1787–1841* (Cracow, 1898), 24, as cited in Opalski, *Jewish Tavern-Keeper*, 37–39.

[61] Regarding the incidence of usury in the Galician countryside, see Leopold Caro, *Lichwa na wsi w latach, 1875–1891* (Lwów, 1893); Pilat, *Wiadomości statystyczne*, 6–7; Kowalczyk, *Zarys historii*, 13; Kącki, *Ks. Stanisław Stojałowski*, 20–21; and Magryś, *Żywot chłopa*, 171–73.

[62] Caro, *Lichwa na wsi*, 4–5; Taduesz Pilat, "Licytacye sądowe posiadłości włościańskich i małomiejskich w latach od 1880–1883," *Wieniec*, November 20, 1884, 207.

a new imperial law against usury in 1877, the absence of alternative sources of credit kept interest rates high. Galicia continued to have the highest rate of usury in the Austrian Empire, and the creation of cooperative lending institutions for small farmers became a common goal of peasant activists as they entered formal politics.[63]

Besides being a source for loans, the tavern was also a medium of information for largely illiterate villagers who learned news about the world or gossip about local affairs. Folk songs reflect the centrality of the inn as a conduit for information from outside the village. "And where did you get all this news?" a traveler asks a local peasant in one tune. "In the tavern from the gossiping girls," is his response.[64] Wandering beggars and other travelers were regular features at the village tavern; in times of war, soldiers were quartered there; and villagers sought advice from their fellow drinkers or from the supposedly more worldly tavern keeper. The taverner received news and information from fellow merchants and from the lord, which he passed on to his peasant customers. Above all, the village inn constituted a common meeting place where all were welcome any time of the day, a democratic institution that accepted anyone regardless of wealth or status and provided an increasingly universal atmosphere for all members of village society to take part in social rituals.

The village tavern thus represented a microcosm of public life in the countryside, and, as such, it was the setting for most business deals and for the resolution of conflicts among villagers.[65] When peasants began to serve in local governmental councils in the 1860s, the work of the village mayor and his councillors became part of the tavern setting. Elections to local offices frequently took place in the pub over vodka, and the council met regularly there to discuss "matters of the common good" over alcohol purchased at the village's expense.[66] In some areas, the circle around the tavern grew into a distinct village faction, often standing in opposition to that made up of the local teacher and other literate villagers.[67]

The existence even before emancipation of a distinct public life in the

[63] *Wieniec*, October 2, 1879, 154–55; September 28, 1881, 162–63; November 20, 1884, 207; Antoni Gurnicz, *Kółka rolnicze w Galicji* (Warsaw, 1967), 140–41; and "System Spółdzielczy F. W. Raiffeisena i galicyjska adaptacja F. Stefczyka," *Spółdzielczy kwartalnik naukowy* 1, no. 4 (1967): 140–41; Magryś, *Żywot chłopa*, 120–21.

[64] Kolberg, *Lud: W. Ks. Poznańskie*, 270–71. See also Burszta, *Społeczeństwo i karczma*, 19–11, 180–81.

[65] Magryś, *Żywot chłopa*, 57.

[66] Ibid., 57.

[67] On splits in Ukrainian-dominated Galician villages over newspaper readership and tavern socializing, see Himka, *Galician Villagers*, 107.

Galician countryside, with its complex set of rituals and diversity of opinion, helped to establish some of the procedures and programs that would guide small farmers in political affairs once they were formally enfranchised. The village council, the church, and the tavern emphasized participation, public service, and inclusiveness. For the most part, these bodies constituted a culture that was largely separate from and independent of the life of the estate and the city. Peasant rules of behavior—the ways in which they observed religious fasts, their network of fairs, markets and saint's day celebrations; the workings of the village councils—had little connection to the conduct of cultural and political life among other social classes in mid-nineteenth-century Poland. The wide array of arenas for debate and discussion highlights the existence of an active sphere for public engagement in the Galician countryside before Polish villagers were included in the formal governmental apparatus. This vibrant, adaptable, and independent set of rural "traditions" are what would guide Galician peasants as they set about gaining access to political life outside their village homes.

The Peasant's Imagined Community

Public conflict prompted by factions and rivalries within the village was frequently put aside or deemphasized when peasants were faced with outside influences. The conceptual framework within which Galician villagers conceived of communities beyond the village was an extension of the larger belief systems that structured and explained elements of their daily existences. Much of the power both to help and to harm villagers came from outside the village setting, extending the boundaries of the villagers' daily experience to other rural communities and beyond.

Villagers frequently addressed problems within the community by calling on extraworldly powers via magical incantations or reference to supernatural creatures. They attributed crop failures and spoiled milk to some combination of black and white magic.[68] They employed black magic to ward off and respond to illnesses.[69] Jewish barbers, the consummate vil-

---

[68] Magryś, *Żywot chłopa*, 39–40; Margaret Paxton, "Defining the Divine: On the Range of the Numinous in Rural Russia," 6th Annual Conference on Cultural Studies of Eastern Europe and Eurasia, April 19–20, 1996.

[69] Apart from the lack of availability and expense of medical doctors during this time, part of the disincentive for employing physicians resulted from the peasants' tendency to turn to them late in the progress of an illness, so that little could be done to save the patient. Peasants thus remained unconvinced of the advantages of medical doctors over barbers, medicine men, or "old women" (*baby*). Magryś, *Żywot chłopa*, 40–41; Pilat, *Wiadomości statystyczne*, 85–86. Bujak, *Żmiąca*, 123.

lage outsiders, administered bloodlettings to adult patients for any range of illnesses. If bloodletting failed, peasants called on supernatural forces by throwing the patient's bathwater "in a place where three fences met," the same cross in the road where witches were said to summon the devil, or placing the patient's hair under an old willow tree, another spot frequented by devils.[70]

Closer to home, local "outsiders" performed a wide variety of rituals "from the cradle to the grave" in the Polish countryside. Wandering female beggars fulfilled the function of medicine women, midwives, dispensers of magical spells, and matchmakers; while male mendicants were responsible for keeping vigil over corpses prior to funeral services. Beggars also brought new information and passed on legends and stories (often featuring witches, devils, fairies, and sprites) collected on their wide travels throughout the countryside. Villagers reportedly respected the "wisdom and unlimited authority" of these visitors, notwithstanding their position as homeless migrants and the widely held belief that they were witches.[71]

Trusted and respected though they were for their magical knowledge, beggars, shepherds, and others with perceived connections to the "other" world also became foils for the peasantry's general ambivalence toward outsiders. Nineteenth-century Galician villagers clearly took as their primary social identity the village of their birth. Despite the splintering of the local population into occupational and interest groups, members of a single rural community continued to stress their internal social cohesion, especially in dealing with "outsiders" of various types. As P. M. Jones has observed in his study of the French countryside, "as soon as an external threat loomed over the horizon, internecine strife ceased and ranks closed."[72] Residents of one's native village were, for example, only rarely believed to be witches, while neighboring parishes were frequently assumed to possess entire "nests of witches."[73] Folk songs reflect mild rivalries between nearby villages as residents of one parish are accused of excessive pride or penury and residents of the singer's village promoted for their virtues.[74]

The village "us" was also counterposed to the outsider "them" in

[70] Magryś, *Żywot chłopa*, 41. See also Stanisław Połączek, "Z podań i wierzeń ludowych, zapisanych we wsi Rudawie pod Krakowem," *Wisła* 5 (1891): 629, 633.
[71] Ignacja Piątkowska, "Żebracy w Ziemi Sieradzkiej," *Wisła* 8 (1894): 784–90; Połączek, "Z podań," 624–35.
[72] Jones, *Politics and Rural Society*, 143–44.
[73] Połączek, "Z podań," 629, 633.
[74] Bystroń, *Pieśni*, 120–22.

regional rivalries taunting members of different geographic regions for their ignorance, poverty, or laziness. Songs of courtship and marriage, in particular, call upon regional associations to satirize different population groups, placing special emphasis on Polish speakers in all regions of the historic Polish lands as potentially eligible mates. Such cultural products tend to be evenhanded in their teasing tone as they chastise Mazurians (in the central Polish lands) and Kujavians for impoverishment ("I married a Mazurian woman and received three-quarters of a sheep as a dowry"); mountaineers (from the Carpathian region of southern Poland) for stupidity; peasants from the Cracow district for arrogance ("Although you are a Krakowianka and I a Wielkopole, I'll not be setting my cap at your knees"); and Wielkopoles for naive simplicity.[75] Songs and theatrical portrayals featuring regions of the historic Polish lands helped peasants construct a mental map of an unseen community of Polish-speaking peasants, creating wider circles of familiarity and foreignness that helped peasants distinguish "us" from "them," insider from outsider. Although marriage to a farmer from the Poznań district might be a comedown for a Cracow girl, such an arrangement was at least deemed within the range of possibilities.

A completely different, and much more critical, tone is reflected in songs, folktales, and other cultural artifacts dealing with non-Polish population groups. The disdain in which many Polish speakers held Ruthenians (Ukrainians) is reflected, for example, in the song characterizing a young girl's fate as being "compelled into slavery, when [she] marr[ies] a Ruthenian."[76] Ukrainian was also typically the language of witches and devils in village theater since "to put the Polish language in the mouth of an unclean spirit would be viewed as profanity."[77] And at least one courtship song concludes with a warning against marrying a Ruthenian, who is compared to "a bearded goat" and whose "clothing is so shabby . . . he's not worth four Czechs."[78] Belorussians from "beyond the Bug" River (*zza Buga*) are characterized as pagans, devil worshipers, and witches, as in the 1825 jingle accusing them of being "worse than the Turks, than the dirty Tatars," because this people (*naród*) "doesn't believe in God" (i.e., are not Roman Catholic).[79]

Germans came in for no better treatment in Polish folk culture. Village

---

[75] See the songs of courtship in Bystroń, *Pieśni*, 120–25; in Kolberg's *Lud: W Ks. Poznańskie*, 267–68; and in Oczykowski, "Szopka w Łowiczu," *Wisła* 7 (1893): 519.
[76] Bystroń, *Pieśni*, 123.
[77] Jańczuk, "Szopka w Kornicy," 738–39, 751–53.
[78] Kolberg, *Lud: W. Ks. Poznańskie*, 267–68.
[79] Jańczuk, "Szopka w Kornicy," 742–43.

songs and theater commonly refer to the devil using the Polish word for German (*Niemiec*) and cast him in the urban clothes (including a short dress coat) widely associated with towns in the German lands. The choruses of songs about Germans are much harsher in tone than those discussing Poles, including regular use of the slang "dogs" and "blowpipes" to characterize them. At least one popular refrain known from the eighteenth century complains of the Germans who "came to our country / According to their custom / With carpetbags / and now they are lords."[80] Village theater reflected the Austrian occupation of Galicia in its featuring of German *ekonomi* or stewards, "the Germans who come to [Galicia] without a cent and force themselves on our citizens as administrators, stewards, and so on, growing rich on our backs."[81]

In general, village cultural output portrays those who lived beyond the traditional Polish lands and "foreigners" within them (such as Jews or Gypsies) as being "of another world." Songs and legends depict Gypsies, Moravians, and Hungarians as having the "power to cast spells." Village theater portrays Jews who mistakenly gain entrance into paradise being "ripped out of heaven" by devils and transported to hell.[82] Thus, the concentric circles of the peasantry's communities reserved a familiar position for neighboring villages and even regions in the historic Polish lands, while placing those who stood outside of this nascent national conception in the netherworld or in various derogatory categories.

The peasantry's knowledge of and conceptions about distant lands and peoples were not limited to the information that found its way to the countryside. Rather, the rhythm of village life, from the annual ritual of conscription to the temporary migration of villagers abroad in search of work, involved the villagers' regular personal exposure to "foreign" settings and non-Polish ethnic groups. These exposures helped them refine and adjust their sense of the boundaries separating their perceived "us" and the "them" against which their own group was defined. The most vitriolic commentary about non-Poles grew out of the rituals surrounding the autumn departure of military recruits for service in the armies of the imperial occupying powers.

The recruits' leave-taking formed an integral part of the village calendar, marking an important moment for the entire community. In the first days of October in almost every Galician village, the conscripts assembled for all-night festivities in the tavern before their departure. In a secular echo of

---

[80] Bystroń, *Pieśni*, 123–25.
[81] Jańczuk, "Szopka w Kornicy," 743.
[82] Bystroń, *Pieśni*, 124–25.

religious processions, villagers marched behind the young men in a hierarchy reflecting their relation to the recruits and, accompanied by hired musicians, proceeded to the edge of the village. Only on the perimeter of the settlement, the mental boundary of "us" in this case, did the procession stop as the soldiers climbed into the awaiting wagons and physically separated themselves from the village of their birth and from their weeping families.[83]

"Foreign" place names took on new and frightening meanings for the conscripts as they complained bitterly of their assignment, for example, in "Moravia, Moravia" where "God has tagged me and people have given up on me!" Recruits throughout the Prussian partition feared their own officers more than the enemy's bullets, as in the frequent refrain "I'm not afraid of the bullets . . . but I am afraid of the nasty German officers" (or, "those German doctors" in another version) who had a reputation for brutality.[84] Even under serfdom, when Galician peasants are reported to have been *kaisertreu*, the Austrian emperor was subjected to verbal attacks from recruits and their families who resented the disruption conscription brought to the rhythms of village life:

> Emperor, Emperor, why do we have to enlist?
> A little rye has been sown, when will you let us harvest it?
> Emperor, Emperor, don't make us enlist anymore,
> Because the girls cry and the earth groans . . . [85]

Another popular tune, also from the preemancipation era, discusses the frequent losses of strong young men and eligible bachelors from village society, as female voices lament the fact that "the war is over, the boys are dead, / Let all the devils take the Emperor."[86] In times of war, songs about Italy, Bosnia, the Turks, France, and Prussia, about Bern, Rome, Berlin, Lwów, Vienna, and others came to the village together with characterizations of the inhabitants of these areas. The mental maps villagers developed of the limits to their various "communities" (Galicia, Austria, Poland, Europe, and so on) thus became closely associated with their own

---

[83] Włodzimierz Hnatiuk, "Pieśni rekruckie," *Lud* (1897): 73–75; Bystroń, *Pieśni*, 100–101.
[84] Michał Rawicz Witanowski, "Pieśni wojackie ze wsi Stradomia pod Częstochowa," *Wisła* 3 (1889): 646–49; Bystroń, *Pieśni*, 100–118; and Kolberg, *Lud: Kieleckie*, vol. 19, no. 2 (Cracow, 1886), 159–61.
[85] Bystroń, *Pieśni*, 118.
[86] Ibid.

personal experiences or with the stories returning soldiers told about the far-off lands they visited. The long-standing Polish tradition of migration for work also fostered familiarity with and conceptions about foreign lands. Even before emancipation, patterns of temporary emigration were well established in many parts of rural Galicia.[87] Among the most popular migration patterns was the tradition of sending male villagers to serve as raftsmen on the huge network of rivers spanning Galicia. Beginning already during the sixteenth-century grain trade boom, whole villages along streams feeding into the Vistula emptied of males in the early spring for the five-month trip down the river to deliver grain to the international port at Gdańsk. The arduous two-month walk back to Galicia helped to acquaint rafters with the geography of the Polish lands and with foreign empires.

By the nineteenth century, raftsmen were among the most knowledgeable about the rivers and towns of the Old Polish Kingdom. They brought artifacts and stories from distant lands to their native villages, introducing their neighbors to German cloth, furs, coral, and tea. The rafting tradition also brought the village closer to events in the outside world. News of the January 1863 uprising spread from Russian Poland to the villages of Galicia partly via raftsmen, who also served as spies for the insurgents. Stories of the November 1830 insurrection were told among raftsmen and repeated in their home villages. Urban habits and increasing distinctions in local status made their way into Galician villages as raftsmen became accustomed to wearing "town clothes" found in Prussia in order to distinguish themselves as having been abroad.[88] Gender divisions within rafting villages also shifted as women were left to take over the bulk of the planting and harvesting responsibilities usually reserved for males.[89]

Other forms of migration for work were well established long before emancipation. By the mid-eighteenth century, the burdens of serfdom had become so great throughout the Polish lands that many peasant families were forced to send male representatives abroad to earn money to pay their feudal dues. They worked as laborers in mills, breweries, or on

---

[87] For the motivation and logistics of peasant emigration for work, see Inglot, *Historia chłopów*, 262–70; Kącki, *Ks. Stanisław Stojałowski*, 19–20; Pigoń, *Z Komborni*, 40–44; Gurnicz, *Kółka rolnicze*, 139–40; and Magryś, *Żywot chłopa*, 53–54; and Bujak, *Żmiąca*, 99–100.

[88] Michal Janik, "Flisacy," *Lud* 10 (1904): 4–10. Also Franciszek Kuś, "Pamietników moich," ZHRL, P-64a, 2–4, 9.

[89] See, for example, Konopka's transcription of the ode to a raftman's wife in *Pieśni ludu*, 143.

manorial farms in the winter and returned in time to till their own fields in the spring. Individual villages established relations to employers in foreign lands via connections made over the course of generations. As one memoirist explained, "one cottager closed his shop in frustration and traveled to Hungary searching for another source of income. In doing so, he prepared for others who later followed in his path."[90] At first the destinations were within the Polish lands or to neighboring Hungary or Bukovina. The folk songs of the "mountaineers" from the Carpathian region of Galicia were particularly thick with references to Pest and other Hungarian cities, areas where this border population could most easily find work.[91]

By the mid-nineteenth century, the horizons of Galician villagers expanded still further with the advent of employment opportunities in the industrializing German lands and in North America. Galician peasants began to work seasonally in Prussia, Saxony, Hannover, Westphalia, Württemberg, and to a lesser extent in Bavaria, generally signing up for a nine-month work period before returning to their home villages. At any given time, some 20 percent of the rural population was abroad working in other European countries or in North America, signed on by agents from foreign firms who promised them bonuses to accept work with their companies.[92] Since wages tended on the whole to be higher in Germany or North America and work was available more steadily than in the Polish lands, the tradition of seasonal migration abroad became routinized for many Galician villagers.[93]

Migration encouraged the factionalization of village public life in its introduction of new sources of cash into the local economy. Old divisions between rich and poor shifted as the lowliest cottager was able, after a few years' stay in America, to buy land on which to build a substantial home, with all the modern comforts learned abroad.[94] Returning migrants often surpassed the older, established families in their wealth and ostentation,

---

[90] Pigoń, *Z Komborni*, 40–41.

[91] Bystroń, *Pieśni*, 111–12.

[92] Those who agreed to travel to the United States received the highest bonuses of twelve crowns; those who enrolled to go to Canada were paid six crowns. Migrants to North America tended to stay for several years before returning home, repeating this pattern of migration and return migration some three to five times until they were too old to find work. Inglot, *Historia chłopów*, 262–66; Pigoń, *Z Komborni*, 42; Józef Nocek, "Wspomnienia," ZHRL, P-17 (n.d), 1.

[93] See Magryś, *Żywot chłopa*, 53–54; Inglot, *Historia chłopów*, 262–63.

[94] Chimneys, larger windows, and tile as a substitute for fire-prone thatched roofs were among the innovations returning migrants introduced. Joseph Obrebski, *The Changing Peasantry of Eastern Europe* (Cambridge, Mass., 1976), 20–23; Pigoń, *Z Komborni*, 28–29; Magryś, *Żywot chłopa*, 22; and Pilat, *Wiadomości statystyczne*, 23–24.

thus disrupting earlier patterns of social hierarchy. Migrants who worked in Hungary were said to engender "all the characteristics of the urban proletariat," including a "reckless air" and a "disdain of all local relations," which undercut preexisting economic and generational divisions.[95]

New factions developed even around the issue of reading, as migrants from the United States acquired literature from Polish publishers in Chicago and introduced written material on a large scale. "As more and more such cases appeared in the village," contemporary sociologist Franciszek Bujak noted, "the entire structural organization of the countryside was altered."[96] On a number of levels, the cash and concepts of returnees contributed to the splintering of village society into new, economic and culture-based factions.

Premodern social institutions and attitudes clearly shaped the ways Galician peasants approached public life at mid-century. The village functioned as a complex, dynamic, heterogeneous community comprising factions, institutions for debate, and constantly shifting public opinions. Moreover, evolving notions of communal boundaries characterized village life. As the rudimentary components of a rural public sphere evolved in the postemancipation village, "premodern," supernatural, and even "irrational" conceptions from peasant society made their way into formal political exchanges. These "Polish," yet strangely "foreign" (to the Polish upper classes), elements would be absorbed into crownland-wide political interactions after peasants joined provincial political life. Once villagers elected to the Austrian Reichsrat and the Galician Sejm brought these issues into larger public fora, they became the objects of negotiation and debate in what was becoming a national, socially inclusive public sphere.

---

[95] Bujak, *Żmiąca*, 99–100. See also Pigoń, *Z Komborni*, 42–44.
[96] Bujak, *Żmiąca*, 100.

Chapter Three

Customs in Conflict:
Peasant Politics in the Viennese Reichstag
and the Galician Sejm

Our peasant, despite the fact that he was born on Polish soil, that he only speaks Polish, is incapable of grasping the concept that he is a Pole. What is still worse, among the peasants the name "Pole" and the word "enemy" are one and the same. The Pole for him is the lord whom he despises—who has power and legal jurisdiction over him—for whom he owed feudal obligations.

Zdzisław Zamoyski, 1848

Although there are such paragraphs in the law, they are cold like you judges who are interpreting it. . . . The discussions here about whether the elections are valid are themselves invalid.

Peasant Deputy Jan Siwiec, 1861 Sejm

Galician villagers' initial forays into formal politics highlighted the disjuncture between rural traditions and upper-class political behavior. Elected in large numbers to the revolutionary Reichstag of 1848 and the 1861 provincial diet in Lwów, Polish-speaking peasants presented an agenda to both bodies drawn directly from the experience of serfdom. At the heart of this agenda was a search for a correction to a whole range of perceived historical injustices. Driven by a sense of moral outrage at their treatment under serfdom, Polish villagers sought accountability from their political representatives and more equitable treatment under the law. Enfranchisement as citizens of Austria and Galicia led ex-serfs to assume that the most egregious abuses remaining from serfdom would be eliminated. Efforts by peasant deputies to resolve the indemnities and servitudes questions, for example, highlighted the violated sense of justice with which newly liberated peasants approached the work of these bodies. Above all, villagers sought the reflection of specific local values in decisions taken both in Vienna and in Lwów.

60

The moral code peasant delegates brought to Galician and imperial politics clashed dramatically with the attitudes and assumptions of upper-class representatives. Even when former landlords invoked the higher goal of national unity, as in the proclamations of the Polish National Council during the 1848 revolution, appeals for social solidarity found little resonance among newly liberated peasants. Just as the early appeals of their newly emancipated counterparts in the Congress Kingdom for more equitable wages and access to easements arrayed them against their former lords, Galician farmers' early activism also pitted peasants against gentry.[1] In Galicia, the peasantry's early legislative experiences involved a number of unresolved conflicts between village norms and written law. The next half century would be spent constructing dialogues that would begin to bridge the divide between particular peasant claims and broader appeals to national interest established in Vienna and Lwów.

At least two types of peasant/lord conflict brought out the distinctiveness of village approaches to the legislative process: differences over leadership credentials and conflicting conceptions of land ownership. The criteria peasants used for selecting political representatives reflected a participatory code rooted in long-standing village perceptions of authority and did not always meet imperial requirements for service in political assemblies. Once chosen as delegates, peasant deputies articulated a conception of usufruct that conflicted with the gentry's reliance on documents to prove ownership, vexing relations between lord and peasant in debates over indemnities payments and the uses of common lands. The deep cultural chasm separating the Polish social strata in these assemblies was revealed in the alternative political agenda peasant deputies advanced, stressing equality of access and the redistribution of public burdens across social boundaries, an agenda upper-class delegates largely rejected.

Village Culture and Peasant Politics

During the March revolution in Cracow and the elections to the constituent assembly in June, Galician peasants displayed an unprecedented degree of social and political distance both from their lords and from their traditional protectors, the Austrian officials. Long before their former lords, Galician peasants realized that emancipation offered them the pos-

---

[1] On protests against Polish landlords in the postemancipation Congress Kingdom, culminating in the revolution of 1905–7, see Blobaum, *Rewolucja*, 115–56.

sibility of establishing a more equitable position for themselves in the provincial power structure. Ceasing on their own to perform feudal services before the end of serfdom in late April, Galician peasants continued throughout the summer of 1848 to promote their interests against those of their ex-landlords. They employed a wide range of tactics, including collective action, boycotts, price fixing, and even violence, to demonstrate their power to an entrenched gentry angered over its inability to find workers.

By July, peasants began to form coalitions in the countryside in order to raise agricultural prices and prevent others from underselling them.[2] One gentry observer described a "social revolution" and a "peasant war" breaking out as farmers came out to express their financial independence and strength vis-a-vis their former lords. Kazimierz Wodzicki, a conservative magnate traveling in the Galician countryside during the summer of 1848, wrote that "the peasants . . . raise prices high and maintain solidarity among themselves, and when strangers with lower prices come around they beat them horribly, just like the workers in France."[3] This "class war" was fought on several fronts as peasants banded together to boycott work on manorial farms and to force estate owners to renegotiate wages on a daily basis.[4] In a stark example of the gentry's failure to read the ethical dimensions of peasant behavior, landlords interpreted the unwillingness of their former serfs to perform manorial services as "demoralization [and] untempered laziness" rather than as a desire for fair wages or longstanding resentment of historical abuses.[5]

The economic battles waged between lord and peasant discouraged village participation in the nationalist activities organized during the 1848 revolution. From the first days of emancipation in late April, the Polish National Council in Lwów (Rada Narodowa Centralna) sought to mobilize Galician peasants behind nationalist activities. Yet despite the circulation of fliers inviting villagers to participate, Galician peasants remained largely uninterested, giving the impression that they would "sleep forever" rather than participate in the national movement.

The "power," "legal jurisdiction," and "feudal obligations" the magnate Zamoyski refers to in his evaluation of peasant/lord relations in the

---

[2] Kazimierz Wodzicki to Henryk Wodzicki (July 25 and August 27, 1848), as reprinted in Stefan Kieniewicz, "Obrazki wiejskie 1847–1849. Z korespondencji Wodzickich," *Ze Skarbca Kultury* 2, no. 1 (1952): 49–50.
[3] Kazimierz Wodzicki to Henryk Wodzicki (May 3 and July 15, 1848), ibid., 46–48.
[4] Letter from Ksawery Pręk (May 28, 1848), as quoted in Kieniewicz, *Pomiędzy Stadionem a Goslarem*, 69–70.
[5] Letter from Kazimierz Wodzicki, Żółkiewski district, as quoted in ibid., 69–70.

epigraph [6] had also come to represent the gentry's nationalist goals in the eyes of Galician peasants. Unwilling to acquiesce to the implied return to feudal relations represented in gentry images of the nation, peasants refused to join their former lords in National Council activities. The tenets of eighteenth-century aristocratic nationalism, already under revision amongst Polish émigré communities,[7] would have to be thoroughly reshaped and a revised conception of national goals circulated among peasants before villagers would contribute to the movement.

Indeed, the gentry's own insecurity about peasant participation in Polish national events was reflected in a constant fear of a renewed peasant slaughter such as that of the jacquerie of 1846. The Polish National Guard even defined its mission in 1848 as partly that of "defending the Polish enlightened classes . . . from the peasantry and the [Austrian] bureaucracy."[8] Ironically, part of the peasantry's unwillingness to take part in national activities arose out of a paralysis connected to the very memory of that slaughter and the two years of unassisted hunger and pestilence following it. The timing of the 1848 revolution during the preharvest famine, and in the aftermath of a cholera epidemic that had taken some 148,000 lives, also contributed to a reluctance to take risks in this revolutionary year.[9]

The peasantry's behavior during elections to the Constituent Assembly also underlined the increasing political independence of former serfs.[10] The National Council and the Austrian bureaucracy competed unsuccessfully for the votes of thousands of newly enfranchised citizens in their first massive electoral experience.[11] Neither appeals to peasant nationalism from the Galician National Council nor assumptions of village loyalty to the empire deterred peasants from supporting fellow villagers as deputies

---

[6] Letter from Zdzisław Zamoyski (June 25, 1848) as reprinted in Kieniewicz, *Pomiędzy Stadionem a Goslarem*, 72–74.

[7] Peter Brock, *Polish Revolutionary Populism: A Study in Agrarian Socialist Thought from the 1830s to the 1850s* (Toronto, 1977).

[8] Kieniewicz, *Pomiędzy Stadionem a Goslarem*, 111–29.

[9] Plechta, "Rada Narodowa," 45–46; Kieniewicz, *Pomiędzy Stadionem a Goslarem*, 59–62.

[10] The majority of the electoral battles in 1848 were between peasants and their former lords in the countryside (only nine of the hundred seats allotted to Galicia were reserved for burghers), thus giving ex-serfs their first opportunity to challenge formally the preemancipation power structure.

[11] The May 9, 1848, election ordinance gave suffrage rights to all but the poorest male residents of Galicia above the age of twenty-four, excluding from the franchise landless laborers, servants, and those receiving public charity. The electoral law included no literacy requirement, making it easier for the inexperienced peasantry to be misled. See Włodzimierz Boryś, "Wybory w Galicji i debaty nad zniesieniem pańszczyzny w parlamencie wiedeńskim w 1848," *Przegląd Historyczny* 58, no. 1 (1967): 28–29; and Józef Plechta, "Chłopscy

in the June elections. The Polish National Council promoted the election of "bearers of Polish nationalism," such as priests, landowners, the rural intelligentsia, and even tavern keepers. Council instructions forbade the election of officials or soldiers who were deemed "people from a foreign land and . . . not your brothers." Only in cases where the local landlord "could not be trusted" did the Polish National Council advise peasant voters to seek a "sensible, unprejudiced peasant" to represent them. "Unfortunately," it complained dismissively, "there are not many" of these.[12]

By contrast, Austrian officials presented imperial civil servants as "political instructors" for new peasant citizens. Using the rhetoric of paternalism, they advised villagers to support the election of imperial officials to the Reichsrat. Uncertain peasant voters responded by sending delegates on foot to Vienna to seek advice from the emperor, a reflection of patterns of earlier dependence on the empire.[13] Rebuffing all paternalistic efforts to "guide" their political behavior, however, in the end Galician peasants relied on local attachments to make their choices. Rural voters selected fellow peasants as deputies in a total of thirty-two out of the hundred seats allotted to Galicia in the revolutionary assembly.[14] For the first time in East European history, villagers were able personally to send a message to a political assembly demanding that their interests be formally represented.

The conduct of peasant voters reflected patterns of abuse they had experienced at the hands of landlords during generations of serfdom. Suspicious even to paranoia of upper-class intentions, peasant voters resorted to a wide range of customary techniques to defend themselves against upper-class pressure and perceptions of trickery. Fearing an elaborate ruse to reinstitute feudal obligations, for example, many illiterate and insecure rural voters either avoided the election or refused to place their "X" on the ballot, thus invalidating the results.[15] In several districts, peasant electors refused to appear at the second round of voting, or participated on one

---

posłowie z obwodu sądeckiego w sejmie wiedeńskim w 1848 roku," *Rocznik Dziejów Ruchu Ludowego* 8 (1966): 277.

[12] Plechta, "Chłopscy posłowie," 278–80. Instructions to national councils in Tarnów, Wadowice, Tarnopol, etc. (May 28, 1848), as cited in Kieniewicz, *Pomiędzy Stadionem a Goslarem*, 80–83.

[13] Plechta, "Chłopscy posłowie," 278.

[14] The peasant deputies were split between 18 Poles and 14 Ukrainian representatives. They were joined by 27 large landholders; 20 members of the intelligentsia; 14 priests; 4 burghers; 2 Jews and 1 official. Putek, *Pierwsze występy*, 8–10; Boryś, "Wybory w Galicji," 30; Kieniewicz, *Pomiędzy Stadionem a Goslarem*, 81–83.

[15] Putek, *Pierwsze występy*, 8–10; Plechta, "Chłopscy posłowie," 280–81.

day only to retract their votes and their signatures the next, afraid that they had committed themselves to a new form of feudal services.[16] Far from serving as the automatic ally of either the Polish gentry or the Austrian regime, newly emancipated peasants sought at every turn to act independently, to avoid simplistic offers of upper-class protection, and to deflect perceived threats to their newly won rights. Relying on the tools and techniques available to them, Galician peasants sought to defend what they had gained by decree from the emperor in this first, brief democratic experience. Yet the defense of their newly won rights proved difficult as upper-class deputies repeatedly challenged the very presence of peasant delegates in the Reichstag.

Customary versus Written Law: The Clash over Leadership Credentials

After generations of dependence on outsiders, Galician peasants moved quickly to seize power from church and governmental officials in the village, and to legalize the transfer of power through legislation in the Reichsrat. Representatives from Galician villages submitted petitions seeking local control over clerical appointments and the selection of military recruits. Peasant deputies pleaded for legal guarantees against removing cultivators from their farms (another right of the landlord under serfdom), and they sought a more equitable division of tax burdens.[17] The formation of a more egalitarian tax structure and a reassessment of public rights and responsibilities would become major issues in negotiations between peasant politicians and representatives of other classes until the collapse of the Austrian Empire.

Peasant political convictions arose to a great degree from a sense of historic moral violation. This ethical basis of peasant politics was also reflected in the anti-Austrian rising in the village of Chrzanów in April of 1849. The crisis was a direct response to the reversal of one of the laws passed during the Reichstag session replacing the personal selection of military recruits by lords with a lottery system.[18] Under the new system, all

---

[16] Galician governor Gołuchowski's records indicate that in 17 of the 100 total election districts, contests had to be repeated for lack of quorum. The number of peasant electors who did appear was often strikingly low—8 of 41 in Jaworów district; 19 of 70 in Jasło; 15 of 51 in Drohobycz. In the district of Sambor, peasants expressed their suspicion of the elections by returning empty ballot sheets. Boryś, "Wybory w Galicji," 30–31.

[17] Kieniewicz, *Pomiędzy Stadionem a Goslarem*, 97–99.

[18] On the Chrzanów rising and the general conscription system in Galicia after 1848, see ibid., 130–47.

male residents of the crownland between the ages of twenty-two and thirty were eligible for the draft, and exemptions were available only for the fee of five hundred zlotys. Most villagers welcomed the new system, since it eliminated the use of military conscription as a punishment for village "idlers and troublemakers." Residents of Cracow itself were less enthusiastic about the new law, however, since as a free city Cracow had never previously been subject to the draft and the cost of a nobleman's buying his freedom was viewed as exorbitant.

The debate over conscription had a special immediacy in 1849 since troops were still being sent to quell the nationalist rising in Hungary. Polish burghers (among them democrats and intellectuals) resented the prospect of being ordered to put down a nationalist rebellion with which they sympathized. They feared that once the landlords gave up their right to select recruits, the regime would use conscription to punish those who were deemed "politically suspect" for their activities in 1848.[19] The imposition of the new legislation was thus greeted with considerable passive resistance, with only about 16 percent of those drafted from the Cracow district reporting for duty.[20] Partly as a result of the massive silent protest from Cracovians, the Austrian government granted a petition to exempt the Cracow district, including the villages in its hinterlands, from the new legislation. Outraged by this violation of the egalitarianism that they viewed as integral to the postemancipation order, ex-serfs began pouring into Cracow from the surrounding villages to protest. By late February 1849, imperial officials had established a policy of arresting peasants within Cracow on their way to the bars, and forcing them into military service on the premise that they were "idlers."

Such was the background to the spontaneous rising of the residents in the small town of Chrzanów, thirty kilometers west of Cracow. Here peasants, who felt little gratitude toward the Austrian state since they had been voluntarily released from serfdom by the local landlord, and village leaders fled into the woods en masse to escape the threat of conscription. Several hundred local residents, among them village teachers, craftsmen, manorial officials, and a returning émigré, remained in the forest for several months before they were arrested and convicted of treason by Austrian courts. Of the forty-eight arrests made, five were sentenced to death (one teacher, two cobblers, and two "intellectuals"); fourteen (mostly craftsmen) received jail sentences; and the remainder, predominantly peasants, were drafted into the army. Others remained hidden,

---

[19] Those in the "politically suspect" category were not permitted to buy their way out of conscription.

[20] Kieniewicz, *Pomiędzy Stadionem a Goslarem*, 132–33.

supported by the local population, and were never found by the authorities.

For the peasants of Chrzanów, the perceived violation of the emancipation contract between the citizens of Galicia and the Austrian government merited the risk of incurring capital punishment or conscription for treasonous activities. Neither an economic protest nor the result of fear of army service alone (since conscription was the predictable penalty for protest), the Chrzanów rising demonstrates the lengths to which the peasantry would go to express resentment at the indignity associated with a return to the hated system of selection by landlords. From the first moments of emancipation, Galician peasants sought both accountability from their government and control over their own internal affairs. The reversal of Austrian conscription decisions and the events of 1849 in Chrzanów violated both these expectations.

In a further example of clashes between moral norms and written law, village representatives faced difficulties pursuing their political agendas in both the Reichstag and the Sejm because of challenges to their right to sit. Many upper-class deputies viewed as interlopers the thirty-two peasant delegates from Galicia who attended the constituent Reichstag. At least one representative characterized them as merely "sheepskin coats to which the constitutional flower was pinned."[21] Uncomfortable with the villagers' idiosyncratic approach to political debate, upper-class deputies ridiculed their rough-hewn clothes and muddy boots, interrupted their speeches, and refused to accord them the formalities due to them as official representatives. Speeches by peasant deputies were regularly interrupted by loud murmuring, drowned in a sea of laughter, or cut short by the marshall. Fellow deputies refused to address them by the titles accorded to their colleagues ("Mr." or "Deputy") but rather referred to them as either "deputy peasants" or simply by their last names.[22] The peasantry's almost complete ignorance of the German language meant their exclusion from most parliamentary proceedings in the 1848 assembly. Linguistic limitations also provided an opportunity for gentry politicians to distort the content of legislative debates when providing translations for peasant deputies.[23] More salient than this humiliation, however, were the efforts

---

[21] Deputy J. Starkel, *Rok 1848* (Lwów, 1899), 267, as cited in Boryś, "Wybory w Galicji," 33–34.

[22] See *SsSK* (1861), and Boryś, "Wybory w Galicji," 33–34.

[23] The few peasant deputies with competence in German had their credentials challenged by the Reichstag. These included Stanisław Pawlikowski, mayor of Biały Dunajec, who had studied German in grammar school, Jan Sawka, who had picked up German while serving in

taken to evict peasant delegates from the parliamentary proceedings or to dupe them into alliances that violated their interests.

Investigations into the credentials of peasant deputies brought into sharp relief the clash between the leadership priorities of Galician villagers and the legal requirements for formal political engagement. Rural voters supported the most politically experienced candidates for the 1848 Reichstag, many of whom had played leading roles in the antigentry rising of 1846.[24] Yet complaints were lodged against three newly elected activists based on criminal records that had resulted specifically from their participation in the rebellion. After a lengthy investigation all three were permitted to serve, yet another peasant whose fluent German meant he was initially very active in Reichstag debate was disbarred.[25] Thus the very qualities that had recommended these candidates to their village constituents—organizational experience and linguistic competence—were often the cause of their eviction by politicians familiar with imperial law. Reliance on village criteria for selecting national leaders and the tendency to ignore formal legal strictures thus limited the success of peasant political representatives at the imperial and crownland levels.

The Case of Jan Siwiec

Nowhere was the clash of interests more apparent than in the battle over leadership qualifications during the 1861 Sejm in Lwów. With its expanded electoral base, the Sejm had the potential to play a new, socially integrating role in Polish political life. Meeting for the first time since emancipation,[26] the Galician Sejm (formerly the Sejm of the Estates) was recreated with expanded powers and broadened representation,[27] includ-

---

the imperial army, and Bartolomiej Garbryś of Nowy Sącz district. Pawlikowski's very election was hindered when members of the National Council advised illiterate peasant voters that his name was spelled S-t-o-b-n-i-c-k-i. Plechta, "Chłopscy posłowie," 280–81; Boryś, "Wybory w Galicji," 34–35.

[24] The election districts that had been most active in the massacre of 1846 (Bochnia, Tarnów, Bobowa, Kwęczyn, Brzostek, Pilzno, Dębica, Dąbrowa, and Nowy Sącz) all elected peasant delegates in 1848. Kieniewicz, *Pomiędzy Stadionem a Goslarem*, 86–88.

[25] Deputies Tomasz Bodaś and Wojciech Wójtowicz from Dąbrowa were permitted to remain in the parliament. Deputy Jan Sawka, an active participant in the indemnities debate, was disbarred. Boryś, "Wybory w Galicji," 30; Plechta, "Chłopscy posłowie," 280–81.

[26] The last formal meeting of this historic Polish institution had been in 1845. National Sejms and provincial *sejmiki* were held regularly during the pre-1795 Polish Republic. See Jacek Jędruch, *Constitutions, Elections, and Legislatures of Poland, 1493–1993: A Guide to Their History* (New York, 1998).

[27] The Galician provincial Sejm was constituted through the February Patent of 1861. The patent also established two houses of parliament in Vienna. The Sejm had jurisdiction over matters of commune administration, church governance, primary and secondary schools, the

ing peasants for the first time in its deliberations. Thirty-nine peasants traveled to Lwów, many expressing fear of noble conspiracies to reinstate serfdom at the legislative session. Rumors of the restoration of feudal service had resurfaced, prompting the boycott of Sejm elections in a number of precincts.[28] Despite reassurances from gentry deputies that "feudal relations . . . neither now nor in the future can be returned to," and that "relations of equality and the guarantee of property to the peasant" would not be violated, resentment, mistrust and sharply conflicting worldviews continued to separate delegates in this assembly.[29]

Peasant voters' lack of formal political experience led to the appearance in Lwów of a handful of rural deputies who unknowingly lacked the credentials to sit in the Sejm. The debate over their legitimacy highlights the tension between written law and local customary practices in public decision making.[30] Emblematic of these contradictions was the highly publicized case of Jan Siwiec, whose life story itself is symptomatic of the breadth of meaning subsumed within "peasant" identity. Siwiec's relative prosperity and education earned him the respect and votes of the villagers of Łas, in the district of Slemian.[31]

Siwiec was from a prosperous peasant family owning some 45 morgs (61 acres) of land. Although born into serfdom, both Jan Siwiec and his younger brother attended primary and secondary school. Jan was later among the few peasant sons at the University of Lwów when, inspired by the revolution of 1848, he quit school to return home and defend the peasants in their battle over access to common lands. Siwiec's life and experiences familiarized him with many of the problems common to postemancipation peasant communities and yet provided him with a background atypical of most peasant farmers. He fought actively for compensation for lost forest and grazing land, even traveling to Vienna in 1849 with a petition for the emperor. His efforts at popular agitation led to his conscrip-

---

supply and quartering of soldiers, and agricultural and forestry production. See Konstanty Grzybowski, *Galicja, 1848–1914: Historia ustroju politycznego na tle historii ustroju Austrii* (Cracow, 1959), 219–20.

[28] Nonetheless, thanks partly to a government campaign to encourage rural electoral activity, voter turnout was higher in these elections than it had been in 1848. The newspaper *Czas* led a campaign to get voters to the polls, the Galician provincial government circulated fliers encouraging electoral participation, and the Catholic clergy appealed to the peasantry from the pulpit. Stefan Suchonek, "Poseł Jan Siwiec: Karta z dziejów ruchu ludowego w Galicji," in *Studia dziejów kultury* (Warsaw, 1949), 546–47.

[29] Deputy Potocki to the Galician Sejm, *SsSK* (1861), 10.

[30] For information on Galician electoral laws, see Grzybowski, *Galicja*, 192, 237; and Bohdan Winiarski, *Ustrój polityczny ziem polskich w XIX wieku* (Poznań, 1923), 241.

[31] This district is now known as Żywiec.

tion into the imperial army, where he served from 1850 to 1860, traveling extensively throughout the empire and becoming proficient in German. Following his military service, Siwiec worked as a secretary in a law office, where he familiarized himself with Austrian politics and jurisprudence and even wrote a brochure proposing a series of reforms to Austrian civil and criminal law.

Jan Siwiec was clearly not a typical peasant. His education, income, occupation, and experiences all set him apart from the villagers who elected him as their delegate to the Sejm. Yet, as we shall see in chapter 7, Siwiec may have been a typical peasant leader. His roots lay in the village, his consciousness of peasant problems was formed during the revolutions of 1848, and his education and later experiences taught him how to interact with Austrian bureaucrats and Polish gentry alike. His combined sympathy for the peasant plight and understanding of the legal and political system brought him overwhelming support from the peasant communes during the elections of 1861.[32] Siwiec was by far the strongest voice in support of peasant interests during the 1861 Sejm, arguing for a resolution of the servitudes conflict, for a revision of the flawed Austrian land survey, and defending the interests of other peasant delegates whose credentials were challenged.

Yet despite Siwiec's commitment to represent the interests of his constituency and his thorough knowledge of parliamentary procedures, the Sejm credential committee questioned his credentials and his election was ultimately declared invalid. The irony of Siwiec's popularity among his peasant supporters and his subsequent rejection by the Sejm points to an important disjuncture between popular perceptions and upper-class legal restrictions. In response to the accusation that he did not pay sufficient taxes to qualify as a voter (he had not inherited a substantial enough plot of land to ensure adequate annual land taxes), Siwiec argued that his mandate came not from tax records, but from his moral attachment to the peasantry. He described himself as "a child of the people," who possessed "the heart and the skills" to sit in the Sejm regardless of the amount of taxes he paid. "Perhaps my only crime is that I love the people," he concluded.[33] Siwiec's credentials for service were based on community support of his candidacy, which in turn rested on customary interactions and a moral code distinct from the written law governing nonpeasant society. In the formal negotiations of the Sejm, however, deputies' credentials were

---

[32] Report of correspondent from the district of Slemian, *Czas*, April 7, 1861, as cited in Suchonek, "Poseł Jan Siwiec," 548.
[33] Deputy Siwiec to Sejm, *SsSk* (1861), 75–76.

not based on mere "moral judgments or the virtues of deputies." Instead, Austrian law required that the Sejm seek "the establishment of Siwiec's [legal] mandate," a concept of only secondary importance to Siwiec's constituents.[34]

In a similar vein, peasant deputy Antoni Błaż was also ultimately evicted for lack of credentials since he neither owned land nor paid taxes in the commune from which he was elected.[35] In accordance with peasant custom, Błaż had ceded his land to his son five years previously, when the latter came of age and started a family.[36] The son then became the legal owner and paid taxes on the family plot, although father and son continued to work the land together.[37] Ironically, the elder Błaż's age and life stage probably earned him the authority that prompted his nomination by the commune. Since age brought both high status and the necessity of bequeathing land, the very individuals to whom villages looked for leadership—elders such as Błaż and those with worldly experience like Siwiec— were barred from service by the dictates of state law.

Siwiec himself pointed to this disjuncture between written law and moral authority in defending Błaż, commenting on how "sad" the discussion of credentials was. "Although there are such paragraphs in the law," he admitted, "they are cold like you judges who are interpreting it." Written law, Siwiec charged, was indifferent to peasant customs and hence not morally defensible. "The discussions here about whether the elections are valid," he concluded, "are themselves invalid. The only requirements should be that the elector have the trust of the people . . . and be selected by the entire community."[38] Błaż himself expressed frustration with the election criteria, arguing that he was "not at fault in this" and could not be guilty of breaking a law since "they chose" him. Community values held a privileged position in this village conception of leadership criteria, standing above the written laws of the state.

The dispute over credentials in the 1861 Galician Sejm represented an important contradiction between village customs and the upper-class code transcribed in crownland law. The outcome of this dispute—the eviction

---

[34] Deputy Potocki to Sejm, *SsSk* (1861), 81.

[35] Błaż was elected from the village of Orzechów in the Sanok district. *SsSK* (1861), 197.

[36] Land was often ceded when a son reached draft age, since land ownership often saved peasant sons from army service. Jan Siwiec's father, for example, tried unsuccessfully to prevent his son's conscription by ceding him two morgs of land in 1849. Suchonek, "Poseł Jan Siwiec," 542.

[37] "I am a farmer and my son is by my side," explained Błaż by way of characterizing his role on the farm. Deputy Błaż to Sejm, *SsSk* (1861), 198.

[38] Deputy Siwiec to Sejm, *SsSK* (1848), 198.

from the assembly of both Błaż and Siwiec—drove home to village representatives the lack of sympathy for customary practices in formal political fora. Peasant leaders continued in this and other assemblies to seek the reflection of rural traditions in written laws. Yet these early political efforts failed to establish a basis of accommodation among Polish social groups. As long as public debate revolved primarily around issues of economic concern, such as the emancipation settlement, the potential for understanding across the social spectrum was limited. Only a shared national discourse that incorporated elements of the peasantry's vision of the "good life" would make possible open political exchange between social strata be in the Galician context. Common ground in shared experience or goals would be necessary in order to transform the tension between village norms and positive law into a working dialogue.

Customary versus Written Law:
The Indemnities and Servitudes Debates

Debate on the details of the emancipation settlement also revealed the distance separating peasant from upper-class agendas in the Reichstag and the Sejm. Disputes over the question of indemnities payments in the 1848 assembly and the division of common lands (*serwituty*) in the 1861 Sejm demonstrated the level of mutual resentment and economic fear that still drove a wedge between the Polish social classes. The issue of whether and how much indemnity emancipated peasants would pay to their former lords in exchange for their farms brought out the contrasting conceptions of land ownership in the Polish countryside. Peasant Reichstag delegates stressed the immorality of serfdom and demanded compensation from the landlords for generations of oppression. They argued that their usufruct was just compensation for their suffering and even suggested that the scars inflicted by the landlords' "rods and whips" on their "toiling frames" should "serve forever as indemnities."[39]

The gentry countered that they should be compensated for the "voluntary" elimination of feudal institutions during the Sejm of the Estates in 1842–45.[40] Aristocratic politicians had the gall to claim that the upper

[39] Deputy Kapuszczak to the Reichstag, as reprinted in Boryś, "Wybory w Galicji," 34–36. See also Putek, *Pierwsze występy,* 12–13.
[40] Emancipation was discussed but no action taken during this last session of the Sejm of the Estates. Nonetheless, Franciszek Smolka presented this fallacious argument to the Reichstag and was greeted with "tumultuous applause" from the upper-class delegates. Boryś, "Wybory w Galicji," 36–37.

classes had protected peasant society from its inherent laziness by forcing ex-serfs to make indemnities payments. Without the discipline required by these financial hardships, one gentry delegate argued, "it [would] no longer be necessary for [the peasant] to work," and the strength of rural society would consequently suffer.[41] Sharply conflicting visions of public morality in these debates meant that little accommodation was possible between the two sides.

Peasants were also concerned about the ownership of common lands (servitudes or *servituty*), a debate over which was to rage in the countryside for almost a half century, starting with the articulation of opposing claims in the 1861 Sejm. Landlords had long regarded the use of forests, pastures, and meadows held in common by serf and lord as compensation for the serf's work in the fields. Once corvée labor ceased to exist, according to this view, so too did the lord's responsibility to make these lands available for peasant use. In contrast, the newly emancipated peasants argued that the *servituty* were a communal right beginning even before serfdom, and evolving through centuries of customary use. At the very least, they argued, villages should be awarded monetary compensation if their traditional lands were to be confiscated. A similar debate over easement rights flared up in the Congress Kingdom following the 1863 emancipation there. Although negotiated agreements between peasant and lord and state intervention resolved many of the disputes in favor of the peasants, some village communities remained dissatisfied and resorted to massive illegal trespassing and even the use of force during the 1905–6 revolution in the countryside.[42] In Galicia, the Sejm debate on the allocation of forests and pastures revealed a new duality separating the gentry discourse of social accommodation from the true convictions held by gentry policy makers.

The servitudes debate opened with a series of platitudes stressing the supposed importance of the peasant perspective in achieving a satisfactory resolution of the servitudes question. Over a decade had passed since the enfranchisement of Galician peasants. Upper-class Poles had begun to court village public opinion, partially to ensure their own election. Bishop Leon Sapieha, president of the Sejm, emphasized the need to begin the debate with the proposal of the recently evicted Jan Siwiec since it was a

---

[41] Deputy Borkowski to the Reichstag (August 19, 1848), as cited in Boryś, "Wybory w Galicji," 34–35.

[42] See Blobaum, *Rewolucja*, 135–42, Lewis, "Revolution in the Countryside," 1–3, 24–27; and Brodowska, *Ruch chłopski*, 86.

"peasant's petition coming from the village commune." The bishop stressed that "none of us can have devoted quite as much consideration on this account" as Deputy Siwiec, whose opinion was "the more important for us because it comes directly from the understanding of a farmer."[43] In rhetoric very different from that used in the Reichstag emancipation debate, Sapieha explicitly credited Galician peasants with a legitimate perspective on the division of servitude lands.

The apparent harmony between lord and peasant dissolved, however, as delegates became better acquainted with and increasingly frightened by village priorities. Representatives discovered conflicts between their views of property rights and those of the peasant delegates. The latter proposed, for example, that the right to common lands depended not on official documents of ownership or inheritance but on established traditions of use. "He who works the land possesses it," explained a Ukrainian peasant deputy. For Galician peasants, he stressed, "there has never been a question" about this.[44] Since "the truth has always been that no gentleman works," the disputed land, according to this view, clearly belonged to the villagers. In a society where tilling a plot of land over generations established ownership, customary practice was violated when servitudes claims were settled in favor of the lords. "The gentlemen took . . . the fields where our fathers, our grandfathers, our great-grandfathers plowed," complained another peasant deputy, emphasizing the extent to which the confiscation of this "inherited" land conflicted with their understanding of ownership.[45] For the vast majority of peasant land claims, written documents were unavailable. Gentry representatives sarcastically noted that although it would be "far easier" if peasant land "were allocated based on documents, such is not the case." Instead, they complained maliciously that "for every hundred communes, only five possess documents" and that "all others depend on use."[46]

For Galician estate owners, property rights based on usufruct were illegitimate. Gentry landholders were accustomed to official deeds of ownership, which for the most part they but not the peasantry possessed. Nonetheless, in a small percentage of cases, neither side possessed written documentation, and ownership had to be determined by other means. Even in the process of arbitration itself, however, peasants and lords found

[43] The slightly more elevated term "farmer" (*włościanin*) is used here rather than the often derogatory *chłop* (peasant). Sejm president Sapieha to Sejm, *SsSK* (1861), 300–301.
[44] Deputy Krawców to Sejm, ibid., 348.
[45] Deputy Kołbasiuk to Sejm, ibid., 317.
[46] Count Wodzicki to Sejm, ibid., 324.

themselves at odds with one another. Village claimants, accustomed to legal powerlessness, approached the judicial system with profound mistrust. They complained that small farmers "could not penetrate this process," since the gentlemen "know the best lawyers," had the ability to bribe officials, and possessed the connections to delay the machinery of arbitration. The result was the perception that "even when a peasant has a paper, that does not allow him to collect wood," since gentry lawyers were always able to "find excuses" to deny the village its "rights."[47]

Conditioned by centuries of legally sanctioned abuses, Galician peasants were reticent to acknowledge the legitimacy of judicial verdicts. Instead, they sought a system for resolving disputed claims that (unlike the imperial court system) took account of land usage as a basis for ownership. They specifically proposed the inclusion of village participants on arbitrational boards, which of course gentry parliamentarians steadfastly opposed. Conservative gentry delegates argued that poorly educated villagers were ill equipped to recognize "the difference between rustical property and demesne property," to understand the Josephine agricultural survey of 1820, the 1860 cadastral survey, or the "various decrees [that] have been issued on the basis of these documents."[48] The peasantry's legal understanding was also marred by an "irrational" approach to property rights, based on the "convenience" of the commune rather than on "the [written] law." Gentry spokesmen failed to understand the consistency in peasant perceptions of land ownership, charging villagers with "getting giddy in the head and coming up with demands that are illogical." They are like children in a candy store, commented one deputy. They "cry . . . when they see candy that they want and that is not given to them."[49]

Unable to reconcile peasant land claims with their own understanding of document-based written law, gentry deputies were increasingly struck by the sharp differences separating Polish classes. Many upper-class Sejm deputies regarded the peasantry's unwillingness to recognize property rights as a violation of the fundamental basis on which European civilization was built. Peasant efforts to incorporate elements of rural traditions and customary practices into the Galician law code were thus rejected by upper-class representatives frightened by the implications of these legal shifts. Compromise legislation proposed by peasant deputy Szpunar, for example, declaring forests and pastures a "public good" owned by no one, was greeted with utter derision from conservative representatives. Count

---

[47] Deputies Szpunar, Kowbasiuk, Procak, and Bielewicz to Sejm, ibid., 317–50.
[48] Deputy Count Dzieduszycki to Sejm, ibid., 313–14.
[49] Deputy Father Sanguszko to Sejm, ibid., 308–9.

Potocki summarized this view, pronouncing the proposed compromise tantamount to "the abolition of the right to property, the foundation of all societies." Acceptance of the peasants' community-based conception of property rights as a foundation of written law in Galicia would, in the view of gentry leaders, lead to "the ruin of the countryside [and] the ruin of the entire country."[50]

Although initially more sympathetic to the village agenda than the 1848 parliament, this first Polish assembly to include representatives from the lower classes concluded by recommending that peasant input should simply be ignored. "As a simple person," conservative deputy Ziemiałkowski declared, the peasant lacked "the ability to differentiate" between (written) legal and (customary) illegal practices. Far from attempting to integrate the rural perspective into crownland law codes, Ziemiałkowski characterized the village attitude toward property rights as a "social ill . . . [and] a cancer" that, if not excised, would affect the whole "body of society."[51] The village "code" of conduct was officially declared a legacy of feudalism that needed to be purged from the peasantry's consciousness as it entered public life.[52] The judgment of upper-class legislators notwithstanding, elements of such thinking would continue to inform peasant politics for some years to come.

Village delegates to Polish and imperial representative institutions discovered in the early years following emancipation that their new status did not guarantee legal equality with their former lords. Their experiences in representative bodies helped underline the extent to which social and cultural attitudes formed under conditions of serfdom still had a powerful influence on political interactions with the gentry. Despite what may initially have been good-faith efforts to resolve the deeper tensions remaining from serfdom, the cultural divide separating Polish social strata constituted an insurmountable barrier to workable political negotiations in this period.

After a disappointing lack of progress on their reform agenda in the Sejm and Reichsrat, peasant leaders retreated to their village homes and pursued an often vigorous program of reform through local political and

---

[50] Deputy Count Potocki to Sejm, ibid., 356–57.

[51] Deputy Ziemiałkowski to Sejm, ibid., 335.

[52] For a counter example, see Peter Czap's characterization of the development of two distinct law codes in Russia after emancipation, leading to the development of a separate system of rural administration and justice in Russia between 1861 and 1912. Peter Czap Jr., "Peasant-Class Courts and Peasant Customary Justice in Russia, 1861–1912," *Journal of Social History* 1, no. 2 (winter 1967): 149–78.

economic institutions. They devised strategies to make their agenda heard, including the eventual formation of working relations with influential nonpeasants. The public sphere as it was constituted in the village would thus take shape first among reform-minded villagers, then incorporate the help of urban intellectuals. Only in the last years of the century would rural civil society reconnect with the national political process, forming a socially inclusive national public sphere.

Chapter Four

Making Government Work: The Village Commune as a School for Political Action

In the past thirty years . . . as a result of active participation in *gmina* and district matters, a new generation has come up in the countryside, a generation significantly different from earlier ones. The horizon of its thinking has broadened; its subjects have diversified as familiarity with the laws under which the people live and the relations in which they live has come from an expansion and clarification of familiarity with the outside world—the larger world. Through energetic activity, their ideas have become sharper and their capability for thought and understanding has improved.

Stanisław Tarnowski, head of Galician Conservative Party, 1896

Despite the passion and moral outrage with which peasant delegates pursued their agenda in the Reichsrat and the Sejm, a combination of linguistic barriers, inexperience, and a lack of allies prevented them from establishing an influential presence in political life outside the village. Instead, for the generation coming of age after 1861, participation in the institutions of communal self-government represented the crucial training ground in which to familiarize themselves with modern political life. In combination with debate in rural newspapers and the increased use of crownland law courts, active engagement in local government helped create a public sphere, in which all villagers could openly contest political decisions. The growing vitality of these institutions helped establish a pattern of debate and negotiation in the countryside, signaling the transition to modernity in public affairs. Peasants began to find value in written law as a basis for conflict resolution and public interaction, bringing them one step closer to finding a common language with which to communicate with upper-class Poles.

The challenge to traditional practices involved in the peasantry's increased reliance on law codes and governmental apparatus had the effect of displacing certain members of village communities and promoting the interests of others. Participation in commune self-government and the use of law courts to resolve neighborly disputes prompted the formation of increasingly rigid and hostile factions, with those perceived to have access to power and influence pitted against the self-proclaimed impotent. Although these factions remained fluid and mutable in the early period of self-government, the more formalized nature of peasant conflict represented by electoral campaigns and legal proceedings served to shut out large numbers of villagers from access to power. As a result, the mobilization of smallholders into national associations and institutions would be selective and incomplete, drawing initially on villagers with experience in local governmental affairs and other leadership positions.

The Evolution of the Self-Governing Commune

Service on village councils was particularly important to the evolution of peasant politics in this period because it was one of the few types of formal participation available to peasants in the face of noble attempts to exclude them from crownland politics. After the Polish gentry formally pledged its loyalty to the Austrian emperor in 1866, Galicia's autonomous government was placed firmly in the hands of the conservatives.[1] Led by a group of nobles from Cracow, known as *stańczycy*,[2] these conservatives worked for some two decades to remove peasant and burgher representatives from their positions in crownland government and to maintain a monopoly on political power. Using a number of elaborate polling tricks (see chapter 9), the *stańczycy* prevented the reelection in 1867 of any peasant deputies from the 1861 Sejm. Not a single smallholder was sent to the Sejm in either the 1876 or 1883 sessions, and only in 1889 did peasant influence gradually return to the Lwów assembly. Peasant representation in the Viennese Reichsrat also dropped sharply from its high in 1848 of

[1] The new administrative structure consisted of two parallel hierarchies of governance, one branch comprising the provincial Sejm, its Governing Board (Wydział Krajowy), the School Council (Rada Szkolna), and district councils (rady powiatowe); and the other, a branch of the Austrian imperial bureaucracy, made up of the governor general (*namiestnik*) in Lwów, district governors (*starostowie*), and the local commune governments (*gminy*). Kieniewicz, *Galicja*, xiv–xv, xxv–xxviii.

[2] Named after the sixteenth-century court jester under King Sigismund I whose name their 1869 pamphlet bore (*Teka Stańczyka*), the *stańczycy* broke with the tradition of national uprisings and advocated loyalty to the Habsburg emperor as a means for political reform. See Lawrence D. Orton, "The *Stańczyk* Portfolio and the Politics of Galician Loyalism," *Polish Review* 27, nos. 1–2 (1982): 55–64.

thirty-three to a mere two smallholders elected in 1873 and one each in 1876 and 1886.[3] With ever-diminishing opportunities for representation in crownland government, Galician peasants retreated to the countryside, turning away from national concerns and focusing instead on local issues and activities.

The promulgation of the Austrian Commune Law of 1866 coincided closely with gentry attempts to exclude peasants from imperial and crownland political bodies. The new law effectively eliminated the subordination of village government to manorial administration, creating instead a separate administrative structure for every single settlement unit—villages, towns, cities—with officers elected by local citizens. All landed estates not administratively tied to a village commune at the time the law came into effect were to be governed and financed separately from the villages.[4] Unlike the system of rural administration established in the Congress Kingdom after emancipation, which joined several villages and estate lands into an administrative unit (also called a *gmina*), the Galician reform introduced single-village governance.[5] Although many complained that the *gminy* were too small to be efficient and lacked qualified people to fill village offices, the system provided political experience for new peasant citizens. First, the new law placed the entire financial burden for supporting rural facilities on the shoulders of villagers since manorial farms were exempted from all taxes and fees within the commune.[6] Second, it disqualified gentry, government officials, clergy, and teachers from holding positions in village government, forcing peasants into leadership roles.

After the law came into effect, commune treasuries were expected to take over responsibility for the building and repairing of parish churches, the maintenance and staffing of rural schools and hospitals, and primary responsibility for the repair of roads and bridges.[7] The disqualification of

---

[3] Stanisław Rymar, "Chłopi polscy w Parlamentach i Sejmach, 1848–1939," unpublished manuscript, ZHRL, O-158, 115, 140–42, 152–53; Dunin-Wąsowicz, *Dzieje Stronnictwa Ludowego*, 29. On the activities of Polish representatives to the Austrian Parliament, see Philip Pajakowski, "The Polish Club and Austrian Parliamentary Politics, 1873–1900," Ph.D. diss., Indiana University, 1989.

[4] Pilat, *Pogląd historyczny*, 31–32.

[5] On the administration of the Congress Kingdom countryside, see Lewis, "Revolution in the Countryside," 9–12; and Brodowska, *Ruch chłopski*, 112–17.

[6] Virtually all landed estates separated from adjacent villages administratively in order to absolve themselves from financial responsibility for maintaining the village infrastructure. The census of 1869 shows an almost twofold increase in "rural communes" in comparison to the census of 1857 because of the number of estates separating off from the villages. Pilat, *Pogląd historyczny*, 50–51; Inglot, *Historia chłopów*, 241–44; Bujak, "Wieś zachodnio-galicyjska," 334–36; Kieniewicz, *Galicja*, xix.

[7] The Road Law, in particular, demanding a set number of labor days from each peasant household, was a source of discontent among the peasantry. Villagers viewed the labor

the upper classes from serving in village government forced inexperienced peasants into political and leadership positions. The immediate effect of the new Commune Law was thus the isolation of Galician villagers both from their former lords and from the protection of the Viennese government. In the course of fifty years of rural self-administration,[8] however, participation in the organs of village government helped create a more politically active stratum of peasants with increasing expectations for public life.

Participation in commune government stimulated the peasantry to reevaluate its attitudes toward authority and to redefine its public service expectations. Although elected leaders were frequently guilty of corruption, abuse of power, and mismanagement in the early years of commune self-government, villagers soon reformed local government and made it more accountable to their needs. They were often assisted in their efforts by outside authorities, such as district governors, members of the clergy, and editors of peasant newspapers, who were able to pressure village officers into compliance with the law. Peasant mayors in Galicia tended to be more responsive to the wishes of their rural constituency, even where it meant challenging higher authorities, than their counterparts in the Congress Kingdom, where Russian authorities frequently replaced disloyal rural administrators.[9]

The process of challenging local authorities, including peasant mayors, meant a transition from the villagers' deferential attitudes toward administrators under serfdom. Partially as an inheritance from their subject position prior to emancipation, ex-serfs looked on their local administrators with attitudes ranging from "deference," "respect," and absolute "obedience," to "fear" and even "hatred." As late as the 1880s, contemporary researchers noted that "in general, the peasantry . . . exhibit the deference for all forms of authority . . . found among the serfs" and that they often felt "at the mercy of the arbitrariness" of the authority figure.[10]

The self-governing village commune (*gmina*) consisted of a village mayor (*wójt*), two or more assistants, a secretary (*pisarz*), sometimes a

---

requirement as reminiscent of serfdom and objected to the repair of roads and bridges near estates that they rarely used. Several incidents of peasant resistance to the Road Law and frequent efforts in the Sejm to reform it failed to bring about a satisfactory resolution.

[8] Attempts were made to reform *gmina* administration in the Sejms of 1868, 1871, and 1873/74; however, no comprehensive alternative was ever approved. Inglot, *Historia chłopów*, 241–42.

[9] The tight control Russian authorities maintained over village officers in Russian Poland led many peasant governors of the Congress Kingdom to oppose their fellow farmers' agitation for greater independence from the Russian empire. Brodowska, *Ruch chłopski*, 132–34; Blobaum, *Rewolucja*, 123–35.

[10] Bujak, *Żmiąca*, 134–36; Pilat, *Wiadomości statystyczne*, 82–84.

treasurer (*kasjer*), and a village council ranging in size from eight to thirty-six members, depending on population. The most important figure in the new village administration was the village mayor or *wójt*. Although law limited his official duties, tradition and the structure of rural society endowed the *wójt* with extensive local power and authority. Officially, the *wójt* was responsible for enforcing all crownland and imperial laws in the village, including assessing, collecting and paying taxes; organizing peasants for roadwork; assisting conscription agents; and sometimes serving as the local sheriff.[11] In theory, many of these activities were to be conducted in conjunction with the village council, which was charged with controlling financial matters, overseeing the *wójt*'s activities, appointing *gmina* officials, conducting elections, and determining punishments for lawbreakers. However, in practice, the council members' lack of familiarity with the machinery of government (and initial lack of interest) meant that the mayor himself often had a free hand in village administration. During the first several years of *gmina* self-government, many village mayors were reluctant to call council meetings in which their authority might be challenged and, instead, in the absence of a village police officer or treasurer, tended to matters of discipline and finance on their own.

In the 1860s and 1870s, very few village mayors were literate or had a clear understanding of the laws they were charged with enforcing. Local authorities judged less than 12 percent of the crownland's village mayors to be qualified in 1876. Although about 20 percent of mayors had a weak ability to read and/or write, many did not have "a minimal familiarity with the law," "know what was expected of them," or "understand what the secretary presented them to sign."[12] The early years of communal self-government were characterized therefore by a haphazard administration at best, and at worst a reign of chaos and corruption. Rural government was placed in the hands of "uneducated, inefficient, and impractical" individuals who led the *gmina* to "disorder" and governed based on inability and "bad will." Survey respondents characterized fifty-seven of the eighty-eight village mayors in Limanowa district, for example, as "lacking in energy," and seven as habitual drinkers. Elsewhere, "not a single trace of orderly work" was accomplished because of badly qualified mayors. Even those officials with some reading knowledge were said to "have no sense of the spirit of the law and make absolutely no use of legal books."[13] Council sessions were rarely called in the early years of self-government.[14]

[11] Inglot, *Historia chłopów*, 242–43.
[12] Józef Kleczyński, *Życie gminne w Galicji* (Lwów, 1878), 127–29, 140–42.
[13] Kleczyński, *Życie gminne*, 134.
[14] Some 27 percent of the communes held no meeting in 1874, and only 8 percent called more than six meetings. Kleczyński, *Życie gminne*, 169–72.

Wójt from the village of Wola Justowska in the traditional dress of the Cracow district. Photograph by J. Eder. Courtesy of the Ethnographic Museum, Cracow. Inventory number III/44908/F. Reproduction by Jacek Kubiena.

When meetings were held, councillors reportedly met in the tavern and drank at the *gmina's* expense.

Yet within a decade after the inauguration of the self-government system, villagers began to take action to correct their mayors' administrative ineptness and financial corruption. Bucking the tradition of infrequent council meetings and casual assemblies in the inn, they called to account mayors who did "not even assemble the *gmina* council."[15] They challenged those guilty of misappropriation of village funds or having "a night on the town" rather than conducting official business. They expressed embarrassment at the behavior of their leaders who "set a horrible example" and failed to demonstrate that emancipated peasants could conduct themselves in an "enlightened and progressive manner."[16] In one egregious case in 1876, the villagers of Kopki complained not only that their mayor "conducted all his business in the tavern," but that "the poor farmers had to buy him a drink to get business done."[17]

From a practical point of view, village critics argued that such neglect of official responsibilities could have severe consequences for the welfare of the commune. When a *wójt* did not "do in good time" what the district governor ordered him to, the result could be forced conscription of villagers into the imperial army,[18] the ruin of local fields and forests, or the disappearance of money from *gmina* coffers. Appeals from constituents complain of the neglected *gmina* roads, schools falling into disrepair, mills in disorder, the embezzlement of funds, and the abuse of public lands.[19] In 1890, the peasants of Szlachtowa wrote, for example, to the Nowy Targ district governor that their *wójt* and his officers had not only failed to protect their woods and fields but reserved these lands for the exclusive use of their friends. And members of the Czarny Dunajec and Jaworki communes wrote "with a sick heart" that those who stole firewood from the local forests did not fear fines for their behavior since the *wójci* "had never punished anyone in the past."[20]

---

[15] Maciej Gaźda, Mykita Hołowacz, Antoni Sroka, and Hrehory Burztyka (near Jarosław) to *Pszczółka*, March 13, 1879, 41–42; F. K. (Jazłowiec) to *Wieniec*, March 24, 1876, 5.
[16] Letter from near Sambor to *Pszczółka*, May 2, 1878, 4.
[17] Kopki, June 23, 1876, to *Pszczółka*, August 24, 1876, 3. District officials in the Sanok district also complained of government sessions being conducted in taverns. Kleczyński, *Życie gminne*, 134–35.
[18] Maciej Gaźda et al. (near Jarosław) to *Pszczółka*, March 13, 1879, 41–42.
[19] Villagers of Szlachtowa (1890) and villagers of Groń to *starostwo* (district governor) in Nowy Targ, Archiwum Państwowe Miasta Krakowa i Województwa Krakowskiego (hereafter APKr), ST.NT.18, Pl. 13.
[20] Complaints from the communes of Szlachtowa (1889), Groń, Czarny Dunajec (1879), and Jaworki (July 2, 1885), Nowy Targ Starostwo, ibid.

The potential for corruption was increased by the tendency for the village clerk or *pisarz* to amass more power than his nonelective position warranted. The *pisarz* was responsible for all official (and often unofficial) correspondence between the village and the other political institutions in the crownland. In theory, the *pisarz* was to serve the *wójt* and the village council that appointed him, but his powers frequently surpassed this subordinate position for at least two reasons. First, whereas crownland law prohibited the election of government officials, teachers, or clergy to the office of village mayor, members of these social groups were permitted to serve as *pisarz*.[21] An experienced and literate secretary could actually govern the village in the absence of a qualified *wójt*. Since the vast majority of village mayors were chosen from among the smallholders themselves,[22] the clerk was generally more worldly than his peasant superior. Second, since very few *wójci* were themselves literate,[23] the *pisarz* could easily submit documents against the mayor and councilmen's wishes, while the latter remained unaware of any inconsistency. So great were the apparent responsibilities of the village *pisarz* that he was seen by many as the most important actor in autonomous village life.[24] Yet clerks too came in for strong criticism as poorly qualified, "simple" people unfamiliar with the law and "barely literate." District governors from among the gentry attacked commune secretaries for their perceived inaccuracy, laziness, selfishness, "greed," "disobedience," "abuse of power," and tendency to "take advantage of the incapabilities and trust of their superiors." By some accounts, rural clerks were simply "bad people" who exploited the population and "wasted away the *gmina* property," or even "drunks" and "rowdies," who were "morally ruined."[25] Clearly those outside the village saw room for improvement in the conduct of rural self-government. Rural

[21] Crownland law was not able consistently to displace local custom, and the appointment of nonpeasant intellectuals as clerks continued in many rural areas. As of 1875, only 47 percent of village scribes were full-time farmers. Some 22 percent were teachers, 4 percent were officials, 3 percent were large landholders, 3 percent were merchants, and 2 percent were priests. Kleczyński, *Życie gminne*, 118–23.

[22] Some 99 percent of Galician village mayors were professional farmers in 1875. Kleczyński, *Życie gminne*, 123–26.

[23] During the period 1874–77, only 20 percent of all Galician *wójci* had even a weak reading knowledge. Yet village mayors appear to have been chosen from among the better-educated farmers, since the literacy rate among mayors was higher than for the rural population as a whole. The best-educated officers were elected in the western part of the crownland, while over 90 percent of commune officials in eastern Galicia were illiterate. Many mayors may also have learned to read once they were elected, as in the Congress Kingdom countryside. Kleczyński, *Życie gminne*, 127–32; Brodowska, *Ruch chłopski*, 154.

[24] Kleczyński, *Życie gminne*, 117–18, 135–36.

[25] Bujak, *Żmiąca*, 134; Kleczyński, *Życie gminne*, 140–43, 155–57.

residents themselves soon learned to make use of governmental machinery to eliminate the worse abuses of their local officers.

Grassroots Reform and Local Accountability in the Village Commune

The Galician village of the 1860s and 1870s was governed according to an administrative system that initially had difficulty policing itself. Its participants were unfamiliar with the appropriate channels for reform, and most were disinclined to challenge the authority of officeholders. As villagers gained experience in local government, however, many of them sought to bring their administrative bodies more in line with local needs, relying increasingly on the village council as an instrument of social and economic improvement. Customary village practices and long-standing social attitudes began to wane, as the benefits of formal law became apparent to peasant reformers. The shift to a more active political approach thus involved an increased willingness to challenge traditional forms of authority and a more critical relationship to the social and political sources of power.

The structure of crownland administration provided numerous opportunities for the oversight of local governors. Commune mayors were required to transmit information about local administrative activities to the district governor and to the governor general in Lwów. Election results for *gmina* positions were sent to the district office for approval. Other administrative matters, such as the appointment of a new postmaster, treasurer, or secretary, required formal acceptance by the district governor. District officials processed requests for exceptions to crownland law and complaints about election results. Villagers employed this hierarchy of accountability to challenge *gmina* election results or procedure and to complain of dishonest or inefficient village officers. In time, traditional deference toward officeholders eroded.

The respect and awe in which many villagers held their *wójt* under serfdom (because of his important position as arbitrator between village and manor) was transformed after emancipation by a new set of responsibilities. No longer at the mercy of the landlord's arbitrary will, the village mayor now represented a link between the village and the entire imperial administration. As such, the *wójt* was increasingly perceived as a spokesman for villagers' concerns at the same time that he was expected to implement the will of the state.

Within a decade after the introduction of the self-governing commune system, smallholders made use of written law to question the credentials of village officers and to replace them with commune officials more responsive to the wishes of their constituents.[26] They sought allies elsewhere in the Galician administrative structure, appealing to district governors, to the governor general in Lwów, to peasant editors, and occasionally even the emperor himself for assistance against intransigent and dishonest local rulers. Activist villagers became sophisticated and discerning in their tactics and in the alliances they forged to make local government more accountable to their interests.

The first line of attack for frustrated villagers was the district office, which annually received hundreds of complaints about the activities of commune officers, often dictated by illiterate peasants to local secretaries or priests. Carefully detailing the nature of the alleged violation, the complaints display detailed knowledge of imperial and crownland laws in their frequent and accurate citation of relevant legal passages.[27] Greater comprehension of crownland election laws allowed villagers to submit petitions assessing the legal eligibility of village councilmen to serve (a far cry from their custom-based discussions of eligibility as recently as the 1861 Sejm). In 1886, a complaint from Odrowaz, Nowy Targ district, argued that all eight recently elected members of the village council were legally ineligible to hold *gmina* office because they "paid no land taxes" and thus were not legal members of the commune.[28] Similarly, six villagers from nearby Mizerna complained in 1882 that their new *wójt* could not legally take office since he owned no property in the *gmina*.[29] The electors of Kęty, Nowy Targ district, also requested a reelection in 1870 because of a violation of election laws.[30]

In a volte-face from the behavior of peasant representatives in the 1861 Sejm, villagers had begun to use written law to their own benefit, even where it overturned traditional practices. As will be demonstrated in chapter 7, attitudes among some villagers evolved in the postemancipation period to challenge election abuse, governmental corruption, alcohol abuse, and other well-entrenched village practices. Written crownland or

---

[26] Pilat, *Wiadomości statystyczne*, 82–84.

[27] As in the 1885 complaint from Groń, Nowy Targ district, accusing the *wójt* of campaign violations in inaccurately transcribing the names peasants called out for their (oral) votes and similar complaints from the communes of Czarny Dunajec, Jaworki (July 1885) and Szlachtowa (1890), Nowy Targ district. APKr, ST.NT.18, Pl. 13.

[28] Józef Ostręba, *gmina* Odrowąż to the *starostwo* in Nowy Targ (February 12, 1886), APKr, ST.NT.18, Pl.13.

[29] Mizerna to *starostwo* in Nowy Targ (November 24, 1882), APKr, ST.NT.18, Pl. 13.

[30] Kęty to *starostwo* in Biała (1870), APKr, St.B.51.

imperial law was often employed as an instrument for reinforcing one faction or the other as "traditional" practices went through periods of transition.

Elected officials also began to police one another in an effort to bring about responsible local government. In some cases these protests were supported by a large majority of village leaders, as when the entire council of the *gmina* of Jaworki requested the replacement of their mayor in 1883 for "not conducting commune affairs in accordance with the law." According to the complaint, the current *wójt* had embezzled funds from the *gmina* treasury, failed to protect the *gmina* forest, neglected the roads and the school, and "used various official functions for his own good."[31] The following year, ten council members from the nearby *gmina* of Odrowąż complained to their district governor that the current village scribe, Antoni Łas, "charged too much for his services." Moreover, Łas was said to have fraudulently collected funds for a land tax two years running, only to turn the money over to the *wójt* for the latter's personal use.[32] Clearly, Galician villagers were finding ways to make use of crownland law to challenge practices such as bribery and unfettered use of the woods. Such challenges to activities perceived as damaging to the commune's well-being demonstrate a decline in the preemancipation "fatalism" characterizing many Galician villages and an upsurge of activism as the possibilities for improving local conditions became more palpable.

After rural newspapers began to circulate regularly in the countryside beginning in 1875, disgruntled villagers also employed the press to publicize their complaints about local conditions. Already in 1876, residents of the village of Załośce published a letter in the peasant newspaper, *Wieniec*, complaining of election irregularities committed by the incumbent local mayor, along with a copy of their petition of protest, signed by seven hundred villagers. The district governor "threw the old *wójt* out of office and ordered the newly elected one to begin immediately."[33] Through such published complaints and letters, Galician peasants were able to debate publicly the appropriate uses of village government, both among themselves and with local intellectuals reading the rural press. Such public discussions helped create a critical public in which peasant readers were encouraged to participate. (See chapter 8 regarding the larger role of the press in formulating peasant identity.)

---

[33] Załośce to *Wieniec*, August 17, 1876, 4.
[31] Josafat Surma et al., Jaworki, to *starostwo* in Nowy Targ (July 2, 1885), APKr, ST.NT.18, Pl. 13.
[32] Józef Ostręba et al., Odrowąż, to *starostwo* in Nowy Targ (February 12, 1886), ibid.

Notwithstanding the massive nature of the Załośce protest, newspaper correspondence was a uniquely individual act, requiring a villager visibly to step out from the crowd and express an opinion that, in the case of critiquing local government, was not typically a consensus view. The act of publicly registering criticism of local conditions and village leaders was part of a larger breakdown of rural consensus on public affairs, helping to establish local factions. Though it is clearly difficult to assess which letters were written by small farmers and which by priests or teachers, a high percentage of rural intellectuals were themselves peasant born. As we will see in chapter 7, the boundary between the categories of peasant and nonpeasant in the village was extremely porous.

Rural newspapers also carried discussions reflecting frustration with public drunkenness. Despite the legal requirement that the antidrunkenness law of 1868 be posted prominently in every tavern, its enforcement was extremely lax. Villagers openly expressed to editors their resentment of local officials who allowed many "unsteady folks" to wander the village.[34] Everywhere concerned villagers called upon the unseen public of rural newspaper readers to help reinforce crownland activities in the enforcement of laws perceived as protecting rural society.

Reflecting preexisting ethnic and religious tensions in village life, the rural press often debated methods for removing members of non-Polish ethnic groups, including Jews, from local councils in the belief that they worked against the interests of "real" Poles. Letters suggested that local Catholics were "paid by the Jews" to support certain candidates in elections or that Jewish members of village councils were preventing the enforcement of drunkenness laws. Readers encouraged one another to "elect one of their own" in order to "improve the welfare of the *gmina*," and many attributed the failure to enforce drunkenness laws to the fact that "the entire village council consists of Jews."[35] Remedies for these and other rural "problems" circulated in the peasant press, including at least one request to the emperor himself for an imperial commission to come to the village and investigate the ostensible monopoly on local power by *shtetl* Jews.[36]

Such claims of Jewish monopolies on village councils are difficult to substantiate. Jewish property owners were legally entitled to full membership in the commune and to represent themselves in municipal government after 1867, and Jewish names do appear on communal administrative

---

[34] Near Bochnia to *Pszczółka*, January 9, 1878, 4.
[35] Izdebki to *Wieniec*, May 26, 1876, 5; Jazłowiec to *Pszczółka*, August 8, 1878, 3.
[36] F. K., Jazłowiec, to *Wieniec*, March 24, 1876, 5.

documents in the governor general's office.[37] The fraction of Jewish residents in Galician *shtetl* communities ranged as high as 70 percent, and some 30 percent of the crownland's total Jewish population resided in the countryside. Yet outside of the *shtetl* towns, Jews formed no more than 3–4 percent of total village residents.[38] Regardless of how widespread Jewish council members were, perceptions of increased Jewish control certainly influenced many subscribers to the rural press.

Debate in rural newspapers in turn brought about the evolution of a clearer vision of the qualities preferred in local officials. Peasant leaders sang the praises of upstanding local governors in order to critique unacceptable ones. Stressing moral rectitude and honesty in implementing the state's laws, peasant critics revealed their increased attachment to crownland laws when they corresponded to their changing conceptions of appropriate leadership qualities. Accordingly, state laws were deemed positive when they provided support for local anti-alcohol campaigns or control of usury, negative when they removed villagers' rights to forests and pasture land. Councillors who were "sober and solid" were recommended over those who were "harsh," unfair, and conducted their business in taverns. Villagers found in the pages of the peasant press information on how to prevent the election of "drunks . . . as councilmen and dishonest *wójci*." Although village mayors often used their power in an arbitrary way, by the 1880s and 1890s rural voters increasingly called *wójci* to account via the peasant press and asked for their replacement.[39]

By the late 1870s, literacy was regarded as an asset for village mayors, in contrast to the earlier preference for simple "virtue and understanding" in mayoral candidates. Candidates were encouraged to "at least know how to read" because otherwise the "*wójt* would know only as much as the *pisarz* told him." How could the mayor be expected to punish parents who did not send their children to school, queried peasant writers, if he himself could not read?[40] Rural readers learned of alliances struck between mayoral candidates and village schoolteachers to mobilize voters to support those who were "friends of the school" and who encouraged education in their constituency. The old *wójt* in one commune had always "turned his head away when walking by in order to avoid looking at the

[37] On the lengthy process of emancipating Galician Jews between 1848 and 1867, see Artur Eisenbach, *The Emancipation of the Jews in Poland, 1780–1870* (Oxford, 1991), 344–46, 367–68, 405, 496–504.

[38] Wasiutyński provides information for 131 *shtetlach* (*osady miejskie*), ranging in population from 295 to 5,600 total residents in 1880 and comprising 1.5 percent to 70 percent Jewish residents. *Ludność żydowska*, 106–8, 132–58.

[39] *Przyjaciel Ludu*, March 15, 1891, 88.

[40] Jan Rajda, Wieprz, Jarosławski district, to *Pszczółka*, February 27, 1879, 25–26.

[dilapidated] school building" and avoid repairing it. When he sought reelection, the villagers, with help from the local intelligentsia, disappointed his efforts.[41] By contrast, a letter writer from Łoszniów lauded the "good grace" of his community's recently reelected mayor through whose influence a new school building was being erected and the parish church restored.[42] Local intelligentsia increasingly became part of election campaigns, helping villagers to determine "who was and was not their friend" and to assemble village councils reflecting their education needs.[43]

Newspaper campaigns were also used to publicize suggestions for better organization and use of village funds. One letter suggested that mayors read relevant laws aloud at council meetings in order to educate council members.[44] Others proposed renovation of school buildings, the establishment of savings banks, and the repair of churches. Such suggestions were frequently tied to anti-alcohol campaigns in which the funds villagers spent on alcohol were proposed as contributions to community improvement. "I would prefer to see the tavern closed," penned one peasant from Kopki, who advocated using the same funds to "resurrect our school, which has stood empty for some eighteen years." A peasant from Sambor district argued that "if the *gmina* has so much money" that the entire council can spend its evenings in the tavern, "it should put it into a savings bank."[45]

Peasant letters also helped promote cultural and economic improvements, as in the case of the *wójt* from Brzezina, who discussed his plans to organize a village theater in an 1874 letter to *Wieniec*.[46] Residents of a village in Tarnopol district wrote in 1874 to announce they had constructed a storage facility to help local residents by buying wholesale goods in large quantities at reduced prices.[47] And several *gmina* governments reported in 1875 that they had pledged to stop drinking.[48]

Public Conflict and Rural Litigation

In addition to appealing to district governors and publicizing the transgressions of local officials in the peasant press, peasants turned to the

---

[41] J. L., Brzeziny (June 8, 1876), to *Pszczółka*, August 24, 1876, 3.
[42] M., Łoszniów (July 30, 1876), to *Pszczółka*, September 7, 1876, 4.
[43] Andrzej Batycki, Dynów, to *Pszczółka*, June 16, 1876, 3.
[44] Maciej Gaźda et al., near Jarosław, to *Pszczółka*, March 13, 1879, 41–42.
[45] Kopki (June 23, 1876) to *Pszczółka*, August 24, 1876, 3; Samborski district to *Pszczółka*, May 2, 1878, 4.
[6] Jan Chmura, Brzezina (August 20, 1874), to *Wieniec*, September 17, 1875, 7.
[47] *Wieniec*, May 1, 1875, 66.
[48] Ibid.

courts for redress of their grievances, contributing still further to the splintering of village society into factions and interest groups. After emancipation peasants were permitted to bring their petitions to district courts, where they presented increasingly sophisticated cases both against their former lords and against one another. The imperial court system thus became a central site for negotiation and opinion formation in the postemancipation public sphere. Although imperial law had long granted villagers the right to petition their lords,[49] emancipation brought expanded access to the court system while offering new motives for peasant litigation.

The rapid growth of rural litigation after emancipation resulted from several factors. Land hunger in the early years of emancipation brought about the frequent redistribution of plots and consequent disputes over property lines. New civil procedures for trials meant that cases were often heard on seemingly trivial matters and were permitted to drag on for long periods of time. Finally, official and unofficial scribes (*pisarze*) and official notaries began to view litigation as a means of earning a living, spawning the growth of an entire class of rural "intellectuals," including large numbers of *shtetl* Jews, who grew up around the law courts.[50]

In the early postemancipation period, legal proceedings reflected the social cohesion peasants felt in opposition to their former lords. Entire villages set out to sue their landlords for the injustices and abuses imposed on them under serfdom. Petitions charged that former serfs had been forced to work more days than legally required under serfdom; to provide extralegal services; and pay excessive taxes. The specificity of these early complaints reveals a clear familiarity with the law and with the litigation process.[51] In protest against the continuation of feudal obligations after emancipation, peasants petitioned to be excused from rural road repair,

---

[49] Residents of "royal villages" in southern Poland had possessed this right even under the Polish Republic. See, for example, Podraza, "Ruch Ludowy"; Rozdolski, *Die grosse Steuer- und Agrarreform Jozefs II*, as cited in Inglot, *Historia chłopów,* 191–92.

[50] Pilat, for example, stresses the "marked increase" following emancipation in "neighborly conflicts and the tendency toward litigation." Peasants reportedly "very much liked to sue one another right to the bitter end" and were "very persistent" during the many trials. Pilat, *Wiadomości statystyczne,* 80–81.

[51] One 1857 complaint from the village of Korsów demanded a total of 55,552 crowns from the estate owner to compensate peasants for the excessive labor days the lord had demanded of them between 1820 and 1848 (calculated at 20 crowns per day). The district court dismissed the case. *Gmina* of Korsów to Prince Ignacy Komoroszski [*sic*], May 3, 1857. In Papers of Bolesław and Maria Wysłouch, 50, "Court documents pertaining to servitudes and the regulation of rural commune land in Galicia, 1850–1878." Ossolineum MS 7225/II, case number 9737.

emphasizing the infrequency with which they used many roads and bridges in comparison with their former overlords.[52] Moreover, smallholders continued to attest to their traditional rights to forests and pastures—even in the aftermath of legal verdicts denying them these rights. Peasant complaints in the 1850s and 1860s carefully documented the legal basis (as well as the customary usage argument) for access to gentry forests, citing imperial legislation in support of their cases and complaining of having to perform labor in exchange for preexisting forest rights.[53]

In the second postemancipation generation, however, legal conflicts began to pit villagers against one another for several reasons. Beginning in 1868, the promulgation of two new imperial laws permitting free division of peasant landholdings and removing the limitations on usury prompted a renewed upsurge in peasant litigation.[54] As plot sizes grew smaller through repeated land divisions, villagers began to covet every square meter of land. They applied their experience in litigation to intravillage feuds with their neighbors, with allegedly corrupt Jews, and even with members of their own families in attempts to increase the size of their ever-shrinking holdings. The subtle social divisions existing in preemancipation village society grew into more publicly visible rifts as peasants attacked one another for violating extravillage laws on land ownership. They complained of the growth of "greediness" such that "everyone wants the land of the other, even when it is only a little bit." "Out of this," it was agreed, "came the quarrels and court cases," since "everything [was] brought to court" for resolution. Extended legal proceedings tended to stratify the village community along economic lines leading to increased resentment. As one writer noted, "in the countryside it is more difficult for the poor to obtain justice than it is for the rich." In the case of "wealthier" peasants with greater access to power, the perception was that "the rich have better chances and always win because the *wójt* and the entire *gromada* are pulled in; this is a great injustice."[55]

Nonetheless, jury trials and commissions meeting in the countryside rarely resolved conflicts to the satisfaction of all residents and frequently

---

[52] See, for example, the 1865 complaint from villagers refusing to repair the local bridge, which they rarely used. Ossolineum MS 7224/II.

[53] A commune in Samborski district argued in 1850 that it possessed rights to the use of local forests not by virtue of traditional rights under serfdom, but rather as a result of the "Samborski legislation" of December 30, 1847, February 20, 1849, and April 26, 1850. The commune thus petitioned (without effect) to have its postemancipation payments of fourteen annual labor days waived for the use of the forests. Ossolineum MS 7224/II.

[54] Inglot, *Historia chłopów*, 164–65.

[55] Golcowa to *Pszczółka*, January 28, 1878, 3.

even hurt the village economy as a whole. Such was the case in the imperial commission meeting in the village near Kolbuszowa that erupted into
a riot when local peasant women and children attempted to interrupt the
proceedings. "Even the police were not able to calm the impassioned
people" assembled at the meeting of village officials, where the ownership
of a single piece of farmland was to be resolved. In the end, the commission's decision was delayed and the army was stationed in the village at the
commune's expense.[56] Although the cure for public conflict was often
more debilitating than the disease, peasant willingness to take their fellows to court nonetheless demonstrates the growth of differences of opinion and debate in the Galician countryside and the search for procedures
to resolve these conflicts.

Galician peasants learned several important lessons as they became
involved in public conflict at the local level. First, they discovered that they
were not completely alone in their struggle for accountable government.
Limited attempts at reform in the 1870s and 1880s introduced them to the
channels through which they could act and the groups from whom they
could expect assistance. District governors often replaced corrupt local
officials in response to peasant petitions; editors offered advice and support to commune governments attempting to reform, while publicizing
examples of local accountability through their papers; and crownland law
courts heard their complaints and helped resolve disputes. Second, villagers learned that government by conscientious individuals could help
bring about improvements in rural conditions. As limited economic
improvements began to appear in rural communes owing to the election of
honest and dedicated officers, a link was forged between the abstract concept of government and the more concrete reality of everyday life in the
village. Finally, smallholders saw in these years that it was often within
their power to bring about a change in government if the existing regime
did not represent their interests. This perspective was eventually transferred to the crownland political arena, where peasants would seek
increased accountability from their representatives. Yet in this process of
"becoming political," peasant society was increasingly fractured by conflicts over use of public funds, property lines, and perceptions of power
and relative economic standing. These shifting factions formed the terrain
in which notions of national identity would take root among the villagers.

---

[56] Wincenty J., Kolbuszowa, to *Pszczółka*, April 17, 1878, 3–4. This is one of the few
instances of collective action on the part of peasant women and children that we have
recorded for this period in Galicia.

PART II

The Construction of a Peasant Pole

Chapter Five

The Peasant as Literary and Ethnographic Trope

A nation at peace with its political situation can calmly research its folklore from the *purely scientific perspective* . . . a race deprived of its independence must [focus] . . . on the question: to be or not to be.

Jan Karlowicz, editor of *Wisła*, Warsaw journal of ethnography

History teaches us that nations do not die off so long as their *lud* (peasantry) continues to live, making it possible to revive the half-dead members of a nation and pour new life into it via the activities of its intellectual work.

Antoni Kalina, editor of *Lud*, Lwów folklore periodical

Postemancipation political contests within and beyond the village were played out in an atmosphere of ongoing crisis in the Polish nationalist movement. The upper classes, aware that the failure of three mid-century nationalist risings (1830, 1846, and 1863) owed much to an unsupportive peasantry, turned to the countryside after 1864 in the hopes of breathing new life into the moribund movement. A new generation of liberal thinkers—writers, ethnographers, economists, sociologists, and local officials—flocked to the countryside from the cities and estates of the crownland. They brought with them ideas about economic and cultural reform and conceptions of a Polish nation that included the participation of all social classes. They recorded their impressions of village customs and rituals and circulated them in newspapers, novels, and scholarly studies.

The intellectual interest in country life was inspired by a twofold desire to integrate emancipated peasants into educated society and to mobilize them behind the goals of the floundering nationalist movement. The surge in publications about the village helped both draw attention to the plight of the postemancipation countryside and establish the peasant as a focus of debate in the public arena. As the Galician social elite set out to "nationalize" folk culture, selecting, categorizing, and freezing specific components of the village experience in the service of particular reform initiatives, peasants countered with competing images of themselves. Peasant culture was transformed into a discursive battleground, with visions of national progress debated among rural Poles as well as those outside the village.[1] The newly enfranchised peasants became a trope through which the social elite and peasants alike could discuss and debate the nature of Polish society and each group's role within it.[2]

Galician peasants possessed a long-standing sense of boundaries separating themselves from the "others" both within and beyond the village. Through popular cultural motifs and public debate, they shaped specific conceptions of "foreigners" and used those references to help reinforce their own evolving feeling of group identity. By the 1860s, more sustained contact with upper-class Poles prompted peasants to adjust certain aspects of these group attachments. Visions of "peasantness" and "Polishness" produced outside the village among upper-class scholars and writers were debated later by villagers, and eventually absorbed and internalized by a significant minority of Galician smallholders. Village leaders would employ this amalgam of upper-class literary images and peasant folk impressions to help carve out a place for peasants within the national movement.

In time, the trope of the peasant would become a tool of reforming villagers themselves. Depictions of the peasantry were easily accessible to village readers. Stories, anecdotes, and reports of country life—many of them containing clear ethical prescriptions for peasant behavior—filled the pages of village newspapers, bringing new models of "peasantness" to the public arena. Spanning the spectrum from romantic notions of pre-Christian primitivism to realist visions of rural poverty, drunkenness, and illiteracy, these representations of rural life provided a range of peasant "types" among whom literate villagers could choose in constructing and refining their own vision of peasant identity. Examples of "appropriate" peasant behavior became the focus of debate in rural journals, and contention arose among villagers over the qualities exhibited in the model peasant.

In this way, villagers themselves took part in selecting and rejecting cultural symbols, internalizing portions of outsiders' impressions of rural life and adjusting that vision where it did not fit their views. Even as intellec-

---

[1] For an examination of this process of selecting and adapting national symbols in the Swedish case, which challenges Hobsbawm's notion of inventing national traditions, see Orvar Lofgren, "The Nationalization of Culture," *Ethnologia Europaea* 19 (1989): 5–23.

[2] Kathy Frierson has argued convincingly that in the Russian case, questions about the character of the peasant were deeply embedded in larger concerns about the nature and fate of Russia itself. See *Peasant Icons*, esp. 6–9.

tuals and officials sought inspiration for their programs of national rejuvenation from village values, peasants coopted upper-class rural imagery as a strategic maneuver to write themselves into national life on terms acceptable to upper-class Poles. Yet this process of selection and cooption effectively excluded certain segments of the rural population who were unwilling or unable to subscribe to the image of the hardworking, God-fearing, sober peasant. As literate landowning peasants drifted toward alliances with the lower gentry, who shared their (constructed) vision of peasantness, landless laborers would fail to see themselves in public references to peasant values and would search elsewhere for political solutions.

From Idealization to Scientific Realism

In the aftermath of emancipation, images of the peasant appeared on the cultural scene in Galicia as never before. Former serfs were transformed during the post-1848 period from distant but inspiring vessels for the essential features of Polishness to a more "scientific" subject characterized by poverty and ignorance, but capable of cultural improvement. Polish society in this period debated whether the peasant was to be a source of national strength, as romantic writers wished, or an asset to be trained, updated, and employed behind an agenda of modernization and social reform, as the Polish liberals believed.

After the late-eighteenth-century partitions of the Polish Republic, a romanticized notion of the Polish "folk" arose in educated circles as a source for national renewal. Drawing on the ideas of German romantics, Polish intellectuals constructed an image of "their" peasantry as the guardians of a "national spirit" uncorrupted by the cosmopolitan Western influences of the aristocracy and the Catholic Church.[3] Scholars such as historian Joachim Lelewel (1786–1861) searched for remnants of an earlier and purer "Slavic" culture preserved in remote peasant communities.[4] Research expeditions to the countryside, such as Hugo Kołłątaj's systematic study of Lithuanian villages in the early 1800s, set out to document the customs, language, and buildings of the peasantry in order to demonstrate the uniqueness of Polish culture in contrast to those of the occupy-

---

[3] Dirk Hoerder, Horst Rössler, and Inge Blank, eds., *Roots of the Transplanted* (Boulder, Colo., 1994), 1:60–67.

[4] Andrzej Walicki, *Philosophy and Romantic Nationalism: The Case of Poland* (Notre Dame, 1994), 4–5; Anna Kutrzeba-Pojnarowa, "Kultura ludowa w dotychczasowych polskich pracach etnograficznych," *Dzieje folklorystyki polskiej, 1864–1918*, ed. Helena Kapeluś and Julian Krzyżanowski (Warsaw, 1982), 26–27.

ing powers.[5] The romantic project of transforming Poland from a political nation based on citizenship rights into a cultural nation that could survive in the absence of state structures relied on perceptions of the essentialness of the peasant experience as a symbol of Poland's cultural continuity.[6]

In the aftermath of the failed January Rising of 1863–64, the peasant image was reappraised. Polish intellectuals began studying the peasantry as part of their reevaluation of the nationalist movement. Whereas the "discovery" of the folk as an element of cultural nationalism had been a romantic enterprise, improving the peasantry's educational and economic circumstances was a realist or positivist project. Writers and scholars of the post-January period reflected a general shift toward greater realism as they emphasized the work that needed to be accomplished in the countryside. A new exposé trend in prose revealed the fatalism, superstition, ignorance, and blinding poverty of the countryside, but also brought forth hope in a future transformed through expanded rural education and land reform.[7] The moral regeneration of the nation was perceived to depend on working "at the base of society" to correct the poverty and physical shortcomings among peasants.[8] These "realistic" reports and literary depictions of rural poverty would pave the way for concrete reform initiatives in the next generation as gentry and intellectual volunteers flocked to the countryside to introduce agricultural improvements, promote education, and encourage the development of a peasant national identity.

The Ethnographic Construction of the Polish "Folk"

The formal study of folklore and ethnography was one of the earliest scholarly projects reflecting the shifting orientation of national agitation in

---

[5] Kutrzeba-Pojnarowa, "Kultura ludowa," 25–27. See also Mieczysław Piszczkowski, *Obrońcy chłopów w literaturze polskiej* (Cracow, 1948). For a characterization of the peasant trope in Enlightenment literature, see Andrzej Woźniak, "Źródła zainteresowań ludoznawczych w ideologii polskiego Oświecenia," *Etnografia Polska* 15, no. 2 (1959): 37–51.

[6] Walicki, *Philosophy and Romantic Nationalism*, 64–73.

[7] On the tensions within Polish intellectual circles at this time, see Jerzy Jedlicki, *A Suburb of Europe: Nineteenth-Century Polish Approaches to Western Civilization* (Budapest, 1999). Doris Sommer has approached a similar transition from heroic portrayals of patriotic fighters to an emphasis on national "civilizers" in Latin American literature in her study of "foundational fictions" in nineteenth-century novels. See "Irresistible Romance: The Foundational Fictions of Latin America," in *Nation and Narration*, ed. Homi K. Bhabha (London, 1990), 71–98.

[8] On the basic tenets of the positivist program in the countryside, see Henryk Markiewicz, *Literatura pozytywizmu* (Warsaw, 1989), 24–40; and Stanislaus Blejwas, *Realism in Polish Politics: Warsaw Positivism and National Survival in Nineteenth-Century Poland* (New Haven, 1984).

Poland toward more concrete improvements for the lower classes. Ethnography was virtually invented as a field of scholarly interest throughout Eastern Europe in the 1850s and 1860s and quickly developed into a distinct discourse for the promotion of national interests through research in peasant culture.[9] Under conditions of heavy censorship, ethnographers played a major role in transforming the image of Poland from that of a nation represented only by its elite to a more organic, socially inclusive ideal in which peasant and lord were thought to share a common cultural bond. The systematic study of peasant culture by ethnographers thus played a key role in the transformation of nationalism in Eastern Europe and elsewhere to a more "modern" conceptualization that included participation by peasant farmers.

Founders of Polish folklore studies, such as Oskar Kolberg (1814–90) and his successor Jan Karłowicz (1836–1903), carefully documented the peculiarities of what they characterized as specifically Polish peasant culture, contrasting the songs, folktales, rituals, and costumes of the inhabitants of old Poland from those of its neighbors. By depicting the characteristics linking rural communities with one another, ethnographers consciously sought to define the cultural boundaries of the "nation" even under conditions of foreign rule. Ethnography, as it developed in the Polish lands, thus had a clear national agenda from its very inception. The search for "Slavic" folk culture became, in the censored atmosphere of the partitions, a search for clear markers of Polishness—though this identity was frequently applied to the other residents of, for example, the eastern *kresy* (borderlands).

In an effort to define culturally the borders of the postemancipation "popular" nation, early ethnographic studies gave special attention to the peripheral areas of Polish territory, those characterized by ethnically mixed populations. The Warsaw ethnographic journal *Wisła*, founded in 1887, focused much of its early material on Chancellor Bismarck's Germanization efforts in the Polish countryside. Its Lwów contemporary, *Lud*, published numerous articles on Ruthenian, Lithuanian, and Belorussian traditions. Confessional differences alone did not deter early ethnographers in their search for the pre-Christian essence of Polishness. Kolberg himself, in correspondence about the Polish district of Mazuria

---

[9] Oskar Kolberg and his friend Józef Konopka, two music students from Warsaw, were responsible for inaugurating the field of Polish folklore studies when they set out in 1841 to collect songs, legends, and homilies in the Polish countryside. See Elżbieta Millerowa and Agata Skrukwa, "Oskar Kolberg (1814–1890)," in Kapeluś and Krzyżanowski, *Dzieje folklorystyki polskiej*, 25–48.

Oskar Kolberg, father of Polish ethnography. Courtesy of the Ethnographic Museum, Cracow. Inventory number III/79682/F. Reproduction by Jacek Kubiena.

north of Warsaw, categorized local peasants as "still Slavic" (i.e., Polish) despite their preponderant Protestantism.[10] The boundaries of the Polish nation were manipulated in much of this work using selective examples from peasant culture—pre-Christian rituals rather than formal religious affiliation, material culture rather than dialect or language.

Led by scholars such as Kolberg, the new field of ethnography quickly mushroomed into a project for the officially sanctioned preservation and promotion of Polish culture.[11] For much of the nineteenth century, the field of ethnography hovered on the thin line between idealization of peasant society and the realistic study of village material and social culture.[12] Kolberg's early efforts to force eastern Slavic peasant customs into his preconceived notion of "Polishness" or "Slavicness" suggest an awareness that the basis for defining national boundaries was changing. Ethnographers worked to establish a commonality of "traditions" that effectively linked the lands and peoples of the area perceived as "Polish." Folk customs, many of relatively new vintage, were promoted and highlighted as the essence of a homogeneous national culture with its roots in the countryside.

One component of the selection and freezing of ostensibly age-old peasant "traditions" was the founding of regional and local official folklore institutes and ethnographic museums in the last quarter of the nineteenth century. All over Eastern Europe, among peoples lacking independent political institutions, ethnography evolved into a field dedicated to the promotion of subaltern cultures as the foundation of national communities. Ethnographic exhibits at the Paris World's Fair of 1867 marked the "discovery" of peasant art and folk crafts among the urban elite of Western and Eastern Europe. The Vienna World's Fair in 1873 provided an

---

[10] Correspondence with Karol Claudius, March 20, 1876, as cited in Millerowa and Skrukwa, "Oskar Kolberg," 68.

[11] The occupying empires themselves made use of ethnographic research to prove their own claims over contested populations. See Austin Lee Jersild, "Ethnic Modernity and the Russian Empire: Russian Ethnographers and the Caucasian Mountaineers," *Nationalities Papers* 24, no. 4 (1996): 641–48; Susan Layton, "The Creation of an Imaginative Caucasian Geography," *Slavic Review* 45, no. 3 (fall 1986), and Layton, *Russian Literature and Empire: Conquest of the Caucasus from Pushkin to Tolstoy* (Cambridge, 1994); and Nathaniel Knight, "Science, Empire, and Nationality: Ethnography in the Russian Geographical Society, 1845–1855," in *Imperial Russia: New Histories for the Empire*, ed. Jane Burbank and David L. Ransel (Bloomington, 1998).

[12] On the tension between romanticism and realism in East European ethnography, see Tamas Hofer, "The Perception of Tradition in European Ethnology," *Journal of Folklore Research* 21, no. 1 (April 1984): 137–38; and Józef Burszta, "Kultura chłopsko-ludowa a kultura narodowa," *Etnografia Polska* 2 (1959): 391–415.

opportunity for the small nations of Eastern Europe to export images of their national heritage to the imperial capital.[13]

Ethnographic museums displaying the "primitive" creations of "national" folk culture opened in Budapest in 1872, Warsaw in 1888, Lwów in 1895, and Cracow in 1905; a Czech ethnographic exhibit arrived in Prague in 1895. At the same time, ethnography blossomed as a university subject throughout the Habsburg monarchy and beyond. The Jagiellonian University in Cracow began regular lectures on ethnography in 1851, and the University of Lwów would establish a permanent chair in Polish ethnography in 1910. Cracow's anthropology commission established a separate ethnographic section in 1874, headed by Kolberg. Temporary international exhibits of Polish folklore were held in Kołomyja in 1880 and Lwów in 1885.

Each of these associations made it clear that their raison d'être was the use of peasant culture as a medium for promoting nationalist political programs. Even Jan Karłowicz, leader of a second generation of more systematic Polish ethnographers (a generation willing to acknowledge trans-European influences on native peasantries), argued that ethnographic research in Poland could not afford to remain objective in its analyses. "A nation at peace with its political situation," he proposed, "can calmly research its folklore from the purely scientific perspective," yet "a race deprived of its independence" must instead focus on the question "to be or not to be."[14] In marked contrast to West European anthropology, with its treatment of peasant societies as marginal groups in larger cultural systems, Eastern European ethnography located its cultural center not in cities or at aristocratic courts, but rather in the native creations of the countryside.[15]

The conception of the peasantry as a component part of Polish national identity faced renewed contestation in the last decades of the nineteenth century as a widening debate over the origins of folk customs was played out in the pages of ethnographic journals. *Wisła*, published in Warsaw beginning in 1887, and *Lud*, a Lwów journal inaugurated in 1895, represented contrasting tendencies in the new field, helping to direct the uses of peasant culture in the redefinition of the Polish nation. These journals were

---

[13] Tamas Hofer, "The Creation of Ethnic Symbols from the Elements of Peasant Culture," in *Ethnic Diversity and Conflict in Eastern Europe*, ed. Peter Sugar (Santa Barbara, 1980), esp. 112–16. On the ways in which "national" exhibits revealed divisions within a single national entity, see Lewis Siegelbaum, "Exhibiting *Kustar'* Industry in Late Imperial Russia/Exhibiting Late Imperial Russia in *Kustar'* Industry," in *Transforming Peasants: Society, State, and the Peasantry, 1861–1930*, ed. Judith Pallot (London, 1998), 37–63.

[14] As cited in Kapeluś and Krzyżanowski, *Dzieje folklorystyki polskiej*, 5–9.

[15] Hofer, "Creation of Ethnic Symbols," 112–20.

founded in an atmosphere of sharp contention over the status of peasant culture in reforming and strengthening Polish national society. Although many members of the positivist intelligentsia believed that the essence of the nation lay in village traditions, few educated residents of Warsaw had any real knowledge of peasant culture. *Wisła,* edited by Jan Karłowicz, appeared as a response to the challenge posed by the theories of Jan Popławski, who contended that the Polish nation was made up of two separate civilizations, one consisting of *szlachta* traditions and the other of peasant folk culture. Karłowicz established the journal with the goal of acquainting gentry readers and members of the urban professions with the life of the Polish peasantry.[16] The journal's implied agenda was clearly to draw upper-class and village culture closer together in order to meld the two separate Polish cultures into a single homogeneous civilization.

Wisła focused on three key ethnographic formulae. First, the journal worked to define broadly and defend vigorously the geographical boundaries of the Polish cultural nation. In articles and editorials, the journal emphasized the threat represented by Germanization efforts in Polish Mazuria and Poznań. Karłowicz printed regularly updated material on the policies of the German government, often accompanied by maps and diagrams showing the expansion of the German school system or the colonization of Polish lands. Second, *Wisła* editors portrayed ethnographic research as the study of national origins and presented Polish-speaking peasants as the true representatives of the Polish nation, their customs and culture as the central elements defining the *naród*. The professionally trained ethnographers who contributed to *Wisła* were careful to acknowledge both the trans-European influences on and the modern variations of the legends and ballads of the Polish *lud*.[17] Christmas plays (called *szopki*) were, for example, shown to have incorporated contemporary images of Jewish taverners, Gypsies, German administrators, and attorneys—characters clearly not drawn directly from the biblical Christmas story.[18] Rural culture thus appeared in *Wisła* as representative of the essence of Polishness, an essence that was neither static nor immune from outside influences.

---

[16] On the intended audience of *Wisła*, see Helena Kapeluś, *"Lud,* Organ Towarzystwa Ludoznawczego we Lwowie," in Kapeluś and Krzyżanowski, *Dzieje folklorystyki polskiej,* 338–40.

[17] As, for example, in the variations of King Lear tunes and Grimm adaptations recorded in *Wisła* 8 (1894): 444–49.

[18] *Wisła* published a wide range of *szopki* adaptations from regions as diverse as Lublin, Radom, and Łowicz. Jańczuk, "Szopka w Kornicy," *Wisła* 2 (1888): 729–51. Variations are recorded in *Wisła* 6 (1892): 464–86; 7 (1893): 518–23; 8 (1894): 281–303; and 10 (1896): 465–89.

The third component in *Wisła*'s deployment of ethnography to redefine national membership involved a pattern of linking traditional peasant culture to the life of Poland's historic *szlachta*. Contributors drew consistent links between the songs and poetry of the peasantry and similar tunes or legends circulating in manorial estates. They emphasized especially peasant renderings of historic moments in the life of the nation such as the seventeenth-century defense of Vienna by the Polish king Jan Sobieski and the exploits of King Zygmunt Wasa.[19] The work of Zygmunt Gloger (1845–1910), a regular contributor to *Wisła*, made perhaps the greatest contribution to promoting the concept of Polish culture as a shared tradition, crossing socioeconomic lines and geographic boundaries. Gloger, an archeologist, ethnographer, and folklore specialist, traced the elements uniting *szlachta* and peasant culture especially during Poland's "golden age." In researching Poland's sixteenth and seventeenth centuries, Gloger found evidence of songs sung in manor houses and, with only a few small adaptations, in peasant huts. Gloger argued that folk tunes labeled as pure peasant "creations" typically showed elements of gentry influences as well.[20] Through his ethnographic research, Gloger managed to communicate the impression of a Poland that crossed political boundaries and a Polish people united in culture, language, architecture, and history. In the pages of *Wisła* and in separate monographs on the history, ritual, architecture, and material culture of old Poland, Gloger recounted the details of local customs as a means of presenting his vision of an integrated nationwide culture.[21]

In contrast to the highly trained scholars with a European-wide perspective who contributed to *Wisła*, many of the folklore specialists associated with Lwów's ethnographic journal *Lud* were of peasant background. Aimed at a more popular audience than its Warsaw competitor, *Lud* was

---

[19] Peasant ballads of the 1683 defense of Vienna are recorded in *Wisła* 2 (1888): 350–57; 4 (1890): 426–29; and *Lud* 3 (1897): 155–57. The legend of King Zygmunt is recounted in *Wisła* 2 (1888): 603–4.

[20] The scholarship of both Glogar and Karłowicz reflected the claim, later made by Peter Burke in *Popular Culture in Early Modern Europe* (London, 1978), that components of premodern rural culture were shared by peasant and landholder alike. See also Kutrzeba-Pojnarowa, "Kultura ludowa," 31–32; and Helena Kapeluś, "Wisła," in Kapelus and Krzyzanowski, *Dzieje folklorystyki polskiej*, 267–68.

[21] Gloger's studies of folk culture helped to sidestep the Russian censor while reinforcing popular images of shared peasant and *szlachta* culture. His major works included *Rok polski w życiu tradycji i pieśni* (1900), *Encyklopedia staropolska* (1900–1903) and *Budownictwo drzewne i wyroby z drzewa w dawnej Polsce* (1907–9). On Gloger's position in the development of Polish folklore studies, see Teresa Brzozowski-Komorowska, "Zygmunt Gloger i popularyzacja folkloru," in Kapeluś and Krzyżanowski, *Dzieje folklorystyki polskiej*, 104–9.

established by Cracow's Folklore Society and edited by Dr. Antoni Kalina (1846–1906), himself a peasant's son.[22] The journal sought to serve the needs of Galician secondary and primary schoolteachers. Contributors included rural elementary teachers and young intellectuals of peasant origin, many of whom sympathized with the peasant movement beginning to stir at the time of the journal's founding in 1895.[23]

In contrast to *Wisła*'s efforts to construct a Polish peasantry out of the population of civilizations on the periphery of the old republic, *Lud* unabashedly emphasized the immense variety of nationalities occupying Galicia, even promoting folklore studies as a basis for legitimizing minority nationalist claims. As a trained linguist, Kalina encouraged contributors to research linguistic differences among the people of Old Poland, focusing on the linguistic borderlands of Lithuania, Belorussia, and Ukraine. Indeed, the Lwów Folklore Society had a number of Ukrainian members who were also contributors to the journal. Chief among these was Ukrainian playwright and political activist Iwan Franko.

Whereas *Wisła* worked to highlight the commonalities shared by peasant and educated culture in Poland, contributors to *Lud* focused on the boundaries of cultural differences separating particular peasant cultures. Understanding the details of peasant culture for its own sake was important, Kalina emphasized, because folk culture

constitutes the eternal source of strength of the *lud* and at the same time an important element in the life of each nation. [Folk culture] represents the very nativeness [*rodzimość*] and resistance of the *lud*, of which the first is a source of the continuity . . . and purity of the national spirit, and the second affirms and protects its life and its tradition. History teaches us that nations do not die off so long as their *lud* (peasantry) continues to live, making it possible to revive the half-dead members of a nation and pour new life into it via the activities of its intellectual work.[24]

Peasant not aristocratic culture was key to defining the boundaries of Poland and to making a claim for its right to a separate political existence. The peasantry in this account represented the insulated set of traditions that helped to preserve the purity of the nation, protecting its essence from

[22] Kalina led the Lwów Society of Folklorists and managed the journal *Lud* for its first ten years. He was a trained specialist in Slavic linguistics, old Polish language, and Slavic culture and filled the Slavic chair at Lwów University from 1888 on. Kapeluś, "Lud," 344.
[23] Kapeluś, "Lud," 338–40.
[24] Reprinted in Kapeluś, "Lud," 346–47.

corrupting outside influences over centuries of invasion, occupation, and foreign borrowings. Kalina and his colleagues described a complex mosaic of ethnic cultures coexisting in the former Polish lands, only a limited portion of which could be characterized as culturally "Polish." Less scholarly in their approach to ethnographic research, *Lud*'s articles tended to generalize across time within peasant culture, freezing wedding customs and the texts of songs in a vague timelessness. Though descriptions of peasant clothing, songs, and rituals clearly noted their ethnic source (as being typically Polish or Ruthenian), the evolution of folk culture over time received less attention here, and influences from outside the village were deemphasized.

Folklore research and the new science of ethnography offered a point of access into village life and provided the basis for a renewed respect for the peasant lifestyle among upper-class readers and peasants alike. Journals such as *Wisła* and *Lud*, together with the publication of Kolberg's hugely popular sixty-four-volume collection and dozens of other minor studies of peasant customs, brought village traditions to the attention of upper-class Poles as never before.[25] Ethnographic researchers provided the first wave of detailed and documented information about the structures of village life to a public thirsty for insights into a portion of society long shrouded in mystery. Yet despite a penchant for colorful illustrations and bawdy lyrics, ethnographic research was accessible only to a relatively limited audience. Much more widely disseminated were the literary renderings of village life painted by novelists and poets, which were often based on readily available folklore studies.

The Peasant as a Statistical Subject and Literary Icon

From the earliest days of Kolberg's wanderings in the Polish countryside, contact between ethnographers and writers helped establish the peasant as a literary icon in Polish belles lettres. The father of Polish ethnography corresponded regularly with writer Józef Ignacy Kraszewski, even sending

---

[25] In Galicia alone, a flurry of publications on peasant customs in particular regions appeared in the last years of the century, including B. Sokalski, *Powiat sokalski pod względem geograficznym, etnograficznym, historycznym i ekonomicznym* (Lwów, 1899); Jan Aleksander Bayger, *Powiat tremblowelski. Szkic geograficzno-historyczny i etnograficzny* (Lwów, 1899); Zofia Strzetelska-Grynbergowa, *Staromiejskie. Ziemia i ludność* (Lwów, 1899); Karol Falkiewicz, *Monografie powiatu grodeckiego* (1896); Father Władysław Sarna, *Opis powiatu krośnieńskiego* (1898); and Stanisław Połączek, *Powiat chrzanowski* (1898).

the novelist a copy of his first book, *Pieśni ludu polskiego* (1857).[26] Polish novelists borrowed ethnographic material to support two new literary conventions of the second half of the nineteenth century: the historical novel and the realistic novel.[27] The picture positivist authors painted of peasant life was both richer in detail and gloomier than the atmosphere portrayed in folklore studies. In their search for the essence of folk customs, ethnographers were willing to overlook much of the poverty, ignorance, malnutrition, and disease common among the peasants. By contrast, the published work of other outsiders studying the village often revealed an atmosphere of despair, fatalism, or bitterness. Popular writers were better able to capture the overall atmosphere of country life, drawing as they did on a wide range of economic, sociological, and pedagogical studies as well as on their own personal observations.

Among the more depressing accounts of the peasantry circulating among educated Galicians in the last decades of the century was a genre of statistical studies assessing conditions in the postemancipation countryside. Largely commissioned by the Crownland Governing Board (Wydział Krajowy), this social science research (details of which are discussed above in chapter 1) brought into sharp relief the chaos of local administration, the ravages of rural alcoholism, high death rates, and widespread peasant dependence on usury. Studies such as Tadeusz Pilat's *Statistical Information* (*Wiadomości statystyczne*, 1881) and Józef Kleczyński's *Conditions of Farmers in Galicia* (*Stosunki włoscian w Galicji*, 1878) exposed the illiteracy, incompetence, and corruption that plagued village government.[28] Sejm deputy Stanisław Szczepanowski's publication of *The Misery of Galicia* (*Nędza Galicyi*) in 1888, with its drastic vision of the poverty and economic stagnation plaguing the countryside, struck the educated public like a bombshell.[29]

---

[26] We have correspondence between Kolberg and Kraszewski dating from 1857. Ethnographic material also appears in Kraszewski's peasant novels of the 1840s (*Ulana* [1843], *Ostap Bondarczuk* [1847], and *Chata za wsią* [1854]), including the author's own observations on the Lithuanian peasantry gathered while he worked as a tenant farmer and landowner in Volhynia. Regarding Kraszewski's literary work, see Czesław Miłosz, *The History of Polish Literature* (Berkeley, 1983), 256–57. Millerowa and Skrukwa, "Oskar Kolberg," 64.

[27] On connections between ethnographic research and writers of the positivist period, see Markiewicz, *Literatura pozytywizmu*, 112–15.

[28] Pilat headed the Galician Crownland Bureau of Statistics, while Dr. Kleczyński was a professor at Lwów University.

[29] On the reception of Szczepanowski's studies among the Galician public, see Edward Wierzbicki, "Poglądy Stanisława Szczepanowskiego na rozwój oświaty i wychowania w Gal-

Taken together, these studies presented a picture of the Galician countryside that contrasted sharply with both romantic literary depictions and the folklore images previously circulating in the popular press. They described the crownland countryside as "one of the most densely populated in Europe,"[30] possessing the highest rate of rural auction in the Habsburg Empire (due largely to defaulted usurious loans).[31] They portrayed Galician peasants as unable to attend school in winter for lack of shoes to wear, and they situated the province near the bottom in imperial educational rankings (superior only to impoverished and remotely settled Bukovina).[32] The data compiled by Pilat in the early 1880s showed that almost half of all Galician villages had no school and that, as late as 1875, over 80 percent of village mayors could neither read nor write.[33]

Circulated widely in the contemporary press and the subject of passionate debate in the Sejm, statistical research demonstrated steadily decreasing plot sizes, increasing numbers of landless laborers, and the continuation of primitive cultivation techniques.[34] Some of the most damning studies of rural economic conditions were written under pseudonyms, including Leopold Caro's examination of village credit needs and the effects of usurious interest rates in the countryside.[35] Thirty years after emancipation and ten years following the granting of Galician autonomy, rural economic and cultural conditions showed little improvement over those of the preemancipation village.

These and other images of rural hardship were typically omitted from published folklore accounts of village culture. Only the private correspondence of ethnographers offers a glimpse into the depressing realities and "sadness" researchers encountered. As Kolberg recounted, "oftentimes I came to [the peasants] in filthy cottages, in fear of their very skin, among thick smoke . . . dense with people, practically without light."[36] Such mus-

icji," *Rocznik Przemyski* 21 (1979): 273–82, and Wierzbicki, "Wpływ 'Nędzy Galicji' Stanisława Szczepanowskiego na rozwój ekonomiczny Galicji," *Rocznik Przemyski* 22/23 (1983): 473–78.

[30] Szczepanowski, *Nędza Galicyi*, 1–2.
[31] Report by Dr. Tadeusz Pilat, National Bureau of Statistics, cited in *Wieniec*, November 20, 1884, 207.
[32] Report of the Galician census of 1880, published in *Pszczółka*, November 9, 1881, 171–72.
[33] Dr. Tadeusz Pilat, cited in *Wieniec*, July 17, 1884, 113.
[34] Pilat, *Wiadomości statystyczne*, 6–8, 25–26, 58–60; Jadwiga Dawidowa, *Kółka rolnicze w Galicyi* (Warsaw, 1890), 3.
[35] *Lichwa na wsi w latach, 1875–1891* (1893).
[36] Millerowa and Skrukwa, "Oskar Kolberg," 64.

ings about the harsh realities of everyday life soon found their way into popular literature. As a consequence, a parallel trend developed alongside ethnographic accounts of village customs—a trend toward painting a realistic and often fatalistic account of peasant society as a basis for the reform projects and the long-term cultural integration of the peasantry into Polish life.

Polish literature of the 1880s and 1890s provided the narrative framework to bring alive the images that statisticians and folklore specialists had introduced earlier. Indeed, the novel in particular, more than any other discursive form, could weave together the disparate symbols that had come to be associated with national folk culture—the peasant expressions (*gwara*), the calendar of harvest and planting rituals, fields of rye dotted with toiling laborers.[37] The late-nineteenth-century peasant novel helped sharpen the popular contemporary image of the peasant in his dual role as both the tragedy and the hope of the Polish nation. Images of peasant families struggling to overcome poverty and darkness established a balance between the misery of the rural situation, on the one hand, and the salvation offered in the peasant character, on the other. Novelists such as Bolesław Prus, Eliza Orzeszkowa, Maria Konopnicka, and later, Władysław Rejmont painted in the darkest colors the hate, mistrust, fatalism, and demoralization found in peasant relationships with one another and with the gentry. At the same time, these writers emphasized the self-sacrifice, piety, and work ethic exhibited by exemplary village characters. The tension between crisis and inspiration found in fictionalized accounts of village interactions came to represent a crucial dichotomy in educated notions of the peasantry's role in the Polish nation.

Characteristic of a confidence in the peasantry's ability to shoulder the burden of moral responsibility for rebuilding Poland was the literary work of Eliza Orzeszkowa. Orzeszkowa herself had taken part in the uprising of 1863, seeing the revolt as a struggle for democracy and the emancipation of the peasants as well as for national independence. Her novels display a strong didactic and moral quality, bringing out the peasant characters' ability to persevere despite obstacles thrown up by social conditions. For example, Krystyna, the young female protagonist in *Dziurdziowie* (1885), the story of a peasant family in a Belorussian village, elicits pity and indignation even as she is burned to death as a witch by superstitious villagers. Krystyna's character reflects the dignity of hard work and generosity of

---

[37] On the role of the novel in helping to build national solidarity, see Sommer, "Irresistible Romance."

spirit as well as demonstrating affection and responsibility toward her children. In drawing out the character traits of industriousness, self-sacrifice, and piety, Orzeszkowa articulates the elements of a new peasant-based morality. In the case of the village of Dziurdziowie, only a select group of characters possess the qualities necessary to save rural society. Orzeszkowa has little sympathy for the cruel, superstitious rabble that takes Krystyna's life, but appears to see some hope for rural redemption in the values she gives her protagonist. Orzeszkowa's work reflects the process of social and moral differentiation taking place in rural society. While some peasants can be perceived as possessing the qualities essential to the protection of Polish land and traditions, others are painted as representatives of a greedy, fearful, self-serving, preemancipatory past that would need to be eradicated for the peasants to make a positive contribution to Poland's future.

The nobility comes in for particularly critical treatment in Orzeszkowa's work. In her *On the Banks of the Niemen*, gentry landholders are portrayed as unconcerned with the fate of their country (represented here by the graves of insurgents from 1863) and preoccupied with dreams of moving abroad.[38] The peasant farmer holds the key to national preservation and resurrection here. This variegated hierarchy of morality, with the pious peasant occupying the top rung of the ethical ladder and the village masses and treasonous gentleman farmer placed well below him, was closely reflective of a self-conception developing among Galician villagers themselves. Indeed, images circulating via such novels helped carve out the outlines of a superstratum consisting of peasants who displayed "moral" traits in contrast to the mass of "immoral," impious, or ignorant villagers.

The literary commitment to peasant society as a regenerative national force is most optimistically reflected in the poetry of Maria Konopnicka (1842–1910), a close friend and contemporary of Orzeszkowa. The themes in Konopnicka's work echo the metaphoric treatment of peasants as a source of national strength found in other literary works of the time. The blackest descriptions of peasant misery, darkness, and demoralization are found, for example, in her series *In the Mountains* (*W gorach*, 1876–78). Konopnicka purports here to "take into [her] frame the sadness of millions" by training her lens closely on "this land that is in the throes of pain." Yet this rural misery is portrayed as stemming mainly from the economic oppression of the upper classes and is therefore remediable

---

[38] Miłosz, *History of Polish Literature*, 306–7; Markiewicz, *Literatura pozytywizmu*, 71–78.

through active participation in village life. Konopnicka even presents in *Imaginie* (1884–87) an apocalyptic vision of a peasant uprising that brings national independence, the elimination of misery, and freedom from ignorance.[39]

In all her work, Konopnicka relies on ethnographic material to acquaint her readers with the rhythms of folksongs, bringing alive the richness of the peasant cadence to educated readers. She carefully distinguishes between positive and negative peasant traits, juxtaposing the pious character and the quarrelsome; the energetic worker and the one resigned to passivity; the pessimistic personality and the hopeful one. Especially by the writing of her *Mr. Balcer in Brazil* (*Pan Balcer w Brazylii*, written in 1892–1909, published in 1910), Konopnicka clearly reveals her belief in the strength of character possessed by certain representatives of the village. The tragedy and misfortune encountered during Mr. Balcer's attempts to emigrate and his ultimate decision to return to his native soil are stark reminders of the obligation Konopnicka believed the peasants owed to the national cause to remain on their farms.[40]

The Internalization of Peasant Tropes

Literary images of village life circulated widely among all strata in Galician society. Peasant novels and populist poetry were read by residents of the village as well as by educated Poles. Intellectuals went to great efforts to adapt historical and realist novels for peasant readers and publish them in brochures or in the columns of peasant newspapers. The works of Kraszewski, Orzeszkowa, Prus, and others circulated in this way throughout all three Polish partitions, were incorporated into the curriculum of many country schools (see chapter 7), and were adapted for the peasant stage. Polish classics were even published in serial form in the peasant press.[41] Country markets and fairs sold popular literary adaptations for inexperienced readers, village reading rooms stocked classical literary works beginning in the late 1870s (see chapter 6), and traveling vendors

---

[39] Accusations that Konopnicka was attempting to incite a peasant rebellion against the landlords drew the special attention of tsarist censors and Polish conservatives alike, making the publication of her work increasingly difficult. Miłosz, *History of Polish Literature*, 318–19.

[40] Maria Konopnicka, *Poezje* (Warsaw, 1969); Markiewicz, *Literatura pozytywizmu*, 169–84.

[41] Both *Wieniec i Pszczółka* and *Przyjaciel Ludu* published major Polish literary works in serial form. See Markiewicz, *Literatura pozytywizmu*, 187–98.

supplied major works of Polish prose along with heavy-handed didactic and morality pieces.[42]

The thematic content of these works would soon make its way into the literary creations of villagers themselves, which often echoed the ethical sentiment introduced by upper-class writers. The characterization of peasant "types" found in scholarly and literary prose was reflected in the writing of many peasant authors, who emphasized the themes of self-improvement, hard work, and respect for the land in their literary work. The vision of the Polish peasantry that would be produced in the countryside represented an adaptation of the tropes available in upper-class literature with an admixture of village ideals. Drawing alternately on romantic and realist traditions, village writers would portray the peasantry as the source of national strength (as the romantics argued), but also its future (as realists suggested). They would reject images of isolation and insulation as overdrawn, and depictions of rural misery, darkness, and superstition as relics of the past (see chapter 8).

Peasant poets and prose writers would draw on iconographic portrayals of self-sacrificing small farmers devoted to church attendance, personal improvement, and the protection of the land to construct a new patriotic village superstratum. In contrast to outsiders' portrayals of the peasant as a passive symbol of uncorrupted Slavicness or as defining the boundaries of Poland through language and custom, villagers would choose a more proactive prescription for national participation. No longer content with being used as icons for a nation that offered them little active role, rural leaders sought to redefine the contribution the village could make to Polish political culture. They presented themselves—or at least the minority for whom village authors spoke—as prepared to engage actively in national life, whether by fighting to protect Poland's borders or by imposing rural standards of morality on a corrupt and selfish aristocracy. It was these perceptions and this village-based imagery that would drive the political fortunes of peasant leaders as they entered public life in the coming decades.

---

[42] Markiewicz, *Literatura pozytywizmu*, 189.

Chapter Six

The Gentry Construction of Peasants: Agricultural Circles and the Resurgence of Peasant Culture

Anti-Semitism is a great sin—it contradicts the teaching of Christ, because it is cruel, inhuman, and arouses low instincts. Judaism is to be combated through Christian means—economic measures. Let us be patriots!

Count Tarnowski, Catholic Conference of Conservatives, Cracow, 1893

Stojałowski was a fanatic of the medieval type, and the more dangerous because he resorted to any and all means of demagoguery to attract the poor masses. The peasants regarded him as their defender against the despotism of the magnate-landowners. But the cunning priest followed the customary strategy of the Christian Socialists, and he steered the discontent of the people against the Jews.

Simon Dubnov, *History of the Jews*

The circulation of ethnographic and literary images of peasants encouraged upper-class Poles to initiate rural reform projects. Beginning in the 1870s, a wide array of village-based associations, including agricultural circles, reading clubs, credit societies, and farming cooperatives, sprouted up "like mushrooms after a warm rain, transforming the face of the Polish village—often suddenly and radically."[1] Parish priests, members of the landed gentry, and urban intellectuals appeared in the countryside armed with programs intended to promote cultural and economic improvement. These associations and organizations helped introduce a sociological restructuring of rural community life. New affiliations prompted alliances between activist villagers and their upper-class benefactors, while poorer villagers continued to drift away from civic participation. At the same

---

[1] Memoirs such as Stanisław Rymar's frequently reflect on the sudden emergence of associational life in the countryside. "Pamiętniki z lat życia, 1880–1962," 1, ZHRL, P-183/I, 17–18.

time, the programs guided by village outsiders were heavily revised in contact with rural customary practices. The budding organizational life in the
Galician countryside thus encouraged a melding of upper-class visions of
peasant priorities with the agenda of activist villagers, resulting in the
beginnings of a new alliance system cutting across and uniting members of
previously antagonistic social classes.

One component in this realignment of rural political forces was a sharp
shift in the position of rural Jews. Functioning as pawns and frequent
allies of the landed gentry under serfdom, *shtetl* Jews saw a demotion in
their status as landlords began to see benefit in assisting Catholic peasants.[2] As Polish landholders struggled to convince former serfs to take part
in reform programs, attacks against Jewish establishments often represented a basis for cooperation between peasant and lord. Jewish tavern
keepers and shop owners found their positions gradually undermined by
Polish Catholic commercial competition aimed at displacing them and
building links between Polish Catholics of different social strata. The forging of this new anti-Jewish alliance represented the first example of the
gentry's formal invocation of an ethnic "other" as a means of attracting
peasant support behind a nationalist program. Over time, anti-Semitic
rhetoric would become a potent and often uncontrollable weapon in the
ongoing battle to engage peasant interest and electoral support.

Even among upper-class organizers themselves, conceptions of peasant
needs remained heavily contested. Gentry activists clashed over organizational priorities and the limits of peasant independence within associational life. Liberals and conservatives, priests and landowners butted
heads over the best methods for funneling money and information into village society. One of the most prominent tensions that played itself out in
the agricultural circle movement and its subsidiary organizations was the
conflict between large landholders, who sought to maintain control over
the operation of village associations, and the village intellectuals who promoted increased peasant independence. Ultimately, the two groups disagreed about the extent to which local farming institutions should reflect
the rhythms of village culture as opposed to gentry perceptions of peasant
needs. In short, who would guide the postemancipation countryside—
local notables, gentry outsiders, or village farmers?

Of the maze of Galician rural associations founded in the 1870s and

---

[2] On the shifting position of Jews within Galician political culture, see Kai Struve, "Die
Juden in der Sicht der polnischen Bauernparteien vom Ende des 19. Jahrhunderts bis 1939,"
Zeitschrift für Ostmitteleuropaforschung 48, no. 2 (1999); Zygmunt Hemmerling, "Stronnictwa ludowe wobec żydów i kwestii żydowskiej," *Kwartalnik historyczny* 96, nos. 1–2
(1989): 155–81.

1880s, the largest and most influential was the Agricultural Circle Society (Towarzystwo Kółka Rolniczego or TKR). It was officially chartered in 1882, but its first stirrings appear as early as 1877. The circle movement sparked the emergence of a number of branch institutions, including Christian stores, reading rooms, farmers' cooperatives, and credit associations. At its peak just before World War I, the agricultural circle movement boasted over 82,000 peasant members in close to two thousand separate village circles.[3] Many of the subsidiary institutions originally sponsored by the circle organization later developed independently, unfettered by circle administrative regulations and supervision. Each circle thus represented both itself and the organizations it spawned; each influenced its own members and the nonmember villagers who shopped at its stores, rented its farm machinery, made use of its credit institutions, or participated in its regular parades and holiday celebrations. The agricultural circle movement thus played an important role in establishing new patterns of rural organization in the last quarter of the nineteenth century.

The Contestation of Agricultural Circle Administration

At least three distinct factions competed for control of the agricultural circle movement in its early years: intellectual and gentry advocates of "organic work," the rural intelligentsia led by Father Stanisław Stojałowski, and the peasants themselves. Conservative gentry and more liberal intellectuals formed the first part of this power triangle. They set out to "work at the base of society," integrating peasants into the "organic structure" of the nation. The movement's founders sought to disseminate information on modern methods of cultivation and civic responsibility to the peasantry through individual circle cells.[4]

Rural clergy and teachers led by Father Stojałowski, an ex-Jesuit and parish priest, represented a second corner of the triangle. These rural intellectuals worked to promote peasant membership in economic and educational societies on a decentralized model.[5] Stojałowski, who was responsi-

---

[3] Gurnicz, *Kółka rolnicze*, 78–80. The Galician agricultural circle movement was modeled on a similar network in Prussian Poland, founded in 1862 to help protect Polish land from Prussian colonization. By 1903, Poles in the German Empire had established 100 circle cells, 6,000 dairy cooperatives, and 6,000 lending banks. Andrzej Zakrzewski, *Od Stojałowskiego do Witosa* (Warsaw, 1988), 45–50.

[4] For an introduction to the philosophy of organic work as it applied to the Polish peasantry, see Blejwas, *Realism in Polish Politics*, 25–28.

[5] Stanisław Stojałowski, the son of a customs official, was born in 1845 in the village of Zniesienie, near Lwów. His father's family was descended from middle-level gentry in the largely Ukrainian section of eastern Galicia. Stojałowski became a Jesuit in 1863 but was dis-

Father Stanisław Stojałowski. Archive of the Institute for the History of the Peasant Movement. Courtesy of the Ethnographic Museum, Cracow. Inventory number III/7126/F. Reproduction by Jacek Kubiena.

ble for a host of publishing and organizational enterprises in the country-side, carefully encouraged input from the village population, calling for letters and reports from peasant subscribers. Yet he too had a hierarchical conception of the social order, which he maintained even as he promoted patriotism and service to the nation among the peasants.[6] The third component was made up of peasant members of village associations, who straddled a tenuous line between village culture and the reform packages introduced by outsiders.

It was the organizational energy and creativity of Father Stojałowski that prompted the creation of village agricultural circles. The impetus came in 1877 at a crownland-wide assembly in Lwów's town hall attended by some two hundred peasants along with representatives from the Sejm, university professors, and members of the church hierarchy.[7] Signs of tension among the movement's factions were already apparent at this first meeting as villagers complained that upper-class spokesmen misrepresented their interests. Maciej Szarek, a frequent correspondent to Stojałowski's newspapers, complained that he and his fellow villagers felt the founders of the Agricultural Circle Society had little concern for the most serious problems of the countryside, including usury and drunkenness.[8]

The agricultural circle movement was formally organized under the guidance of the Society for People's Education and Work (Towarzystwo Szkolnictwo i Prace Ludowe) at another assembly during the summer of 1878 attended by some three hundred persons. At both of these founding meetings, Stojałowski made clear his desire to "awaken the interests" of peasant circle members and "give peasants the possibility of influencing in some way the administration of the society" through participation in regular mass meetings.[9] Indeed, the priest stressed the grassroots sources of

---

missed in 1875, partially as a result of his organizational activities among the peasantry. Father Stojałowski is best known for launching two popular peasant journals in 1875, *Wieniec* and *Pszczółka*, and publishing them until his death in 1911. Stojałowski's organizational efforts among the peasantry often challenged the authority of the episcopate, prompting bans of excommunication on the priest and his followers. See Kącki, *Ks. Stanisław Stojałowski*, 22–32.

[6] Several studies have tackled Father Stojałowski's somewhat conflicting attitudes toward the peasants, including Kącki, *Ks. Stanisław Stojałowski*; Antoni Gurnicz, "Ks. Stanisław Stojałowski a rozwój myśli chrześcijańsko-społecznej w Galicji," *Międzyuczelniane zeszyty naukowe: Studia z historii myśli społeczno-ekonomicznej*, no. 4 (1964): 127–35; Kieniewicz, *Galicja*, xxxiv–xxxvi; and Stefan Suchonek, "Działalność polityczna ks. St. Stojatowskiego w Żywiecczyźnie," *Gronie* 2 (1939): 127–42.

[7] *Pszczółka*, October 4, 1877, 1–2.

[8] Ibid.

[9] *Wieniec*, April 19, 1885, 30.

the organization, noting with approval that villagers had begun, on their own initiative, to "advise themselves about their own matters" and "to solve their own misery."[10] Even while acknowledging the grassroots impetus of much of the early activities in village farming clubs, however, Stojałowski and other members of the Galician elite persisted in their efforts to guide and direct these dispersed local activities. The priest himself stressed the need for education to be conducted in a cooperative spirit, making use of alliances among social groups. "Education," the editor advised, should be offered to peasants "in the name of brotherly love," with an eye toward building ties between social strata rather than promoting class divisions and mutual hostilities.

Stojałowski's concern about the possible eruption of an independent peasant organization was faint compared with the suspicions of the conservative gentry. The crownland's leading conservative journal, *Czas*, referred derisively to the agricultural circle project, complaining that "under the cloak of a town meeting," peasants were "becoming involved in ignorant and antisocial work . . . against the national interests."[11] Editors of *Czas* accused Stojałowski of encouraging "separatism" among the peasants and "acting against the interests of the peasants and those of other classes."[12]

The agricultural circle movement was the product of negotiation among individual clerics such as Stojałowski, members of the Galician political establishment, and the village activists who attended early meetings. The movement was split from its inception among Stojałowski's efforts to decentralize operations in order to empower villagers, the often-grappling attempts by political leaders to assume centralized control, and the disparate activities of local peasant farmers. This three-cornered power struggle continued during the entire history of the agricultural circle movement, allowing peasants space to refine their ideological stances and to articulate their interests.

The tension within the movement was heightened in 1882 when the conservative Galician gentry asserted its political and economic authority over the organization's operations. Father Stojałowski had long been plagued with financial problems, including indebtedness and accusations of tax violations.[13] His petitions for Sejm subsidies were repeatedly denied, and attempts to collect private contributions met with

---

[10] *Pszczółka*, May 30, 1878, 1.
[11] *Czas*, July 2, 1888, as cited in Rymar, "Chłopi polscy," 184.
[12] Ibid., 184.
[13] Stojałowski discusses these in *Wieniec*, June 1, 1881, 92.

little success.[14] In the hopes of buttressing the financial security of his own organization, the Society for Education and Work, Stojałowski turned to the Galician Farmers Society (Towarzystwo Galicyiskie Gospodarskie).

At a mass meeting held on the symbolically important date of May 3, peasants and gentry met both to celebrate the anniversary of the signing of the stillborn Polish constitution of 1791 and to negotiate increased financial support for the society. Stojałowski agreed to merge the Society for Education and Work with the Galician Farmers Society and to accept "certain changes in the statutes" of the new organization in exchange for the financial backing of the conservative society. The convention elected a new slate of influential conservative board members, among them Sejm marshal Prince Adam Sapieha,[15] member of the Crownland Governing Board (Wydział Krajowy) Piotr Gross, and the bishops of Cracow, Przemysł, and Lwów.[16] The formal name of the newly merged organization was the Agricultural Circle Society (Towarzystwo Kółka Rolniczego or TKR).

The programmatic differences between Stojałowski and his new benefactors became clear almost immediately after the TKR's conception. Stojałowski lobbied hard both at the May assembly and again during a mass meeting held in Przemyśl the following September for increased decision-making power to be allocated to individual circle cells. The large landholders, however, suspicious of Stojałowski's efforts, sought instead to centralize the society's activities.[17] Conservative leaders of the TKR argued that permitting village circles to set their own agenda reinforced the cultural isolation peasants experienced under serfdom and did little to integrate villagers into the larger society. Rather, they held, the Polish peasant needed to be taught to be a citizen. Afraid lest Stojałowski encourage independent peasant control over local circles, the board transferred the new society's headquarters away from the priest's editorial offices in 1884 and forbade peasant delegates from participating in general assemblies. From this point on, peasant influence declined, and conservative gentry dominated the TKR's administrative apparatus.[18]

---

[14] Gurnicz, *Kółka rolnicze*, 51–52.
[15] Prince Sapieha was a longtime opponent of Stojałowski's rural schemes. As head of the Farmers Society, he had refused in 1877 to entertain the priest's proposal for the formation of agricultural circles. *Pszczółka*, May 31, 1877, 3; Kącki, *Ks. Stanisław Stojałowski*, 52.
[16] On the centennial celebrations for the constitution in Lwów and the meeting merging the two organizations, see *Wieniec*, May 5, 1882, 73–74; Gurnicz, *Kółka rolnicze*, 52–57; Rymar, "Chłopi polscy," 191–92.
[17] *Pszczółka*, September 14, 1882, 145–46.
[18] Gurnicz, *Kółka rolnicze*, 57–60.

Many village organizers and peasant members, already chafing at Father Stojałowski's mild attempts to suggest reading material and speakers at meetings, resented the TKR leadership's insistence on centralization. As the gentry-led farmers' organization began to receive more attention in governing circles and in the mainstream press, villagers expressed annoyance that their earlier efforts at self-improvement and organization somehow lacked legitimacy since they were not pursued in close association with large landholders. One village correspondent, who called himself "Tuszowiak" (resident of Tuszów), complained of the publicity surrounding the mass meetings after the TKR was formed. Galician villagers, commented this correspondent, have been meeting in such assemblies since 1877, but "so what? No one paid any attention to that because it was only peasants. . . . If there had been any gentry, princes, counts, or representatives of the crownland . . . if there had been any of these at [the earlier] meetings, they could have seen the poverty in which the peasant lived." The writer, perhaps a village notable himself, complained that all this time the upper classes "did not bother with the peasants." Even after estate owners and other upper-class politicians became involved with organization in the rural areas, many villagers still refused to trust their activities. "Neither the Sejm nor any farmers' society does anything in the name of all the farmers," Tuszowiak concluded. "Take this to those good gentlemen living so far from us," he instructed Stojałowski.[19]

Conservative politicians sought throughout the 1880s to integrate the peasants into mainstream Polish culture through a paternalistic agenda. Yet the rural reforms the central board of the Agricultural Circle Society proposed had an element of hypocrisy to them. Conservative deputies in the Sejm slashed the educational budget year after year, defeating efforts to expand the network of rural schools,[20] while state expenditures on alcohol production exceeded those for education by a factor of ten to one.[21]

Conservative leaders in the TKR and in the Sejm also refused to support Franciszek Stefczyk's efforts to establish a system of rural cooperatives offering low interest loans for peasants to purchase land and farm equip-

---

[19] "Tuszowiak" to *Wieniec*, January 17, 1886, 15. Although it is difficult to determine with any degree of certainty the exact social background of correspondents to rural newspapers, the details included in the letters suggest most were written by those closely familiar with village life, including rural intellectuals, craftsmen, or small farmers.

[20] Efforts by liberal Sejm deputies to raise governmental support for building schools and training and compensating teachers met with resistance from crownland conservatives. See Edward Wierzbicki, "Poglądy Stanisława Szczepanowskiego na rozwój oświaty wychowania w Galicji," *Rocznik Przemyski* 21 (1979): 273–75.

[21] Wierzbicki, "Poglądy Stanisława Szczepanowskiego," 276.

ment. Despite his position on the central board of the TKR, Stefczyk was unable to convince the organization's leadership or government officials in the Sejm to enact the alternative system of rural credit. Stefczyk's proposal to an 1889 meeting of the Agricultural Circle Board in Lwów was greeted with "barely veiled mistrust" and a refusal to grant support.[22] The unwillingness of conservative politicians in the diet to support rural schools, educational programs, and credit institutions demonstrated the disparities between their agenda and the grassroots efforts in the countryside.

Conservative TKR leaders relied on the promotion of local gentry and clerics to replace peasants as heads of individual circles in order to facilitate centralization.[23] Upper-class members of the society, however, were far more eager to serve on regional administrative boards than to be active in individual circle cells.[24] This preference for regional over village activity left the leadership of village organizations to the rural intelligentsia, many of whom had strong sympathies for the peasant cause. In time, the leadership shifted to a cadre of active small farmers. The number of peasant officers in local circles increased dramatically as the organization expanded its reach and widened its range of activities. In 1889, peasants led 49 percent of the total of 529 circles submitting reports; by 1908, 55 percent of the presidents and 83 percent of the vice-presidents of 1,340 reporting circles were peasants.[25] Estate owners headed only 8 percent of all circles in 1889 and served as secretaries in only 0.5 percent.[26] Parish priests and schoolteachers formed the majority of the other officers in the countryside.

Despite the unwillingness of the TKR leadership to consider schemes for decentralization, the sheer growth in the number of local circles and the lack of interest estate owners displayed in the day-to-day operation of individual cells led to ever-increasing independence for village officers. As the split between center and periphery grew, a rural reform movement was born in which local initiative and social independence were fostered. Indeed, rather than breeding national solidarity and social cooperation,

---

[22] Antoni Gurnicz, "System spółdzielczy, F. W. Raiffeisena i galicyjska adaptacja F. Stefczyka," *Spółdzielczy Kwartalnik naukowy i*, no. 4 (1967): 143–48. For details of Stefczyk's cooperative system, see *Przyjaciel Ludu*, February 1, 1891, 40, and April 1, 1891, 103–4.

[23] See Gurnicz, *Kółka rolnicze*, 20–26, 37–40.

[24] TKR district boards were headed by large landholders, officials, priests or attorneys. See transcript of the activities of the TKR for 1891 (Lwów 1892), as cited in Gurnicz, *Kółka rolnicze*, 106.

[25] *Czasopismo dla spółek rolniczych* (August 1, 1909); transcript of the activities of the TKR for 1908 (Lwów, 1909), as cited in Gurnicz, *Kółka rolnicze*, 107.

[26] Transcript of the activities of the TKR for 1889 (Lwów, 1890); *Tygodnik Rolniczy*, no. 25 (1890), as cited in Gurnicz, *Kółka rolnicze*, 106.

the policies of the TKR administrators encouraged greater independence of rural circle members from their gentry "leaders."

The Roots of Peasant Activism

Long before gentry farmers became interested in promoting rural education, peasant activists were molding agricultural circles to fit the traditions and rhythms of rural society. The 1877 organizational meeting of the Agricultural Circle Society in Lwów sparked the formation of dozens of circles and subsidiary reading rooms throughout the countryside. Clerics and other village intellectuals relied on customary forms of organization to gain the attention of the peasantry in the early years of the movement. At the first mass peasant meeting in Lwów, for example, Stojałowski himself stressed the close ties between traditional and modern forms of mobilization, portraying the educational circles as extensions of village meetings held during serfdom. "Now, instead of such meetings under open skies," the priest explained, "there are organizational meetings such as those of the agricultural circles."[27]

Cultural linkages between the circles and traditional occasions played a key role in the founding years of the peasant movement. Later, peasant assemblies were scheduled to correspond with important saints' days or other religious anniversaries, meshing customary forms of association with new political content. Peasant farmers from Kosłowa (Milatyna district) initiated a petition in 1878 proposing a mass assembly for the following summer (1879) on the occasion of the anniversary of Saint Stanisław's death.[28] Throughout the preparation for the May 1879 meeting, the event was publicized as a "religious pilgrimage to the grave of Saint Stanisław" in Cracow that would also, almost incidentally, be the occasion of a mass peasant meeting. Peasant correspondents to rural newspapers composed poetry encouraging their fellows to participate in the pilgrimage.[29] The event itself, attended by thousands, was suffused with the religious and national symbolism appropriate for celebrating the life and death of a Polish saint.[30] In this way, the assembly took on a double valence, the modern political movement merging with potent national symbols.

Events in the countryside in the months following the christening of Stojałowski's Society for Education and Work bore witness to an increasingly

---

[27] Transcript of Father Stojałowski's speech, reprinted in *Pszczółka*, October 4, 1877, 1–2.
[28] Kącki, *Ks. Stanisław Stojałowski*, 49–50.
[29] Such as the poem by Jan Mikoś, from the village of Gwoznica, encouraging peasant participation in the Cracow pilgrimage. *Pszczółka*, March 28, 1879, 50.
[30] See *Wieniec*, May 30, 1879, 85–86.

active and independent peasantry being mobilized into rural associations, even in the absence of significant gentry assistance at the grassroots level. Over one hundred village communes were represented at the 1878 founding meeting in Cracow. [31] Following the meeting, many of these peasant participants returned to their villages to establish a total of some thirty circles with 492 regular members throughout western Galicia in the coming year.[32] These were independent grassroots efforts, pursued without significant supervision from upper-class administrators. Indeed, enthusiasm for rural organization was most marked precisely in those areas lacking a strong tradition of gentry leadership.

The Biała district in western Galicia was a case in point. Two weeks after the Cracow meeting, some 1,500 peasants attended a mass assembly in the small town of Bestwina. The Biała district lacked significant numbers of Polish gentry since it had been heavily colonized by Germans after falling under Austrian rule. The absence of natural leadership among the local gentry and the presence of "foreign" landholders prompted the Biała peasants to cultivate "their own Polish customs more carefully."[33] The greatest and most immediate response to Stojałowski's bid for village organization thus came from an area lacking in natural Polish gentry leadership, but in which peasants maintained strong nationalist traditions. Biała smallholders took the initiative to organize local assemblies, and only later joined the Society for Education and Work.

Father Stojałowski fought desperately to maintain control over the burgeoning agricultural circle movement in the years following its inception. He traveled throughout the Galician countryside, holding meetings with peasants and village notables. He initiated a number of mechanisms to facilitate communication within the growing organization, including establishing a new journal, *The Village Farmer (Gospodarz Wiejski)*, which featured articles on agricultural innovations, grain prices, and currency exchange rates.[34] Here and elsewhere, Stojałowski emphasized the correct procedures for establishing and running agricultural circles.[35] Stojałowski circulated a survey among the chairs of local cells, inquiring about the services each chapter offered and the focus of discussions among mem-

---

[31] *Pszczółka*, July 25, 1878.

[32] Kącki, *Ks. Stanisław Stojałowski*, 51–52.

[33] *Pszczółka*, July 25, 1878, 2.

[34] *The Village Farmer* was published for only about a year and a half. Kącki, *Ks. Stanisław Stojałowski*, 51–52.

[35] See, for example, *Pszczółka*, February 8, 1877, 1. Later articles reemphasized the appropriate procedure for founding and running reading rooms. *Pszczółka*, February 1, 1879, 10–11, for example, carried detailed instructions on how to start up village reading rooms,

bers.[36] Despite these organizational strategies, the grassroots momentum of the movement forced it beyond Stojałowski's guidance and direction and beyond the control of conservative gentry. Instead, the activities of agricultural circle cells were shaped by local initiative, including the interests of peasant members.

Nonfarming village elites, including schoolteachers, parish priests, and merchants, led many of these early Galician agricultural circles. It was a merchant, Franciszek Popiel, who brought together the fifteen hundred peasants in Biała district. And Jan Schnajder, a tailor from Oświęcim, was instrumental in attracting members to the Biała circle.[37] Parish priests and rural teachers, who were in a position to "brush up against the peasants" and "feel their poverty and misery," established reading rooms at first unattached to any larger organizational hierarchy. The parish priest, the postman, and the school headmaster in the village of Ujście Solne, for example, "noticed the lack of education in their countrymen" in 1877 and founded a reading room to help remedy it. They managed to obtain subscriptions to two rural newspapers free of charge, and used Stojałowski's paper to send out an appeal for contributions of more books.[38] And in March of 1879—still before the formal founding of the Society for Education and Work—the village mayor and schoolteacher in the village of Bieńczyce came together to found an independent reading club. Agreeing that "one route out of their poverty was the creation of a reading room," the two called a meeting in the schoolhouse, in which the assembled villagers "unanimously decided to take action." Reflecting later on the founding years of the peasant movement, the village correspondent known as "Tuszowiak" recalled that the teachers and clerics were the only ones who "felt the needs of agriculture just like the peasants."[39]

In the early days of Stojałowski's organizational initiatives, many rural reading clubs remained unattached to the national agricultural circle hierarchy.[40] Rather than simply joining Stojałowski's society, members of the

---

emphasizing that they needed to be constructed "in association with membership in the agricultural circle society."

[36] See sample survey printed in *Wieniec*, July 24, 1879, 113–14.

[37] *Pszczółka*, July 25, 1878, 2; *Wieniec*, October 16, 1879, 167–68; Jan Schnajder to *Wieniec*, October 30, 1879, 175.

[38] The newspapers were *Chata* (The Cottage) and *Nowiny* (The News), both primarily religious in emphasis. Michał Tazbierski and Józef Mroziński (Ujście Solne) to *Pszczółka*, September 20, 1877, 4.

[39] "Tuszowiak" to *Wieniec*, January 17, 1886, 15.

[40] Stojałowski explained the differences between independent rural clubs and agricultural circles, recommending "simply joining the Society" for Education and Work as the easiest method of founding a library (*Pszczółka*, December 19, 1878, 1). Nevertheless, many inde-

club in Bieńczyce, for example, "wrote a request [directly] to the governor general" regarding the founding of a reading room in their *gmina*.[41] The villagers of "C.," near Wieliczka in the district of Cracow, resolved to found a reading room and even traveled to Cracow to visit the offices of the Society for People's Education and Work (Towarzystwo Szkolnictwo Prace Ludowe or TSL). Rather than joining immediately, however, they managed to establish a reading room and library, eliminate the village tavern, open an elementary school, and found a credit society a full two years before joining the TSL.[42]

Customary Interactions in Village Associations

The tension between leaders and members within the circle movement continued to sharpen as the network of agricultural circles and their subsidiary associations expanded. Peasants and village intellectuals promoted local interests distinct from those of gentry benefactors, prompting the village population to pull farther away from the guidance of the central power structure. Center and periphery developed in different directions, and the momentum of the movement remained in the countryside among individual village activists.

The social function of agricultural circles became an increasingly important attraction for peasant members, often overriding the intended educational purpose for which the associations were originally established. Many members were drawn to circle activities because they provided an alternative to congregating in the village tavern. Gathering on Sunday afternoons and holidays to read newspapers, exchange farming information, or participate in various celebratory activities, peasants gradually developed a social group operating outside the jurisdiction of the tavern manager, with his perceived high prices and usurious loans.[43] Stojałowski and other TKR leaders had originally envisioned one of the primary purposes of the organization as that of "improving the moral level of the peasantry" by convincing them to "shun drunkenness and ostentatious celebrations."[44] Although the opportunity to congregate in the circle building as opposed to the tavern was

---

pendent reading clubs continued to exist in the countryside for a number of years after the Society for Education and Work was established.
[41] R. K., Bieńczyce, Cracow district, to *Pszczółka*, March 13, 1879, 47.
[42] *Wiejscy działacze społeczni*, vol. 2: *Zyciorysy inteligentów* (Warsaw, 1938), 340–42.
[43] For more on the role of the Jewish innkeeper in the Polish countryside, see Opalski, *Jewish Tavern-Keeper*.
[44] Cited in Gurnicz, *Kółka rolnicze*, 52–57.

enjoyed, circle meetings still became forums for organizing rural entertainment. One group in Tarnów district, for example, engaged mainly in activities such as "entertainment, carnivals, New Year's Eve celebrations, exchange of wafers [at Christmas] and others. Meetings . . . included [the singing of] patriotic songs, chats, tea, pipes, playing of cards and dominoes."[45] Other circles helped bring together "choirs, amateur theaters [and] . . . fire departments," purposes that soon displaced their intended function as reading circles or centers of agricultural education.[46]

As the circles took over the functions of entertainment and social organization in the village, they soon absorbed responsibility for staging celebrations of various commemorative and patriotic occasions. Agricultural circles coordinated preparations for events such as the anniversary of the Polish Constitution of May 3 (1791), in which the circle building and circle members played prominent roles. As one participant recalled,

> In the morning after the playing of revelry on the trumpet, flags of red and white [Polish colors] flew from the homes of circle members, in the church there was a mass, after the mass a parade passed through the village with music. During the parade, the fire department always walked at the head of the procession. At the statue of the heroes of Grunwald or on the veranda of the circle [building] there was a speech about the constitution of May 3. . . . The windows in the circle building, in the schoolhouse, and along the road were decorated with May 3 banners; in the evening everything was illuminated with lights.[47]

In this and other cases, circle participation served a transitional purpose, offering a customary means of celebrating modern political and patriotic occasions. The parade, led by members of the fire department in their uniforms, lent a military air to the performance, replacing the masks and costumes worn by participants in traditional village processions. The statue of Grunwald represented the peasantry's commitment to serve the nation, as they had by fighting in the fifteenth-century battle to rid the country of Teutonic Knights. Church and school, the pillars of peasant morality, were joined by the circle building, which now symbolically replaced the tavern as the center of community celebrations.[48]

As circle meeting rooms, whether located "in a community building, the

---

[45] *Wiejscy działacze społeczni*, vol. 1: *Życiorysy włościan* (Warsaw, 1937), 229.
[46] Gurnicz, *Kółka rolnicze*, 85–86.
[47] *Wiejscy działacze*, 1: 229.
[48] For more on patriotic celebrations and the role they played in the development of Polish populist nationalism, see Stauter-Halsted, "Peasant Patriotic Celebrations."

schoolhouse, or the home of one of the members,"[49] began to fulfill the socializing functions traditionally met by village taverns, local clergy and the church hierarchy greeted the development with enthusiasm. Neither Stojałowski nor TKR board members raised any initial objections to social activities within village chapters, so long as the economic and educational aspects of the TKR's agenda were also pursued. Meanwhile, in areas where agricultural circles took the lead in organizing rural entertainment, "the tavern next door stood completely abandoned, whereas before it [had] as a rule been full of people."[50]

Although gentry and clerical administrators may have been somewhat chagrined at the transformation of what they intended as a primarily economic and educational organization into a focus for rural entertainment, they could hardly have resented the role circle assemblies assumed in staging celebrations of national anniversaries. Galician newspapers were full of plans for crownland-wide events to commemorate patriotic occasions, and the participation of the peasants—especially in their native villages where they could not interfere with official celebrations—was greeted with general approval by the Galician social elite.

Agricultural circles also began to usurp another function often served by literate rural middlemen, including many *shtetl* Jews, that of legal counselor. The circle building functioned as an arbitration court in many villages, permitting "disputes between members to be heard by upstanding and honest people and [making it un]necessary to wander around the courts of justice."[51] Agricultural circles thus devised an alternative to the time-wasting and expensive procedure of traveling to regional courts to settle local conflicts. In doing so, they partially displaced the position of rural scribes, who earned their living from documenting legal proceedings.

The position of agricultural circles as centers of rural social life came to conflict more with the conception of TKR administrators, however, as tavern functions were more closely replicated through the sale of alcohol to members. Stojałowski reported sadly in 1884 that at least one circle had overstepped its authority by directly opposing the TKR's policy on alcohol consumption, further indicating that local control over circle administration had supplanted the guidance of the central powers.

It is a sad fact that today we must note . . . that a circle in a certain location . . . requested permission from the *starostwo* [office of the district

[49] Dawidowa, *Kółka rolnicze*, 8.
[50] *Wiejscy działacze*, 1: 229.
[51] See, for example, the report of the agricultural circle in Borzęcin, district of Biadolin, to *Wieniec*, November 6, 1884, 201.

governor] to sell sweet drinks [alcoholic beverages]. The *starostwo* denied permission, and the leader of this circle, a *wójt* . . . brought to the *starostwo* a second request for permission to establish a store with a variety of goods, because the meager trade in foodstuffs 'was not adequate for the needs of the residents.' The *starostwo* this time gave his permission— and shortly thereafter the store was enlarged to include 'essential' goods, including sweet vodka in bottles. Reportedly, the store then began to sell vodka in bottles—and secretly to gather people at the store for shot glasses. The *wójt* in this way found a means of getting members of the village drunk and in the evenings even gathered people and served them in his home.[52]

For some circle members, including this enterprising village mayor, the inclusion of alcohol at social gatherings represented a logical extension of the social function agricultural circles had come to serve for their members. Such blatant violations of the TKR anti-alcohol policy indicate the distance from the dictates of the TKR board many individual village clubs had come. Efforts to centralize all aspects of circle life, subordinating their activities to the dictates of the TKR leadership, had failed. Instead, the decentralization that Stojałowski had formally sacrificed to the large landowners was becoming a de facto reality. Peasants were taking the administration of the circles into their own hands, integrating village customary elements into their official functions.

Even more significant for the larger identity of the TKR, its leadership increasingly had difficulty convincing circle members to accept its pedagogical agenda, including the establishment of reading rooms and the teaching of farming techniques.[53] The central board assisted individual circles by sending them books, newspapers, information on agricultural techniques, and religious texts to encourage the peasantry's "moral development."[54] Yet of the half dozen newspapers regularly provided to circle libraries, only two—Stojałowski's journals, *Wieniec* and *Pszczółka*—are ever noted in peasant letters and reports as among those read aloud and discussed at weekly meetings.[55] Stojałowski's papers and a handful of

---

[52] *Wieniec*, December 18, 1884, 225.

[53] The founding program of the TKR placed reading rooms and the dissemination of agricultural information as the two primary aims of the organization. Dawidowa, *Kółka rolnicze*, 4–5.

[54] *Wieniec*, April 19, 1885, 30.

[55] Other papers local circles received included *Niedziela* (Sunday), *Chata* (The Cottage), *Samorząd* (Self-Government), *Nowiny* (The News), and *Rolnik postępów* (The Progressive Farmer). Dawidowa, *Kółka rolnicze*, 9; *Instrukcja dla kółek rolniczych* (Lwów, 1883); and *Wieniec*, February 15, 1883, as cited in Gurnicz, *Kółka rolnicze*, 83.

books did become the focus of discussions at many weekly circle meetings.[56] Indeed, circle membership often provided illiterate peasants with their only opportunity to hear news and information read aloud from the weekly press by better-educated members.[57]

Attempts to promote agricultural education through the circles proved even more difficult. Efforts to "encourage all local farmers to take part in agricultural lessons given by traveling agricultural teachers sent by the central administration" were largely unsuccessful.[58]

Travelling lecturers, who spoke on topics ranging from "moral sciences and economics" to "belles lettres," reportedly failed to connect with their peasant audience.[59] Circle members complained that the instructors presented "only theoretical" sides to agrarian problems, refusing to "demonstrate their lessons on location" so that peasants could see the lessons translated into reality. The language and approach of the instructors frequently made their lessons difficult to follow. One circle member from Wiązownice complained that "it is generally known how difficult it is to get members to attend at the time of the meetings" (as opposed to social occasions). The reason for this was that "the intelligentsia usually don't understand how to address the peasant and generally lecture in the tone of an academic, a style not understandable [to the peasant]. And this is naturally the reason that peasants leave and don't even bother to attend the sessions."[60]

Even in educational matters, then, deemed the highest priority by circle administrators, peasants were not able to "make use of even half the improvements offered them" because of the failure of upper-class educators to take account of local needs and perceptions.[61] As the agricultural circle movement grew, the gap between the tactics of gentry organizers, on the one hand, and the attitudes of the peasants they sought to mold, on the other, continued to widen. Increasingly, villagers simply accepted the materials they were offered and determined based on local needs the uses to be made of them.

---

[56] As, for example, in Krościenko, on the Dunajec river in southern Galicia, where some sixty members met "almost every Sunday in the afternoon" to "read newspapers and useful books and counsel together about the needs of the circle." *Pszczółka*, December 1884, 217.

[57] Occasionally, sections of books were also recited, such as the performance following the inauguration of the agricultural circle in Krzeszowice in March of 1882, where *Twenty Stories from the History of Poland, Lithuania, and Ruthenia* was read aloud to the assembled audience. *Pszczółka*, July 20, 1882, 118.

[58] Reprinted in Dawidowa, *Kółka rolnicze*, 4–5.

[59] From a lecture schedule published in *Pszczółka*, July 20, 1882, 118.

[60] Unsigned letter, Wiązownica, to *Pszczółka*, October 18, 1882, 166–67.

[61] Dawidowa, *Kółka rolnicze*, 9–10.

The tension between leaders and members within the Agricultural Circle Society was manifested most visibly in the system of representation within the organization. From its earliest days, the society maintained rudimentary elements of democracy. Each village circle elected a delegate with voting rights to attend the general assemblies. After the official merger with the gentry Farmers Society, this level of peasant participation gradually eroded. By 1885, three years after the merger of Stojałowski's grassroots circle movement with the Galician Farmers Society, local circles were forbidden to send official representatives to vote at annual meetings. Instead, they were asked to send delegates to the gentry-dominated district meeting, where a single delegate would be chosen to attend the General Assembly.[62]

Stojałowski defended his own and the peasantry's sense of grassroots democracy in response to this new regulation, arguing in one of his most challenging (and ultimately unsuccessful) critiques of TKR leadership that "if the . . . General Assembly of Agricultural Circles takes place without the participation of delegates from each individual circle, it will certainly be invalid and illegal."[63] In a sentiment that echoed the accusations of peasant delegates whose credentials were challenged in the Sejm, Stojałowski represented peasant perceptions of a higher morality, indicating that any assembly excluding them was itself not valid. Driven by a mission to guide and inform villagers in the essentials of farming and a zeal to promote social solidarity on their own terms, conservative Galician nobles inadvertently drove peasants away from one of the few official fora in which they might have developed shared interests.

As the gentry bore down on peasant circle members with impenetrable educators and complicated regulations, villagers withdrew still further from the hold of the TKR administration, ceasing to file annual reports or to correspond with the circle board about local matters. By the end of 1885, the number of new agricultural circles began a sharp decline. The total number of circles had almost doubled each year since the movement began, yet after 1884, barely twenty new circles were founded annually and by 1888 the total membership of Galician circles began to drop.[64] By the winter of 1886, Stojałowski's journals published complaints of the large numbers of circles that had "not given a sign of life" recently or had "fallen, due to misunderstanding their task."[65]

---

[62] By the 1886 annual meeting, only sixty of the over two hundred delegates were peasants; in 1891 even nonvoting peasant members were barred from the meeting. *Wieniec*, April 19, 1885, 30; *Wieniec*, February 21, 1886, 25; *Przyjaciel Ludu*, April 15, 1891, 127.
[63] *Wieniec*, April 19, 1885, 30; and June 3, 1885, 49–50, 60.
[64] Dawidowa, *Kółka rolnicze*, 7–8.
[65] Report in *Wieniec*, February 21, 1886, 26–28.

Curiously, however, even without close ties to the central administration, the circles continued their work in the countryside. Ever more circles opened village stores for their members in the 1880s. By the 1890s, the number of new stores opening annually surpassed the number of new circles.[66] Local cells initiated programs for distributing seed during failed harvests in these years, more circles made use of the society's insurance policy, and many clubs began providing scholarships for peasants enrolling in handicraft schools. Circle members increasingly received the services of society lawyers, and they worked for the removal of tolls on public roads. The circle administration was, if anything, trailing behind the programmatic initiatives of local circles and peasant members. Indeed, so faint were the links joining center to periphery within the organization that many village circle members were reportedly surprised to learn that they were part of a larger organizational structure.[67]

Anti-Semitism as a Basis for Cross-Class Alliances

Of all the projects the circle administration initiated in the countryside, peasant members and gentry administrators cooperated effectively on only one main enterprise—the founding of Christian stores to compete with Jewish shop owners in the village. The organization of a wide network of peasant-run general stores to break the Jewish monopoly on rural trade was one area in which village economic needs could be met effectively via the organizational advantages of the Agricultural Circle Society. Anti-Jewish projects also helped foster the perception among gentry and peasants alike that the two groups could work together on the basis of shared national (anti-Semitic) interests. Financial considerations and a desire to place trusted members of the village community in the position of shopkeepers initially sparked peasant efforts to establish Catholic-run stores. Yet in time members of the gentry also interpreted attempts to compete with Jewish merchants as moves in a patriotic game to exclude those perceived as non-Poles according to a culturally based conception of the nation.[68]

[66] Gurnicz, *Kółka rolnicze*, 249; Dawidowa, *Kółka rolnicze*, 7–8.
[67] Gurnicz, *Kółka rolnicze*, 86–96.
[68] Literature on the interaction between Jews and Poles within the Polish nationalist movement is still limited for the nineteenth century. For access to this literature, see Jerzy J. Lerski, ed., *Jewish-Polish Coexistence, 1772–1939: A Topical Bibliography* (New York, 1986). Magdalena Opalski and Israel Bartal have traced Polish-Jewish relations during and after the January Rising in *Poles and Jews: A Failed Brotherhood* (Hanover, N.H., 1992). For an introduction to conditions among Galician Jews and the "Jewish Question" in Polish circles, see Wróbel, "Jews under Austrian-Polish Rule"; Feliks Kiryk, ed., *Żydzi w Małopolsce: Stu-*

Anti-Jewish sentiment in Galician villages sprang from the economic structure of country life.[69] Polish and Ukrainian peasants, generally uneducated and possessing few financial resources, traditionally depended on Jewish merchants living in the countryside to provide the few cash goods they required (salt, kerosene, candles, tobacco, etc.). Village innkeepers were also almost without exception Jewish, since gentry landowners had sold their concessions for alcohol trade only to nonserfs before emancipation. In the absence of formal credit facilities, peasants were frequently forced to turn to village Jews for emergency loans, especially to meet their new tax burdens.[70] Because of their position within the money economy, Galician villagers viewed rural Jews, whether in their capacity as bartenders, moneylenders, or managers of general stores, as responsible for much of their economic misery.[71] To complete the picture of economic control, Jewish families in the 1870s began competing with small farmers to buy up estate land from impoverished gentry.[72] By 1889, some 10 percent of agricultural land was owned by Jews.[73]

The rural press encouraged an image of rural Jews as foreigners, although Jewish families had resided in Galicia since the fourteenth century. Stojałowski's papers regularly reported on the sale of estate land to "foreigners," arguing that "one must allow neither the sale of land into foreign hands, nor the loss of Polish lands into the hands of the enemies of our nation [i.e., the Jews]." Everywhere the small farmer turned, his way out of penury appeared to be blocked by Jews, an image further promoted by gentry institutions in the countryside. Promoting general stores allowed TKR leaders to establish a rhetorical link between their efforts to reduce the power of "foreigners" in the countryside and a frightened and desperate peasantry seeking greater economic control.

The image of the rapacious rural Jew, extracting huge profits from honest farmers, was, of course, incomplete since peasants too benefited from trade relations with rural Jews. For those villagers living near one of Gali-

---

dia z dziejów osadnictwa i życia społecznego (Przemyśl, 1991); and Majer Bałaban, *Dzieje Żydów w Galicji i Rzeczpospolitej Krakowskiej 1772–1868* (Lwów, 1914).
[69] John-Paul Himka examines the economic bases of anti-Semitism in the eastern, Ukrainian areas of Galicia in "Ukrainian-Jewish Antagonism."
[70] Jan Słomka discusses the amount and variety of imperial taxes peasants were required to pay after the end of serfdom, in Słomka, *From Serfdom to Self-Government*, 182–83.
[71] See, for example, the discussion of peasant perceptions of village Jews in Opalski, *Jewish Tavern-Keeper*, 31–33.
[72] *Pszczółka*, June 9, 1881, 89–90, and *Wieniec*, June 17, 1881, 98–99. On the emancipation process and the acquisition of property rights for Habsburg Jews, see Eisenbach, *Emancipation of the Jews in Poland*, 496–97.
[73] Hemmerling, "Stronnictwa ludowe wobec Żydów," 155.

cia's *shtetl* communities, weekly markets provided important opportunities to sell farm produce, as in the predominantly Jewish settlement of Dobromil, in the northeastern part of the province, where

> Mondays the peasantry of the region round used to come to buy for themselves their various household necessities for the week. At the same time, they would bring into town for sale their geese, their quacking ducks, hens, calves, hogs, horses, cows, wagon loads of wood, and so on. And so the *shtetl* used to provide its livelihood, one day rousing up from its week-long sleep. And for the "Yehudim" there was a lively turmoil, a hollering, a screaming, and a bleating, every Monday until time for the "Mincha" evening prayers. Then once again all became hushed quiet.[74]

Despite the economic interdependency of Catholics and Jews, both peasants and gentry saw benefit in breaking Jewish economic power in the countryside. The anti-"other" sentiment kept alive through folk culture under serfdom was directed after emancipation at village Jews, whose unfamiliar language, customs, religion, and professional practices inspired renewed hostility among Catholic farmers. Long-standing cultural differences and animosity fueled by ignorance prompted absurd varieties of suspicion to be directed toward rural Jews. One villager calculated somewhat arbitrarily that each of the eighty-two Jews living in his community was costing Catholic villagers 20 cents per day, and that the village as a whole was losing some 5,986 zlotys per year by doing business with local Jews. "If one village loses so much on the Jews, how much must a district pay, and how much does the entire crownland pay?" queried the baffled peasant.[75]

Partially encouraged by comments made from the pulpit, many villagers came to view Jewish businessmen as dishonest and unscrupulous in their dealings with their Christian neighbors. As early as the first mass peasant meeting in Cracow in 1878, concern about Jewish trickery was high on the peasant agenda. Upper-class TKR members even criticized village participants for having wasted the assembly's time on "unnecessary and unfruitful" discussions of the Jews. A leading peasant activist, Maciej Szarek, defended the smallholders' priorities at the meeting, arguing straightforwardly that they had nothing against the Jews themselves. "It is just the swindling they have troubles with."[76]

Often peasant leaders used the image of Jewish economic dominance to

---

[74] Miller, *Dobromil*, 4.
[75] Franciszek Drózd, Rajcza, to *Wieniec*, February 9, 1882, 31–32.
[76] Maciej Szarek, Brzegi, to *Pszczółka*, July 25, 1878.

motivate villagers toward greater educational efforts, arguing that the only way small farmers would free themselves from economic dependence on Jews was to obtain the skills they needed to compete. Franciszek Drózd, the farmer who complained about the high cost of keeping eighty-two Jews in his village, pinned the blame for these financial losses on the peasants themselves, who did not always keep careful accounts and refused to take on the functions of rural merchants. Why are we losing this money to the Jews? Drózd asked. "Because the people would rather give themselves up to the advantage of the Jews than learn and improve themselves." Rural Jews, Drózd complained, were able to live at the expense of the villagers only because they took "advantage of the ignorance and stupidity of the people." "We must take over some of the work the Jews are living from," he declared. "And this," he concluded, "requires education."[77] Maciej Szarek, peasant activist from Brzegi, pressed the idea of Christian-run stores to educate peasants in the use of weights and measures and to protect them from being tricked by sly Jewish merchants whose "hands" he believed to be "unjust." The establishment of Christian stores, he suggested, would "reduce the amount of goods sold by Jews according to false weights and measures."[78]

The Agricultural Circle Society, with its scheme of establishing a network of Christian general stores to compete with the existing Jewish-run stores, fit neatly into this atmosphere of frustration at the rising economic influence of village Jews. The idea of founding peasant-run stores in rural areas was initially promoted by upper-class activists, including Father Stojałowski, receiving a very lukewarm reception among the rural population.[79] The movement took off only when the Agricultural Circle Society provided low-cost supplies to peasant shops and helped establish a network of rural storage facilities in the countryside. The Agricultural Circle Administration was in a position to help "local circles connect with merchants and manufacturers in order to obtain goods cheaper than through Jewish stores." Because of the immediate material benefit they could offer and the opportunity for an ideological linkage between the classes, the establishment of Christian-run stores proved to be "one of the most useful activities of agricultural circles," according to one contemporary observer.[80]

[77] Franciszek Drózd to *Wieniec*, February 9, 1882, 31–32.
[78] Maciej Szarek, Brzegi, to *Pszczółka*, July 25, 1878.
[79] For Stojałowski's original scheme for founding the stores and its reception among the peasants, see *Wieniec*, January 1, 1881, 2–3.
[80] Dawidowa, *Kółka rolnicze*, 16–18.

"It is high time that we freed ourselves from the advantage of the Jews," announced the TKR leadership during the negotiations leading to its founding. We must "take to trade ourselves," the leaders argued in tones strikingly similar to those used by peasant leaders, "in order to create a new source of income."[81] Members of local agricultural circles were thus encouraged to turn to the board for assistance in establishing stores in their villages. The circle administration helped interested groups find merchants and manufacturers from whom they could obtain inexpensive goods. By the mid-1880s, they had established a number of district-wide storage facilities, permitting store managers from a single district to purchase products in bulk. The result was that many circle stores were able to sell goods at almost half the price of those available in Jewish stores.

The original motivation behind the Agricultural Circle Society's promotion of Christian stores was probably not solely to pique rural anti-Semitism as a means of attracting peasant support to gentry causes, including the nationalist movement. Indeed, the encouragement of Christian trade centers met many of the basic requirements the society set out for itself on an economic and cultural level. They helped to encourage the evolution of a cadre of successful farmers, and yet required little cash outlay since the society served as a clearinghouse matching up merchants and stores. The stores were widely accepted among circle members and nonmembers alike. In this sense, they promoted cooperative ventures between the Polish classes and social and national solidarity among Polish speakers. The Christian store movement represented the first time in the institutional history of the Galician countryside that anti-Semitism was used to draw two previously antagonistic classes together against an "outside" group. The movement marked a shift away from the centuries-old rural alliance uniting landed gentry and their Jewish estate managers and innkeepers against the enserfed peasants. The nobility now began to turn against rural Jews and forge ties instead with their former antagonist—the village farmer. As the social and political realities of the countryside shifted, Jews came to be resented both for economic reasons and because of their "foreignness." A new weapon of national mobilization was introduced into Polish relations at the expense of people who had lived in the countryside and contributed to its well-being for centuries.

Throughout the early period of the peasant movement, Jews would continue to serve as a foil for conflicting interests among Polish social groups and political factions. As the movement splintered into separate political

81 *Wieniec*, February 9, 1882, 30.

factions around the turn of the twentieth century, Stojałowski's more socially conservative branch would accuse early peasant leaders Jan Stapiński and Jakub Bojko of inappropriately close relations with Jews. According to many accounts, Stojałowski even helped to incite the violent pogroms that spread through thirty towns and villages during the 1898 elections to the Viennese Reichsrat.[82]

Circle stores continued to sprout up in the Galician countryside throughout the 1880s and 1890s, contributing to a heightened pitch of Jewish-Catholic conflicts in areas where mutual resentments had long remained dormant or limited to the realm of rhetoric. In the first five years of the TKR's existence (1882–87), 149 stores were established; in the next five-year period (1888–92), another 376 stores opened their doors. Of a total of 832 agricultural circles in 1892, 524 of them had set up general stores that effectively threatened the livelihood of Jewish merchants.[83] By 1900, 82 percent of all agricultural circles had established at least one village store under circle management. In response, rural Jews sought to protect their control over trade. They worked to establish more shops within the tavern itself, as two frustrated circle members from the district of Nowy Targ complained:

And now, when the Agricultural Circle Society wants to save the peasantry from the bad will of the Jews, particularly through the founding of Christian stores, the Jews have changed their tactics and are opening stores in taverns. Some might say that this competition is good and brings more goods and lower prices. The problem is that there is no competition because of the attraction of the peasants to the tavern. If there is something to be taken care of in the tavern, it is then that much easier to talk him into drunkenness. Then when the *wójt* wants to impose the law on drunkenness, the Jews tell him that the peasants came there to the store and not to the tavern.[84]

The peasantry's sense of economic justice was violated when Jewish merchants behaved "unfairly" by charging prices held to be unreasonably high or when they underbid peasants, making dry goods and other staple items easily available. The sense that things have an intrinsic value rather

---

[82] Dubnov reports that the priest started a rumor that Archduke Rudolf, who had committed suicide in 1889, was alive and had ordered assaults on Habsburg Jews. Dubnov, *History of the Jews*, 5:492. See also Hemmerling, "Stronnictwa ludowe wobec Żydów," 160–61; and Struve, "Die Juden in der Sicht der polnischen Bauernparteien."

[83] Gurnicz, *Kółka rolnicze*, 249.

[84] Józef Janiczak, Podhale, to *Wieniec*, March 21, 1886, 46.

than an exchange value, and that the intrinsic value is part of a larger moral order, created a game the Jews could not win and an easy excuse for hostility. The Jews became the symbol of a cash economy the peasants did not fully embrace, a process that helped reinforce anti-Semitic attitudes. Circle members petitioned the Circle Society to lobby crownland officials for new laws forbidding stores in village taverns. In this matter, the TKR leaders refused to intervene. Instead, gentry members of the circle administration and in the Sejm continued to support tavern managers and collect profits from the sale of *propinacja* licenses and alcohol taxes.

Peasant resentment of rural Jews heightened still further after the latter began to retaliate against the loss of business. Jewish merchants attacked parish priests for their role in founding Christian stores. The Jewish shop owner in the town of Kalwarya reportedly offered to donate 60 *zlotys* year to a cloister of the priest's choosing if the clergyman would convince circle members to close their store, and offered the circle itself 100 *zlotys* to cease its operations.[85] In most cases, peasant entrepreneurs persevered. Occasionally, however, as in the parish of Dąbrowa in 1884, the Jews triumphed and circle activities ceased altogether in response to the "great agitation" Jewish businessmen organized.[86].

Like other forms of agricultural circle activity, the movement to establish Christian stores soon grew beyond the control of central society administrators. Circle stores swiftly became the key manifestation of agricultural circle activity in a given village. In many locations, agricultural circles were founded purely for the purpose of establishing a Christian store (with TKR support). By the end of the century, the founding and operating of village stores was frequently the single form of activity in which a circle engaged. By 1898, 911 circle stores were in operation, yet only 340 agricultural circles were active enough to submit annual reports to the TKR administration.[87] In the last years of the nineteenth century, many stores originally under circle administration were leased out and run privately (rather than cooperatively) under the loose supervision of individual circles. And by the early twentieth century, as the number of stores continued to increase, ever larger numbers of them were sold to independent agents who ran them with no connection to the local agricultural circle or the society administration. The spark lit by the TKR leadership inspired a growing cooperative movement in the countryside, but also helped reinforce a growing division between Jews and non-Jews.

---

[85] Both attempts to eliminate the circle store failed. Dawidowa, *Kółka rolnicze*, 25–26.
[86] *Wieniec*, April 19, 1885, 30.
[87] Gurnicz, *Kółka rolnicze*, 77–78.

The agricultural circle movement, with its educational programs, reading circles, village stores, and credit facilities, offered Galician peasants the opportunity to assess and respond to many of the problems plaguing nineteenth-century rural society. Taking advantage of the institutional framework and financial contributions provided by the gentry and clergy, peasant members of agricultural circles devised methods of guiding the activities of local groups at the grassroots level. They drew on customary forms of interaction, combining peasant with elite traditions to create a new direction in rural activism. Peasants learned to work with administrators from the organization's hierarchy on projects of mutual interest, creating a basis for future alliances. Through participation in gentry-sponsored associations such as agricultural circles, villagers developed an interest in community activities and familiarized themselves with many of the larger issues of importance in Galician public life.

Among these public issues was the ongoing question of how the unified Polish nation would treat ethnic and religious minorities. Though the minority question would play itself out only in the period between the world wars, its precursors lay in the attempts to forge alliances between conservative gentry and activist peasants in explicit opposition to Jewish financial interests. Because the rural economic situation was described in terms of a competition between ethnic and religious groups rather than of economic interdependence among Galicia's populations, the social solidarity on which the new nation was founded would be increasingly volatile and unstable.[88]

The civic attitudes the peasants developed had stronger village roots than many upper-class reformers had foreseen. As peasants grew closer to larger communities beyond the village, they remained reluctant to accept external ideals, goals, and methods of interaction as their own. By creating their own approach to public affairs, Galician villagers indicated that they would not be mobilized via the imposition of unfiltered upper-class ideas, but would contribute their own conceptions to organizational life on a national scale.

One outcome of the negotiation played out among conservative gentry activists, local intellectuals, and peasant farmers for control over the day-to-day operation of agricultural circles was the hardening of village factions, long existing along economic and interest lines. Attending circle meetings, serving as local officers, managing stores and reading clubs, and

[88] On the ways in which anti-Semitism was employed by Polish nationalists, see Brian Porter, *When Nationalism Began to Hate: Imagining Modern Politics in Nineteenth-Century Poland* (New York, 2000).

corresponding via the rural press with other farmers involved in promoting village improvements helped to establish a new cadre of village leaders. This new rural elite, motivated partially by the ideological input of gentry philanthropists, had interests that diverged sharply from those of their nonparticipant neighbors. They soon began to establish links with members of the rural intelligentsia in common cause against the backwardness and cultural isolation of peasant society. Carefully molding village associations to reflect a mixture of traditional culture and outside input, this new stratum of village activists emerging out of the agricultural circle movement represented the future of peasant political organization in the crownland. They would eventually define their own agenda on a nation-wide scale—bringing a politicized version of peasant culture to larger struggles.

Chapter Seven

Education and the Shaping of a Village Elite

So now we have a community newspaper. But what does it profit us, if . . . only a few—I don't know if it's even a dozen or so—proprietors can be found who are interested in knowing what's happening in God's world? The rest avoid listening to the newspaper. In fact, they even agitate among the others, saying: "Brother, don't contribute money for the newspaper, because times are tough as it is. Don't crawl over to listen when they read because that's treason; our fathers didn't read and didn't listen to newspapers and they lived, so we don't have to [read and listen]. . . . Whoever's stupid, let him go listen, but we don't need it!" Then they each hide behind the other, pull their caps low over their brows, put their hands in their pockets, and go as fast as they can to Yankel [the tavern keeper]. There they brag even more about how they are supposedly wiser, while the stupider people remained to listen to the newspaper.

Correspondent from Mshana, Złoczów district, to *Batkivshchyna*, 1884

New rural organizations prompted the rise of new factions in Galician village society.[1] Among the rural social strata during the 1880s and 1890s was a cadre of activist peasant leaders who participated in local associations and subscribed to peasant newspapers. This village elite would guide the peasant movement in its early years, taking part in election committees, serving as electors from rural curia, and functioning as deputies to the Reichsrat and the Sejm. Through their activities within and beyond their rural communities, peasant leaders would come into contact with

---

[1] Rural newspapers report extensively on the social tensions surrounding the creation of new agricultural circles. We are told that in the village of Tuligłowa, "laughter" and "derision" greeted the founders of the new circle. In Rudnik, "several individuals were ill disposed" to the circle's presence. Elsewhere, "constant disputes" broke out "between members of the circle and other inhabitants of the *gmina*." J. P., Tuligłowa, Jarosław district, to *Pszczółka*, January 6, 1881, 7; agricultural circle in Rudnik to *Pszczółka*, April 17, 1884, 58; and report by Stojałowski, *Wieniec*, December 18, 1884, 225. Thomas and Znaniecki stress the importance of the news media in introducing information into the village that effected a disruption in the preemancipation unanimity of public opinion. Their presumption of minimal social conflict under serfdom is probably overdrawn, however. *Polish Peasant*, esp. 147–50.

ideas about the peasantry's public role in postemancipation life. Village leaders would help redefine the political and cultural nation in such a way that their fellow smallholders could imagine a place for themselves within it. Leaders served as cultural mediators, drawing the village closer to the city and the estate, and ultimately contributing to a new national political culture.[2] Yet the image of the Polish nation village leaders adopted represented only one of the many nationalist voices coming from the countryside. This chapter focuses on the creation of a village elite and the ways in which this group's vision of the nation was shaped through educational processes. The less educated, illiterate villagers with fewer connections beyond their rural homes would develop wildly variant notions of the nation, some of which are discussed in greater detail in chapter 8.

The creation of village leaders was closely tied to the expansion of formal and informal educational opportunities for Galician peasants in the 1870s and 1880s. As German gave way to Polish or Ukrainian in crownland elementary schools after the granting of Galician autonomy in 1868, greater numbers of Polish-speaking villagers found their way to the local schoolhouse. Following the passage of the 1872 Imperial Law on Compulsory Education, hundreds of new teachers, many with roots in the countryside, were trained for service in rural primary schools. Education would help define village leaders in a number of ways. Villagers who obtained a minimal level of literacy rose to the top of the social hierarchy, eventually displacing an older generation of local leaders whose status had been based on knowledge of traditional practices. Moreover, those who left the village to pursue professional training in urban areas frequently returned to the countryside in the capacity of educators—either as clerics or as lay instructors—and served as linking figures uniting the interests of the peasantry with the programs of nonvillage activists. As the distribution of power shifted from priest to schoolteacher during the generation following the expansion of Polish-language elementary education, the countryside experienced a concomitant shift in nationalist content. Increasingly, the populist, egalitarian emphases of rural educators displaced the more hierarchical vision of the nation shared by most clergymen.

Village "leaders" consisted of at least two separate groups, the peasant farmers who were promoted by their fellows to positions of power and

---

[2] Geoff Eley argues that such cultural mediators helped constitute a national public sphere in Eastern Europe. Eley, "Nations, Publics, and Political Cultures," 297–309. Robert Redfield refers to these linking figures as "hinges" bridging the "little tradition" of the peasant community and the "great tradition" beyond it and connecting the "inside" and the "outside" of peasant society through their participation in formal and informal institutions. Redfield, *Peasant Society,* 38–43, 67–104.

responsibility, and the educated outsiders who served in influential positions in the village and who often fulfilled a patronage function for local peasants. Most of the leading peasant activists in Galicia pursued their reform programs through some position of formal authority within the village, whether as village mayor, commune secretary, council member, agricultural circle or reading room head, circle store manager, or correspondent to a peasant newspaper. By contrast, those who held positions as parish priests, country schoolteachers, and even village organists can be categorized as nonpeasants since they earned their livings through intellectual activities. The formal training enjoyed by clerics and schoolmasters as well as their institutional ties to centers of power beyond the village helped to shape a somewhat separate identity from that of village farmers. Yet those who filled these positions were increasingly of peasant background. Thus the line between peasant and nonpeasant becomes blurred in any assessment of village leadership.

One of the strategies small farmers used to build support for their reform agendas was to foster a series of patronage relationships with local nonpeasant notables, such as priests and schoolteachers. The experience of Galician farmers suggests that patterns of patronage shifted during the course of the nineteenth century as the public agenda of peasant leaders grew more radical. Rather than eclipsing their traditional relationship with rural intellectuals, peasant activists systematically deemphasized their links to the clergy and promoted stronger ties to village schoolmasters. This shift in alliance systems brought with it a gradual transition in attitudes toward the Polish nation and the peasant position within it. Whereas local clergy often supported a hierarchical model of social organization, with church and nobility governing in the interests of a less active peasantry, country schoolteachers were more likely to promote an egalitarian, populist understanding of social relations. Conflicts between priest and schoolmaster within and around the schoolhouse provide a window through which to view the changing standards of peasant leadership and the budding ideology of those who rose to positions of responsibility within the village. The fight for control over rural education would shape the peasant movement in important ways during its nascent years.

The tension within the village on matters of schoolhouse curricula, newspaper readership, and other education-related issues posed a serious quandary for many pious Catholic villagers. Eager to learn about the wider world beyond the village, peasant pupils chafed at clerical restrictions on the curriculum and yet were often reluctant to challenge the authority of the local cleric. Issues of curricular content and the circulation of progressive journals and books eventually prompted a wave of anticlericalism in the Galician countryside. Although peasants continued to aspire to the priesthood and attended services regularly, the unchallenged authority of the parish priest was compromised in the struggle for the formation of a political identity among emancipated peasants. The conflict between church doctrine and the needs of peasant penitents was particularly poignant for clerics who hailed from the village. Peasant priests would find themselves torn between their loyalty to ecclesiastical authorities and their sympathies for the peasant cause, a tension that often played itself out in the various patronage relationships between activist peasant leaders and sympathetic parish clergy.

A number of structural factors also influenced the composition of the leadership stratum among Galician peasants. Far from being an undifferentiated mass in the postemancipation period, Galician peasants were divided by patterns of landholding, education (some villages had schools while others did not), and traditions of political engagement.[3] As discussed in chapter 2, gender and generation differences were also key determinants in shaping patterns of activism.[4] Village leaders tended to be male (because of the gendered divisions between public and private life), and they typically belonged to the generation of small farmers born after the end of serfdom. The priorities voiced by peasant leaders thus constituted only one set of voices emanating from the countryside, typically the voice of young, literate male peasants from villages or regions with a history of activism. The illiterate and less active rank and file was significantly less articulate and its message consequently less accessible. The study of peasant leaders thus reminds us that just as no single vision of the Polish nation existed in the nineteenth century, after peasant emancipation there could also be no unitary Polish peasant identity.

---

[3] Residents of villages in the sub-Carpathian region south of Cracow, for example, had a long-standing tradition of political and military engagement dating from the antigentry rising of 1846 and the activities during the revolutionary year 1848. The first peasant party, the Peasant Union (Związek Stronnictwa Chłopskiego), was founded in one of the district capitals of this area, Nowy Sącz, by a native son of the Carpathian foothills.

[4] Several villages reported strong opposition from rural women to male farmers' participation in agricultural circles and subscription to rural newspapers. In 1882, farmwives reportedly staged a "women's revolution" against circle membership because they were upset that their men were off "vagabonding or sitting around." Women frequently opposed newspaper readership as a frivolous waste of time or as socialist and anti-Catholic. See, for example, *Wieniec*, February 9, 1882, 30–31, and the exchange in *Pszczółka*, fourth Sunday in February, 1895, 90. Father Stojałowski sought unsuccessfully to diffuse this intravillage tension by expanding the membership of agricultural circles to include women in 1884. However, local circles continued to stress rural custom over formal legislation in barring women from their ranks. See *Wieniec*, June 19, 1884, 100–101.

The Training of a Peasant Elite

Patterns of elite promotion and the factors propelling individual farmers into leadership positions provide an important window into the values most cherished by peasant society at a particular historical moment. In Poland, preemancipation rural communities stressed age and knowledge of traditional practices in the selection of local leaders.[5] In the generations following emancipation, however, as villages began to experience social and economic modernization, rural populations tended to emphasize worldliness and formal education as conditions for local leadership.[6]

Despite the intense concern with plot sizes and land inheritance in Polish rural society, neither landholdings nor overall wealth profoundly affected the social status of peasant farmers. Land shortages and repeated divisions meant that most peasant plots were smaller than four acres in total size by mid-century, and thus little significant variation existed among them.[7] The biographies of early peasant leaders consistently confirm that a poor or even landless background was no barrier to political advancement in the countryside. Jakub Bojko, founding member of the Peasant Party and delegate to the Reichsrat, was born on a three-acre farm and was forced to work on the local estate to help feed his family.[8] Peasant writer Stanisław Pigoń's father was a blacksmith and owned no land. Local activist Franciszek Magryś's family owned a one-quarter-morg, plot on which the family home and textile workshop stood. Longtime correspondent to peasant newspapers and local organizer Maciej Szarek was

[5] Kazimierz Dobrowolski notes that the status of the elderly within preliterate communities such as those in the Beskid Mountains of southern Poland is maintained by selective and restricted transmission of customary practices to the younger generation. See his "Peasant Traditional Culture," *Etnografia Polska* 1 (1958): 19–56, reprinted in part in *Peasants and Peasant Societies*, ed. Teodor Shanin (Oxford, 1987), 261–77. Also interesting, anecdotally, is Jan Słomka's *From Serfdom to Self-Government*.

[6] Similarly, P. M. Jones found in the nineteenth-century French countryside that formal training such as that of a parish priest was the most important marker of peasant respect. Jones, *Politics and Rural Society*, 73–74, 242–71. Prasenjit Duara argues that in twentieth-century China wealth continued as a determinant of local prestige, yet patronage connections to representatives of the new Communist regime were increasingly important. Duara, *Culture, Power and the State*, 158–80.

[7] Antoni Podraza, "Kształtowanie się elity wiejskiej na przykładzie Galicji na przełomie XIX i XX w.," *Acta Universitatis Lodziensis. Zeszyty Naukowe Uniwersytetu Łódzkiego. Nauki Humanistyczno-społeczne* 1, no. 43 (1979): 63. On the size of peasant farms in Galicia, see also Wincenty Styś, *Drogi postępu gospodarczego wsi* (Wrocław, 1947), and Styś, *Współzależność rozwoju rodziny chłopskiej i jej gospodarstwa* (Wrocław, 1959).

[8] Janusz Albin and Józef Ryszard Szaflik, "Listy Jakuba Bojki z lat 1891–1916," *Ze skarbca kultury* 27 (1976): 59.

born to enserfed peasants who possessed only a four-morg (six-acre) farm. Szarek worked as a raftsman on the Vistula (thus helping to build his reputation as worldly and well connected) to support his large family.[9] And Jan Siwiec, who became a peasant hero during the 1861 Sejm, was not even a farmer, but worked as a secretary in a law office. Siwiec's urban experience and close familiarity with imperial law proved more important than his landholding status in his native village to his nomination as a delegate to the Sejm. While some peasant leaders were members of the thin stratum of middling landholders (including Stanisław Potoczek, delegate to the Sejm and cofounder of the Peasant Union in 1894, who owned some forty-five acres of land), other criteria were clearly more important in determining authority and status levels among villagers.

Instead of plot size and overall wealth, formal education, connections to centers of power outside the village, and an air of worldly urbanity increasingly accounted for the selection of local leaders in the postemancipation village. This was true for a number of practical reasons. First, as village communities were converted into self-governing communes in the 1860s, literacy came to be viewed as an invaluable asset in elected officials. Villagers perceived their literate peers, who were increasingly from a younger generation of peasants born after emancipation, to be less likely to be swindled by an unscrupulous *gmina* secretary, an avaricious innkeeper, or a wily district governor. Literate village mayors and agricultural circle secretaries could correspond with officials about local affairs and would not "embarrass" the village by signing state documents with a mere "X."

During the second postemancipation generation of the 1870s and 1880s, literate villagers were increasingly well represented on village councils. Peasant leaders themselves point to traditions of pedagogical excellence in their native villages to account for their own political activism and those of their local fellows. Future newspaper editor and early member of the Stronnictwo Ludowe Jan Stapiński hailed from a village whose social life was based around the village schoolhouse, founded at the unusually early date of 1809.[10] Franciszek Magryś attributed the large number of

---

[9] Szarek married young and fathered a total of ten children, of whom five survived until adulthood. He writes of being constantly hungry, of working on a road crew, rafting on the Vistula, and fishing to supplement his meager farm income. Janusz Albin and Józef Ryszard Szaflik, "Listy Macieja Szarka z lat 1861–1904," *Ze skarbca kultury* 39 (1984): 70.

[10] Stapiński was selected as secretary of both the Central Peasant Election Committee and the Stronnictwo Ludowe in the summer of 1895 at the age of twenty-eight. Education developed such a traditional importance in his village that during the years 1880–1910 this tiny hamlet sent about a hundred children to various institutions of higher learning. "That

civil leaders in his village (a Sejm deputy and the founders of the village store, reading room, dairy cooperative, fire department, credit union, and course for rural housewives) to the four years when the local priest gave lessons to village children.[11] And on a more personal level, Jakub Bojko credited the "few years" he spent attending a village school for his selection as commune secretary, his collaboration with rural newspaper editors, and his eventual election as a deputy to the Viennese Reichsrat.[12] The story of the formation of a postemancipation rural elite in Poland is thus closely tied to the tale of the expansion of village education and the stratification imposed by the rise of literacy in the countryside.

Second, peasants with connections to centers of power beyond the village were perceived as offering potential assistance for fellow villagers or various kinds of aid for the community. In a society where some 89 percent of the inhabitants lived their entire lives in the commune of their birth, personal knowledge of far-off lands such as that gained through emigration for work or service in the imperial army vastly increased the prestige a villager enjoyed among his peers.[13] Seasonal work in the coal mines of Saxony, on the great estates around Warsaw and Łódź, and longer periods of migration to Brazil or North America helped introduce knowledge about the wider world to Galician villages. Émigrés often returned to their native villages after several months or years, bringing with them "not only their wages, but also their social, political, and cultural experience," and subsequently found themselves in the leadership stratum within the village.[14]

The experience of the army recruit brought a particularly pronounced elevation in status. During the neo-absolutist period following the revolutions of 1848 until about 1867, the Habsburg monarchy experienced severe administrative centralization. Polish villagers, aware that their liberation from serfdom had come from the emperor rather than from local landlords, continued to respect the power of Vienna and accordingly

---

Haczów should be active—nothing else was possible under such conditions," commented a fellow villager. "Listy Jana Stapińskiego do Karola Lewakowskiego," *Roczniki Dziejów Ruchu Ludowego* 18 (1976): 129–30; Rymar, "Pamiętniki," 17–21.

[11] According to Magryś, Jan Sobek, deputy to the Sejm and founder of the agricultural circle, village store, dairy, and credit union; Walenty Rajzer, head of the store and the dairy; Jan Lenar, organizer and chief of the fire department; and Jan Rajzer, manager of the store and organizer of a course for rural housewives were all educated during the four years of the schoolhouse's operation. Magryś, *Żywot chłopa*, 77.

[12] Albin and Szaflik, "Listy Jakuba Bojki," 59–60.

[13] Bujak found that 89.4 percent of villagers remained in their native villages their entire lives as of 1880. Franciszek Bujak, *Galicja*, 2 vols. (Lwów, 1908), 1:65.

[14] Podraza, "Kształtowanie się elity," 63.

treated those with contacts elsewhere in the empire with pronounced admiration. The soldier's familiarity with the language and geography of the Austrian Empire helped attract the respect of his neighbors. As village mayor Jan Słomka noted about the returning soldier in the 1860s and 1870s,

> He came home in his uniform, and would put it on for Sundays and holidays as long as it held together. After his military service he would speak bad Polish, and there were some who pretended not to understand their mother tongue, but muttered something of German, or Czech, etc. . . . Right to the end of the Austrian days, it would happen that the soldier on returning home would interject German words into his speech.[15]

So central to the self-image of the recruits was this vocabulary that marching songs performed by Polish recruits as late as the 1890s routinely integrated German vocabulary, even rhyming German terms with Polish words.[16] Stanisław Pigoń's godfather attributed his rise to the top of the social hierarchy in his village to his having "picked up some of the language" while serving in the imperial army in Hungary and Vienna in the 1850s and even once catching sight of the emperor.[17]

Initially, the experience of the relatively illiterate soldier was enough to elevate his status in the village.[18] Rural sociologist Franciszek Bujak noted that "the influence of the illiterate vacationing soldier [was] substantially without comparison [and that] his ideas had more influence than those of the constant residents of the village." On the basis of their experience serving in remote locations, "soldiers who had served were pushed forward into leadership positions." Yet upon the soldier's returning to civilian life, this knowledge was often formalized, and the ex-recruit would "learn to read a bit" to cement his prestige in the village community. Formal and informal training went hand in hand in the shaping of peasant leaders.[19]

Third, educated peasants and those with "worldly" experience were able to communicate to their rural neighbors the excitement and liberating possibilities of the nationalist struggles being waged throughout East Cen-

---

[15] Słomka, *From Serfdom to Self-Government*, 153–57.
[16] German words were transliterated into Polish orthography when the lyrics were transcribed, including terms such as "anslag," "forwec," "antret," "gzicht," and "aufmars." S. Gonet, "Język polski w wojsku," *Lud* (1897): 78–80.
[17] Pigoń, *Z Komborni*, 75–76.
[18] As of 1865, only 4.5 percent of the Austrian army recruits were recorded as able to read and write. This fraction would rise only very slowly over the next half century. Michalski, *Dzieje szkolnictwa*, 258–59.
[19] Bujak, *Żmiąca*, 133.

tral Europe. Service in the Austrian army often sparked an initial recognition of the recruit's ethnic identity—a perception passed on to fellow villagers.[20] Travel and exposure to foreign cultures during military service helped stir an interest in nationalist struggles at home, as in the case of young Maciej Szarek, who was stationed in Hungary during the revolutions of 1848. Rather than honing his loyalty to empire, Szarek's experiences prompted him first to oppose participation in German-language cadet school training and then to become one of the earliest peasant activists and patriotic writers.[21] Another recruit, Michał Rado, who would later be instrumental in founding the Peasant Party, developed sympathy for the Polish cause while serving in the Austrian army and hearing stories about the insurrection of 1863 in Russian Poland.[22]

The peculiarly Galician form of emigration for work—serving as raftsmen on the Vistula River—also played a crucial role in shaping the identity of future peasant activists. Peasants from remote mountain villages, such as those of the Carpathian region where Maciej Szarek grew up, came in contact with wider influences through the rafting tradition. Szarek was raised on stories of far-off lands his father told him upon his return from rafting trips. As a grown man, he was able to keep up contacts with intellectuals in Cracow because his rafting took him through the medieval capital regularly. His reputation as a supporter of the Polish nationalist cause circulated throughout the Polish lands and prompted insurgents to seek Szarek's assistance escorting them down the Vistula and into Russian territory during the 1863 uprising.[23]

With increasing numbers of Galician villagers traveling abroad to work or serve in the army, literacy among those at home was in ever greater demand. The desire to correspond with those who had left and to read the literature they brought back drove formal education into an increasingly prominent position. The schoolhouse began to play a more central role in the daily life of the village.[24] And yet the content of rural education was a matter of constant contestation for most of the late nineteenth century. The ways in which conflicts over curricular issues were resolved tell us a

---

[20] Słomka, *From Serfdom to Self-Government*, 156–57.

[21] Szarek later agreed to attend cadet school after being punished by his superiors. Albin and Szaflik, "Listy Macieja Szarka," 70–71.

[22] Franciszek Śliwa, "Z dziejów ruchu ludowego w powiecie mieleckim: początki myśli klasowej i patriotycznej," *Roczniki Dziejów Ruchu Ludowego*, no. 12 (1970): 29–31.

[23] Szarek was even able to introduce himself to the writer Józef Ignacy Kraszewski during one rafting trip and maintain a regular correspondence with him thereafter. Albin and Szaflik, "Listy Macieja Szarka," 71–73.

[24] The shifting status of primary education in the eyes of Galician villagers is discussed in Michalski, *Dzieje szkolnictwa*, 101.

great deal about the training of village leaders and about the early membership in the peasant movement.

The Parson versus the Schoolmaster: The Influence of Local Notables

Far from being a clear predictor of future political activism, the acquisition of formal education in the village often disguised more than it revealed about peasant pupils. Control over the village schoolhouse and its curriculum was heavily contested in the postautonomy Galician village. Torn between the curricular control of the priest and the secularly trained schoolmaster, and under the jurisdiction of the local landholder, the Galician bureaucracy, and the village *gmina*, the schoolhouse witnessed a series of conflicts that had a tremendous impact on the training of village leaders.

Tensions surrounding the governance of the schoolhouse underline the extent to which Galician peasants were caught between centers of authority in the generations following emancipation. Whereas moral authority among serfs had resided in the person of the parish priest and secular authority with the landlord, the postemancipation sources of power were more contingent on local circumstances. The priest, the organist, the schoolteacher, and the mayor held sway to varying degrees within the village, while a wide range of outsiders began to attract the respect of village residents. To complicate matters still further, both village schoolmasters and rural priests were frequently caught between the sympathy they developed for local peasants and their continued loyalty to their superiors. The delicate relationship between peasant activists and nonpeasant notables, on the one hand, and between rural notables and their regional superiors, on the other, suggests some of the complexities the first generation of peasant leaders faced as they made their way into the minefield of local, regional, and national politics.

In the early postemancipation period, parish priests consistently served as spokesmen for the peasantry, promoting the easing of the burdens remaining from serfdom and encouraging national sentiment among their parishioners. Dozens of parish priests sought to mobilize peasants into nationalist uprisings in 1846 and 1848, even promoting emancipation from the pulpit.[25] Parish clergy often preferred to support the interests of the peasantry and to encourage national sentiment among their flock

---

[25] Parish clergy such as Father Ignacy Zieliński of Radawa, Father Karol Szlegal from near Jasło, and Father Antoni from Łosina agitated in support of emancipation in an effort to win peasants over to the nationalist cause. At least 10 percent of the known conspirators in 1848 were clerics, and over a hundred priests were arrested after the failure of the 1846 anti-Austrian rising. In both cases, as in later attempts to mobilize the peasantry, the church

rather than maintain unquestioned loyalty to the emperor.[26] Indeed, conspirators in Galician nationalist organizations during the 1840s and 1850s
directed much of their efforts to winning over recent graduates of clerical
seminaries on the assumption that the pulpit was the easiest way to reach
the rural population and mobilize them behind the national cause.[27]
Through the early years of the peasant movement, the parish clergy and
even bishops in key districts of Galicia—Cracow, Przemyśl, Lwów,
Tarnów—threw themselves into the work of organizing agricultural circles, village stores, credit cooperatives, and reading rooms.[28]

Yet, as Galician peasants began to organize politically, sending representatives from the village to district councils, the Sejm, and the Reichsrat,
ecclesiastical authorities turned against the movement.[29] Indeed, the very
bishops who had been most sympathetic to the social and economic work
of local clergy began to express their concern about independent peasant
political organizations. By 1893, ecclesiastical leaders such as the bishop
of Tarnów, Father Ignacy Łokoś, would voice fear for the stability of the
social order as a result of independent peasant political organization. In a
letter to the Galician governor general, Łokoś wrote: "In several villages,
in particular in the districts of Nowy Sącz [the birthplace of the Peasant

administration vigorously opposed clerical activism, even invoking papal authority to
strengthen their position. Hanna Dylągowa, *Duchowieństwo katolickie wobec sprawy narodowej (1764–1864)* (Lublin, 1983), 98–101; Stefan Kieniewicz, *Konspiracje galicyjskie,
1831–1845* (Warsaw, 1950), 141, 152, 155.

[26] Parish priests often made impassioned speeches to large crowds of villagers during the
1848 Rising, including those by Father Kitryś from Rychwald in the sub-Carpathian region,
Father Pielowski, and Father Maciej Miętus from Mąkowa. Kieniewicz, *Pomiędzy Stadionem a Goslarem*, 63–65.

[27] Dylągowa argues that after academics and students in the higher classes of gymnasia,
future priests enrolled in the seminaries in Lwów were most involved in the dozens of conspiracies planned in Galicia during the 1840s and 1850s. Dylągowa, *Duchowieństwo
katolickie*, 97–104.

[28] In the Przemyśl diocese one of the first activists to support the peasant cause, Father
Antoni Tyczyński from Albigowa, near Łańcut, founded a village school, a school for
farmwives, public halls, a dairy, and helped send peasant sons on to higher education at his
own expense. In Tarnów district, among the first to engage in socioeconomic activism were
Father Andrzej Mucha of Okulice, Father Stanisław Gajewski from Olszowiec, and Father
Władysław Mentrala from Tuchowa. At the beginning of the twentieth century, over half of
the credit cooperatives were headed by parish clergy.

[29] Church administrators sought instead to establish their own Christian political organizations. In 1893, a short-lived peasant party, the Peasant Union (Związek Stronnictwa Chłopskiego) was established under the guidance of Father Stojałowski. In 1906, the archbishop of
Lwów and the bishop of Przemyśl helped establish the relatively weak Związek Katolicko-
Społeczno (Catholic Social Union). Regarding clerical involvement in social and political
activism, see Jerzy Kłoczowski, Lidia Müllerowa, and Jan Skarbek, *Zarys dziejów kościoła
katolickiego w Polsce* (Cracow, 1986), 256–58.

Union] and Limanowa, illegal meetings of peasants are being held, at which debate in the spirit of *Przyjaciel Ludu* [a socially radical peasant newspaper] takes place and the so-called peasant program is discussed." These meetings were deemed "dangerous not only for clergy, whose authority and moral influence might be undermined, but also for the entire social order."[30] Once peasants began to establish political organizations to promote their own needs, clerical leadership was compromised. Ecclesiastical authorities believed that the peasantry could not both govern itself and also accept the traditional social hierarchy.

Village schoolmasters, by contrast, were among the chief promoters of a more populist egalitarian vision of national renewal in the countryside. As we will see, schoolteachers' professional commitment to instruction in Polish and to presenting lessons on the history and literature of the Polish lands made them natural magnets for villagers interested in cultivating a Polish cultural identity. The presentation of national topics to peasant children confronted schoolteachers with the inequalities of the prepartition social structure. In an attempt to write emancipated peasants into Poland's future, many teachers developed radical notions about the distribution of political power in a reborn Polish state. Curricular debates reflect deep rifts between country schoolteachers and their School Council superiors about the way national history and future political goals were to be taught. The tension in the schoolhouse between the authority of the priest and that of the teacher, on the one hand, and between the rural instructor and his administrative superior, on the other, would help underline the impression of the cleric as an advocate of a bygone conception of Polish society and the teacher as a spokesperson for a new, socially inclusive model of the nation.

The Waning of Clerical Authority and the Rise of Rural Anticlericalism

Before emancipation and in the first two decades after the collapse of serfdom, the parish priest represented the primary source of formal education for Polish peasants. This status would gradually be eclipsed by the advent of formally educated, state-certified secular instructors who would staff

---

[30] This exchange is preserved in records of the correspondence of the governor general's office in Lwów. In this case, the governor general's office wrote directly to the governors of Limanowa and Nowy Sącz, warning them about the dangers of peasant meetings taking place in the villages of their districts. Tsentralnyi Derzhavnyi Istorychnyi Arkhiv u m. Lvovi (TsDIAL), fond 146, op. 4, spr. 2368.

the hundreds of new primary schools built in the Galician countryside after 1868. The rudimentary "winter schools" that functioned in many preemancipation villages typically met in the rectory, and the local parson conducted lessons. Peasant memoirists acknowledge learning the basics of reading and arithmetic in these temporary schools. However, they also complain that the curriculum was extremely limited and that little content beyond the catechism was communicated to the pupils.[31]

Clerical influence over elementary education was reconfirmed after 1849 when Count Leo Thun assumed office as Austrian head minister and began strengthening clerical ties to education throughout the Habsburg monarchy.[32] In Galician villages, education was thereafter guided by a partnership between the Catholic Church and large landowners, with the church responsible for curriculum and staff, and the landlords expected to provide the funding for the schoolhouse itself. As a result of the dependence on private resources, however, rural education grew very slowly in the two decades after 1848. Only with the crownland government's assumption of responsibility for elementary schooling did the role of the church diminish and the number of primary schools gradually increase.[33] After 1868, the crownland School Council legally restricted the clerical role in primary education to religious training, a function that parish priests fulfilled with varying degrees of energy.[34]

Despite formal restrictions on clerical activities within the schoolhouse, the local priest remained the only educational advocate in many rural areas, and it was often only thanks to his initiative that village schools were founded. As late as 1887, memoirist Jan Madejczyk noted that the winter school in his parish was founded and run by Father Radzecki.[35] And until 1895, the few peasants educated in the village of Grabie were

---

[31] Newspaper correspondent Maciej Szarek noted that several years in such a school taught him to read texts only with difficulty, and that he did not learn to write until he later joined the army. Michalski, *Dzieje szkolnictwa,* 261–62.

[32] Ibid., 257–58.

[33] In response to an imperial law, the Galician School Council was established on January 24, 1868, and took over the jurisdiction of the crownland's entire elementary school system. Ann Sirka, *The Nationality Question in Austrian Education: The Case of the Ukrainians in Galicia, 1867–1914* (Frankfurt, 1980), 74, 78.

[34] Memoirist Maciej Czuła recalls that in his village of Grabie the "parish priest was . . . so lazy that religious lessons occurred only about two times per year." When the deacon came from the district capital to test the children on their catechism, he was appalled to discover how little the pupils knew. Maciej Czuła, "Niedola szkolna małorolnego chłopa, 1895–1900," in *Galicyjskie wspomnienia szkolne,* ed. Antoni Knot (Cracow, 1955), 461–63. For Galician conservatives' opposition to the secularization of education, see Szaflik, *O rząd, chłopskich dusz,* 51.

[35] Jan Madejczyk, "Dwa lata w szkółce wiejskiej," in Knot, *Galicyjskie wspomnienia,* 450–51.

sent to the organist's home, where most of them were "none the wiser" for their lessons.[36] Even when a two-class state school was finally founded in Grabie, it was initially housed in the "dark damp rectory building" in an informal continuation of the link between priest and teacher, church and pedagogy.

Notwithstanding an 1872 law making education mandatory for all Galician children between the ages of six and twelve, lessons remained informal or nonexistent in hundreds of Polish villages. Barely 20 percent of school-aged children were attending classes in 1872, and, partly owing to rapid population growth, the percentages increased only very slowly through the next several decades.[37] Funding remained an obstacle to the expansion of the rural school system. The village commune was obliged to contribute to the upkeep of the schoolhouse (along with the local lord) and provide housing for the teacher, whose meager salary was paid by the School Council. Along with these fiscal restraints, however, local residents also opposed the expansion of the public education system because of an ongoing belief that peasant children required little formal schooling to fulfill their obligations as farmers.

Indeed, many villagers appear to have been unaware of the legal restrictions on the clerical role in public education. Memoirists praise activist priests for establishing schoolhouses and teaching full-time in them as late as the 1890s. For the residents of many villages, the priest continued to be the primary and often the sole instrument of education in the community.[38] Clerics were hailed as the chief organizers of agricultural circles and reading rooms, the founders of libraries, and the sole subscribers to newspapers that they frequently made available to their parishioners. A "well-run agricultural circle" was the legacy left by Father Tyczyński, the parish priest in the *gmina* of Albigowa.[39] Elsewhere, peasant writers argue that reading rooms and agricultural circles "would never exist and exist now only thanks to" the efforts of activist parish priests.[40] Above all, village clerics served as the primary provider of books and journals for literate

---

[36] Mr. Kolanowski, the local organist, barely knew how to read and write himself, and pupils learned little more than how to pronounce and write the letters. Czuła, "Niedola szkolna," 461–62.

[37] Sirka, *Nationality Question*, 79.

[38] Father Krakowski taught the peasants of Albigowa throughout the 1890s. Franciszek Magryś to *Niedziela* (1892): 749, as reprinted in Magryś, *Żywot chłopa*, 112–13.

[39] Franciszek Magryś to *Niedziela* (1893): 875, as reprinted in Magryś, *Żywot chłopa*, 113–15.

[40] This is the sentiment of Franciszek Magryś, *Żywot chłopa*, 112–13, as well as of the villagers of Błażowa to *Pszczółka*, July 26, 1877, 3; and of Wzdów, where some two hundred farmers attended the founding meeting of the agricultural circle. Village of Wzdów to *Pszczółka*, December 11, 1884, 216. The pedagogical newspaper *Szkoła* also contains fre-

peasants interested in furthering their education. A priest from the neighboring village provided Franciszek Magryś with a regular supply of books and newspapers in the 1880s and 1890s.[41] In many villages, priests were the first to introduce rural periodicals to the peasants, often sparking ongoing and intense interest in the contents of these journals.[42]

Yet it was controversy surrounding the publication and circulation of certain peasant newspapers—especially the organs of the growing peasant political movement—that helped accelerate a decline in clerical authority in the Galician countryside. Literate villagers, most of them schooled by the local priest, found themselves caught between their respect for the institution of the church and an equally compelling desire to read banned periodicals and inform themselves of movements for rural reform. The internal turmoil rural readers experienced and their struggles with conflicting centers of authority helped in large part to define them as increasingly independent representatives of their communities. Village leaders would ultimately struggle to free themselves from traditional centers of authority in order to defend the interests of the village. The process of growing away from the unquestioned authority of the priest was an important component in the early training of many peasant leaders.

Emblematic of the degree to which clerical control over information flow in the village faced increasing challenge from the peasantry was the controversy surrounding the banning of Father Stojałowski's two very popular peasant newspapers, *Wieniec* and *Pszczółka,* in 1894. On February 28, 1894, the governor general's office forbade the reading of or subscription to these papers in twenty-three districts of Galicia.[43] Imperial police investigated and interrogated subscribers to the papers and confiscated copies of the periodicals, ostensibly for their "anticlerical" positions.[44] Stojałowski himself was imprisoned for short periods beginning in

---

quent announcements of clerical founding of reading rooms, educational societies, and libraries, as well as their service as teachers in elementary classrooms.

[41] Magryś, *Żywot chłopa,* 25–27.

[42] Many Galician memoirists comment on the clerical origins of their first newspapers (some even stolen from the rectory), as do peasant writers from the Congress Kingdom, where a more restrictive publishing atmosphere reigned. Kurczak comments that Father Ludwid Czajewicz, an ex-Siberian exile, loaned him a copy of *Zorza,* a nationalist weekly targeted at the peasantry, in the 1890s, which he circulated among other literate villagers. Kurczak, "Pamiętnik," ZHRL, n.d., 22–23.

[43] Stefan Suchonek, "Działalność polityczna ks. St. Stojałowskiego w Żywieczczyznie," *Gronie* 2 (1939): 130; Kącki, *Ks. Stanisław Stojałowski,* 18–19.

[44] The archives of the district criminal court in Cracow contain numerous descriptions of the contents of confiscated peasant newspapers. A single issue of *Pszczółka,* February 26, 1894, is described as containing three separate anti-clerical articles. Archiwum Państwowe Miasta

1889 until his death in 1911.[45] The church itself soon followed suit and imposed a ban of excommunication on all readers of Stojałowski's papers and, in 1897, on the editor himself if he refused to cease publication. Village priests were instructed to refuse absolution to known subscribers.[46]

The papal interdiction of Stojałowski and his subscribers presented newly literate peasants with a difficult dilemma. Torn between the fear they felt for the church with its powers of eternal damnation, and a growing respect for the editor who offered himself as a spokesman for peasant needs, readers began to question the leadership of the church in secular matters. In a lonely battle with individual consciences, many subscribers chose to follow a path away from the dictates of the established church, one that would lead to an increasingly independent peasant politics, unguided by traditional centers of authority. One memoirist described his own moment of crisis regarding the banned newspapers:

> I began to wonder about the contents of the newspapers I [had previously] read, which were written in defense of the existing social structure. I was intrigued by the very unflattering news [they printed] about Father Stojałowski, that he had stirred up the peasants against the Jews, against the gentry, and committed many abuses. And then my curiosity was heightened when on a certain Sunday in 1897 a letter from the bishop was read out from the pulpit, excommunicating Father Stojałowski and all those who read his papers, brochures, who invited him into their homes— these individuals would not receive absolution at confession—because he undermined holy belief and the church.
>
> "What kind of a priest is that"—I thought—and perhaps rightly too. . . . "But from the other side," I thought, "if he writes for peasants perhaps it's worth reading through. But that's excommunication. Hell . . . a mortal sin. . . . But the priest probably knew more about it than we did and he wrote the newspapers. What kind of a priest is he that he writes

---

Krakowa i Województwa Krakowskiego (APKr), Sąd Krajowy Karny w Krakowie (SKKKr), sygn. 224.

[45] The arrests occurred regularly a few days before each election in which Stojałowski sought to mobilize peasant voters to elect fellow villagers.

[46] Stojałowski's position vis-à-vis the church hierarchy is extremely complicated. A trained Jesuit, he was dismissed from the order in 1875, the same year he began publication of his two journals. Having received direct permission form Archbishop Wierzchlejwski before beginning publication, however, Stojałowski remained in good standing with the church until he began in the 1890s publishing explicit attacks on the recalcitrance of parish priests in matters of peasant politics. The church's attitude toward Stojałowski's activities was also strongly influenced by the close relationship between the church and the Habsburg state. For more on Stojałowski's tense relationship with the church hierarchy, see Kącki, *Ks. Stanisław Stojałowski*, 32–37; and Suchonek, "Działalność polityczna," 130.

for the peasants?" I wondered for a long time with the son of a neighbor. We resolved to try to get hold of one of the forbidden newspapers.

> After a time [someone] brought a copy of *Wieniec*. I picked it up with a beating heart . . . [and] finally decided it was more of a sin to write it than to read it and so I read it.[47]

Józef Nocek and his neighbor were so positively impressed by the contents of the paper that they concluded that the editors of the other Catholic periodicals circulating in the countryside "had lied about this priest" and resolved to continue reading *Wieniec*.[48] Indeed, the very fact that a priest was willing to take up the cause of the peasantry itself drew them to the papers. The young men were supported in their decision by the mail carrier, who "continued to bring [them their] papers, but hid them in her clothing, saying they were forbidden."[49]

The internal turmoil Nocek and his friend suffered over their decision about the newspaper helped shatter the faith the boys had in the authority of the local parson, who had initially forbidden them to look at the papers. Indeed, Nocek traces the birth of his own anticlericalism to a conversation he had with the parson, in which the priest refused to acknowledge the value of Stojałowski's cause:

> When he discovered that I subscribed to these papers, he called me to his office and sat with me and read these forbidden newspapers, along with the lies told by other newspapers about Father Stojałowski. I asked him to show me the sins that were spoken about. [He did not, but] only asked me to promise that I would not read certain issues. I told him I would continue to read them all and left the office.

After this, Nocek reports, he "sat every Sunday listening to the false things" the preacher proclaimed from the pulpit.[50] Questions about the social and political organization of the Galician peasants, questions proposed by Stojałowski in his illicit papers, had begun to wean villagers from ideological dependency on the rural clergy. Ironically, of course, although initially responsible for challenging the restrictions village priests placed on the peasant movement, Stojałowski himself would eventually complain of the social radicalism of the movement he helped to found.

Father Stojałowski soon became a martyr in the eyes of his followers who continued to be "warned from the pulpit" against subscribing to the

---

[47] Jozef Nocek, "Wspomnienia, 1880–," 5–9.
[48] The two other papers Nocek refers to were *Krakus* and *Niedziela*, both of which were edited by priests.
[49] Nocek, "Wspomnienia," 8.
[50] Ibid., 8–9.

forbidden papers and to "come from the confessional without forgiveness." Nonetheless, hundreds of village readers continued to subscribe to the journals.[51] Editorials in the papers encouraged villagers to question the authority of local priests, emphasizing the "harms [the peasant] suffered from the . . . priests."[52] Peasant letters published in the papers encouraged subscribers to challenge the position parish priests occupied as the chief educators in the countryside. Maciej Szarek wrote that rural priests sought to ensure that the peasants "remain dark people."[53] A villager from Bestwina accused the local parson and vicar of "misusing the pulpit and the confessional, relying on them to . . . deride education." These priests were reportedly the focus of "public scorn" in the village since they had decided to "spurn their obligations."[54] Anticlericalism grew to such a pitch in the early years of the peasant movement that even the liberal newspaper *Gazeta Lwowska* began attacking parish priests in this period for their recalcitrance in the face of peasant mobilization.[55]

Attacks against parish clergy in the press, in combination with the self-doubt literate peasants experienced over the issue of reading forbidden papers, helped demote the clergyman's position within the village. The social distance many priests maintained from their flock began to grate on a peasantry charged with a newfound confidence in its own social position. Villagers complained of the need to "go before the priest on bent knees and humbly kiss his hand" when they had some request of him rather than "simply assume respect between individuals and above all for oneself," as Father Stojałowski's newspapers taught.[56] A new tension between the village commune and the rectory arose as literate peasants presented themselves as the leaders of a movement to promote the social and national liberation of the peasantry. The preemancipation hold rural clerics had over village culture would erode in the face of this challenge from peasant leaders.[57]

---

[51] Franciszek Kuś discusses the martyrdom of Father Stojałowski in the eyes of his peasant followers in "Z pamiętników moich," 107.
[52] Nocek notes that one particular anticlerical editorial made him think (metaphorically) about the rabid "rectory dog" in his own village "who wanted to attack us." Nocek, "Wspomnienia," 8.
[53] "Głos ludu przez Maciej Szarka," *Pszczółka*, February 26, 1894, 6–7. Confiscated by Galician police. APKr, SKKKr 224.
[54] Village of Bestwia to *Pszczółka*, February 26, 1894, 8–9. Confiscated by Galician police. APKr, SKKKr 224.
[55] For example, *Gazeta Lwowska*, March 21, 1893. Confiscated by Galician police for its attacks on priests. APKr, SKKKr 224.
[56] Czuła, "Niedola szkolna," 467–68.
[57] Regarding the postemancipation conflict between commune and rectory, see Szaflik, *O rząd, chłopskich dusz*, 23–24 and Edward Ciupak, *Katolicyzm ludowy w Polsce. Studia socjologiczne* (Warsaw, 1972), 54–55.

As the balance of power shifted and rural parsons came under attack for educational shortcomings in the countryside, the schoolteacher came to play a more dominant role in the training of village leaders. New anticlerical factions developed in many communities, often organized around the teacher. Peasants who sought to read banned newspapers were often able to obtain them from the schoolmaster after being rebuffed by the priest. Peasant readers felt their human dignity injured when priests and gentry were permitted to read without censorship, but the peasant's intake was restricted. "Why," challenged one reader of *Przyjaciel Ludu*, who borrowed the paper from the teacher, "can others read what they wish, but not the peasantry? Because he must remain dark like the tobacco in a pipe."[58]

As the tension between priest and schoolmaster increased, village teachers found themselves under attack by the religious establishment. One teacher even had to be moved into a village "with the help of the army" because of the local priest's opposition to the pedagogue.[59] Independent efforts by peasant leaders to establish and staff elementary schools also faced opposition from clerics who fought the hiring of progressive teachers. Maciej Szarek complained bitterly, for example, in 1869 that the school he helped found still did not have a qualified teacher owing to clerical intransigence. "The absence of a suitable teacher is the fault of the priest," he believed.[60]

The Schoolmaster as Populist Advocate

The position of the schoolmaster in the postautonomy Galician village reflected a number of important shifts in the rural power structure and in the training of peasant leaders for public life. From its earlier status as an outgrowth of religious instruction, education began to develop a separate existence in the village after the changed school laws of the 1870s. This new position was reflected in the hiring of permanent, full-time teachers, the erection of freestanding schoolhouses separate from the rectory or the organist's home, and the evolution of the schoolmaster as an independent advocate for peasant pupils. In contrast to the conception of social organ-

---

[58] Adam Klimczak, Jarosławiec, Dąbrowski district, to *Wieniec*, third Sunday in March, 1895, 162–65.

[59] "Instructor Benedykt Wygoda przez Zofię Mankowską-Wygodzinę," *Wiejscy działacze społeczni*, 2:2.

[60] Maciej Szarek to K. Libelit (June 11, 1869), Biblioteka Jagiellońska, manuscript no. 6004, in Albin and Szaflik, "Listy Macieja Szarka," 74.

ization encouraged by parish priests, schoolmasters tended to support a more populist vision of national membership. Their training in pedagogical seminaries encouraged them to treat history and Polish-language literature as components of a more inclusive national identity formation. Through their lessons, schoolteachers helped to shift the components of the nationalist paradigm to make the nation more accessible to peasant children.

The increasing local influence of the schoolhouse engendered important changes in the rural social dynamic. Linked geographically to older loci of power, the schoolhouse was typically built in the center of the community, near the church, the manor house, and the rectory. Frequently constructed on the site formerly occupied by the tavern, the school symbolically displaced (one of) the retrograde centers of sociability with a more progressive center of learning.[61] Once the schoolhouse was erected, each of the preexisting centers of authority sought to claim control over its activities. Competing efforts to affect curricular content made the rural instructor one of the most heavily pressured figures in the village. Peasant activist Jakub Bojko summed up the often untenable position of the teacher, arguing that

> [t]he teacher today is morally influenced on all sides. It has to be this way in order to gain the agreement of the priest, the lord, and the peasant. . . . Those three men in no measure agree, and deplore him when he sincerely seeks to get closer to the peasant, and for this he is rewarded only with being removed from his post [by school council officials].[62]

Indeed, the educator was responsible in some senses to each of these quarters. The village commune "owned" the school building, which was constructed and maintained with a combination of village and manorial funds.[63] The Galician School Council held formal control over curricular matters, staffing of the schools, and training instructors. And the parish priest continued to exercise moral influence over the curriculum, despite

---

[61] See examples of building sites listed in *Szkoła* (1893): 124; Jan Madejczyk, "Dwa lata w szkółce wiejskiej," in Knot, *Galicyjskie wspomnienia*, 453. Wojciech Wiącek, "Wiejska szkoła zimowa, 1878–1883," in ibid., 395–99.

[62] *Dwie dusze*, as cited in Szaflik, *O rząd, chłopskich dusz*, 54–55.

[63] Galician administrative archives contain documents detailing the respective contributions of *gmina*, estate (*obszar dworski*), and crownland government. The commune and estate shared responsibility for the upkeep and heating of the schoolhouse. The commune was responsible for providing a home and plot of land for the teacher, whose salary was paid by the School Council. TsDIAL, fond op. 2, spr. 1, "Documents from 1867–1897."

There Is Still Hope for a Better Future. Sketch of a village teacher by Fr. Kostrzewski. *Kłosy* 13 (1871): 277. Courtesy of the Ethnographic Museum, Cracow. Inventory number III/2259/F. Reproduction by Jacek Kubiena.

legal limitations on his activities within the school itself. As Bojko's comment suggests, school inspectors traversed the countryside assiduously recording deviations from the authorized curriculum and removing violators from their posts.

The choreography of rituals performed in and around the school reflected the delicate interweaving of village influences and the fragile balance of power among interest groups. New schoolhouses were christened in a ceremony involving a full Catholic mass and a procession of secular officials to the building site, bringing spiritual and state authority together in a symbolic representation of the proposed meaning of education for peasants. The Galician clerical and secular elite sought to communicate a hierarchical vision of social organization through these ceremonies, a vision that echoed the sentiments of many parish clergy. Piety and citizenship, humility and patriotism came together in their program of lessons for peasant children and in the model of comportment expected of rural teachers. Ecclesiastical authorities blended religious imagery and advice about the educational mission of village teachers during inauguration ceremonies, bidding teachers first and foremost to "work in the spirit of religion and in accord with the church."[64] The inauguration pageantry was repeated annually during final examinations when pupils were asked to perform before an audience consisting of the priest, the mayor, village aldermen, members of the crownland School Council, and the local landlord.[65] Civic and religious authorities, local and crownland centers of power came together in symbolic form during these schoolhouse ceremonies. In an ongoing effort to blend religious piety with Polish nationalism, schoolteachers were expected to promise to "teach [the pupils] to love God and to uphold his holy commandments" as well as to award them texts of Polish history for high marks on their exams.[66]

Partly as a result of the structure of power within the village, rural teachers complained of living in a fishbowl, constantly observed by their neighbors and on an equal social footing with no one. This lonely, exposed position was described by one rural instructor, Bolesław Marchewski, as standing "as though on a candlestick."

Here all eyes fasten on you; here everyone knows what you do, what you say, what you eat, what you drink, even the smallest thing is known. Let

[64] Examples of inauguration ceremonies appear in *Szkoła,* e.g., January 28, 1893, 45 and 124.
[65] On the pageantry surrounding exam day, see Wiącek, "Wiejska Szkoła zimowa," in Knot, *Galicyjskie wspomnienia,* 396–98; and Dunikowski, "Z tyczowych dni . . . ," in ibid., 349–50.
[66] The commitment to "uphold his holy commandments" was part of a chant performed during the St. Gregory's Day (March 12) procession of the teacher and his pupils through the village appealing for financial support. Jan Jakóbiec, "Szkolna droga syna chłopskiego, 1882–1896," ibid., 406–7.

someone or other sit in your home: already news of this travels from cottage to cottage; the young and the old repeat it; they elaborate and comment on your affairs in their own way. It seems as though the walls have ears.[67]

The isolation of the teacher's position led rural instructors to become models for the rest of the community whether they liked it or not. "Whatever you do," cautioned Marchewski, "do not fall into bad grace and become a negative example for anyone."

Unable to develop normal relationships with villagers, rural teachers struggled to determine the kind of model they could represent for local families. Editors of conservative pedagogical newspapers advised instructors to assume a kind of clerical stance, striving to remain morally above the fray while guiding villagers in virtuous behavior. They were cautioned to "[n]ever stand among the people in a place where the dignity of this position would be affected. . . . You don't fulfill your mission as a teacher through a beer glass . . . nor by attending great feasts and frolicking among the people . . . but in the school itself."[68] Educational authorities used the language of the church to characterize the socially elevated position schoolteachers were expected to assume in the village. "The school is a temple," they were told, "and the teacher is a chaplain."[69] Editors of pedagogical newspapers informed their readers that the mission of the rural instructor was not to "mingle among the people," to "visit cottages, bring books, read newspapers here and there," or to "speak to them about great ideas, about great problems," as many rural educators clearly did. Rather than engaging in ideological struggles with their pupils, teachers were instructed to stand as icons of piety and good works.

School Council officials and the heads of pedagogical associations promoted a vision of national identity that closely corresponded to the nationalist paradigm of the Polish Catholic Church. This model of national progress through education involved a marriage of religious piety, social conservatism, and information about the great deeds of the Fatherland. In a set of instructions that carefully interwove religious imagery with conservative patriotism, rural teachers were told,

You are a good son of the church and a good son of this land, hence you know that we are a nation still because the people never lost their reli-

[67] Bolesław Marchewski, "The Position of the Teacher among the People," *Szkoła*, February 4, 1893, 52–54.
[68] Ibid., 53.
[69] Ibid., 53.

gion. . . . Hence, let the school stand as a protector of our nation; let the young generation bear genuine piety; let the elementary school be for the younger generation a school for genuine patriotism based on piety. And then let the example of the teacher bear witness that for us it is a tradition from way back that piety accompanies the high call of the teacher.[70]

Piety, patriotism, and education: this trinity was the formula rural teachers were asked to apply in their daily work in the classroom. Yet, increasingly, village instructors chose to break away from this mold, seizing the opportunity to lead their pupils in extracurricular enterprises, and eventually challenging the pious, hierarchical image of the nation with which they had been entrusted.

Village instructors rebelled, first, against the curricular constraints imposed upon them. The Galician conservatives who controlled the School Council carefully prescribed an elementary curriculum with extremely restricted content for rural schools. According to curricula available for one-and two-class elementary schools (the vast majority of all village schools), most of the 26–28-hour primary school week was to be devoted to the mechanics of reading, orthography, and arithmetic. Only in the second (and usually last) year of study was a subject called "News of the World" officially introduced to rural students. For five hours per week, village pupils were to examine "natural history, physics, geography, and . . . history of the native land, monarchy, and constitutional government."[71] Maps officially available in Galician elementary classrooms included representations of the Habsburg monarchy, the world, Europe, and the Galician crownland. No map of Poland was legally permitted in the classroom. According to the schedule of lessons prescribed for primary school teachers, national history and culture had little place in the content of village education. And as of an 1883 regulation, only officially approved textbooks could be used to teach these topics even during the limited portion of the week when they were allowed. Teachers were forbidden, on threat of removal from their posts, to use their own materials to teach national topics.

Despite what appeared to be a limited role for Polish topics in Galician primary schools, elementary education represented a key source of Polish

---

[70] Ibid., 52–56.

[71] "Lesson plan for a two-class school" (1892), TsDIAL, fond 178, op. 2, spr. 3054. In fact, only a very small portion of rural Galicians officially studied the second-year subject "News of the World." Two-class schools represented a distinct minority in Galician villages. In 1900, a full 1,200 of the 1,962 Polish-language primary schools throughout the crownland were one-class schools. The majority of the larger schools were situated in urban areas. Sirka, *Nationality Question*, 79.

national identity for large numbers of peasant pupils. Village activists mark the period they spent in the schoolhouse as vital to their "discovery" of Polishness. Memoirists comment on their exposure to Polish history, their memorization of patriotic songs and national poetry, and their assignment to "write out the history of Poland and recite it from memory."[72] In most cases, the national message the children received in the schoolhouse contrasted sharply with the one encouraged by local clergy or conservative pedagogical newspapers.

Curricular Conflicts and the "Two Cultures" Debate

The status of rural education was a topic of heated debate in the Galician diet throughout the 1880s, pitting conservative images of a permanent rural class against liberal conceptions of increased social mobility for the peasantry. Central to this debate were questions about the status of the preemancipation social structure within the reemerging Polish state. Would rural schoolchildren be educated to take their place as equal citizens beside their bourgeois and noble compatriots, or would they continue to occupy a lower social rung, enjoying a "second culture" complementing but not competing with the first?

Conservative deputies, concerned with the erosion of the social hierarchy, sought to bring about a formal division of public primary education into rural and urban curricula. Members of the Conservative Party expressed concern that the "worldly" contents of the curriculum might encourage peasant pupils to seek social advancement. Moreover, the parade of inadequately prepared peasant students arriving at Jagiellonian University in Cracow convinced conservatives that the quality of the Polish intelligentsia would be diluted by the inclusion of large numbers of peasants.[73] Rather, the purpose of primary education in the countryside was to "introduce religious and moral principles, and civil obligations [as well as] to instruct about the conditions of the profession," argued Michał Bobrzyński, conservative Sejm deputy and historian.[74] According to Bobrzyński,

---

[72] Wiącek writes about his years in an informal "winter school" where he was steeped in knowledge about Polish history and culture. "Wiejska szkoła zimowa," in Knot, *Galicyjskie wspomnienia*, 396.

[73] This perspective is perhaps best represented in the work of historian, university professor, and conservative political activist Michał Bobrzyński, who served as a deputy to the Sejm beginning in 1885 and as vice-chairman of the Galician School Council after 1890. See Philip Pajakowski, "History, the Peasantry, and the Polish Nation in the Thought of Michał Bobrzyński," *Nationalities Papers* 26, no. 2 (1998): 249–64.

[74] As cited in Michalski, *Dzieje szkolnictwa*, 268–72.

vice-chairman of the Galician School Council after 1890, the professional duty of peasants was to "tend the herds." Bobrzyński's views echoed those of the older *stańczyk* historian Józef Szujski, head of the Cracow Academy of Sciences, who argued in 1880 that "education is the privilege of the gentry."[75] The Galician educational system, Szujski stressed, should ensure that all "pupils be limited within their social class of origin." According the Szujski, the proposed two-tiered system would help "prepare peasant children to perform their profession of farming and . . . not awaken among them higher social ambitions."[76]

In 1884, the Sejm passed a plan to "limit pupils within their social class of origin." The Galician School Council, in turn, under Bobrzyński's guidance, set out to revise elementary school curricula to mark clear differences in content and structure between rural and urban schools. The outcome of these curricular revisions appeared in a law dated May 23, 1895, entitled "Regarding the Establishment and Governing of Public Elementary Schools." The new guidelines limited the official curriculum in rural classrooms to reading, writing, arithmetic, and catechism. No space in the curriculum of one- and two-class rural schools was allowed for history, geography, or civic education. These were topics reserved solely for urban schools preparing upper-class children for public life. Rural primary schools were to emphasize vocational training in agriculture.[77]

As a result of this legislation, teacher training seminars were restructured, reducing the preparation required for village instructors and ensuring that provincial teachers would "have a minimum knowledge [only] and thus would be less likely to encourage ambition in the schoolchildren."[78] After 1884, rural communities were typically denied state permission to build and staff four-grade schools whose curriculum permitted more worldly contents (and access to higher education, since degrees from two-class rural schools did not allow access to other schools without an entrance exam).[79] The holdings of rural libraries and the content of textbooks used in country schools were also revised.

---

[75] Quoted in Sirka, *Nationality Question*, 79.

[76] Józef Szujski, head of the Cracow Academy of Sciences, *SsSK* (1880), as cited in Szaflik, *Orząd chłopskich dusz*, 53–54.

[77] Pedagogical journals in the 1890s engaged in lengthy discussions about the implications of the 1884 Sejm plan. See, for example, *Szkoła*, January 7, 1893, 10.

[78] Michalski, *Dzieje szkolnictwa*, 288–72, on the curricular changes resulting from the increasing power of the Galician conservatives; see also Pajakowski, "History"; and Sirka, *Nationality Question*, 77–78.

[79] Regarding the social divisions and stratification resulting from this law, see Sirka, *Nationality Question*, 77–78.

In the midst of this debate on the degree to which rural curricula should challenge peasant pupils to surpass their social origins, Galician village schoolmasters worked to undermine the educational basis of the unequal power relations in Polish society. Rebuffing the instructions of their own supervisors in many cases, pedagogues sought to shape a Polish nation that was socially inclusive, leading villagers toward a new variety of national expression. They fought the limitations on the established curriculum by seeking to rewrite socially conservative history texts and, in distinct violation of crownland law, to introduce their own material into lessons on the Polish past.

Conflicts over the way Polish history should be presented were particularly contentious, pitting elementary teachers against School Council officials. Instructors complained that the presentation of the Polish past was too dry or too broad to engage peasant pupils and set out to rewrite history texts to make them more accessible to their students.[80] School Council officials noted "an unusually lively level of activity . . . in the area of writing textbooks" throughout the 1880s "in an effort to create improved models of teaching . . . and to achieve a happier nation."[81] Yet at least one pedagogue commissioned in 1875 to devise a new Polish history text for introduction into the Cracow Teachers' Seminary was sharply criticized by the School Council for his irreverent approach to the Polish *szlachta*. School Council director Schmidt attacked Henryk Stroka's new text for its "criticism of the founding mistakes" of the old Polish Republic, its emphasis on the gentry's role in the downfall of the state, and its attack on the upper classes for their attitude toward the peasants.

Stroka's efforts to write the peasants into Polish history and to raise questions about the gentry's treatment of villagers under serfdom flew directly in the face of the conception of the national past the School Council sought to promote. School Council members expressed concern that this questioning of *szlachta* behavior would lead the "lower classes . . . to learn hatred and disgust for their nation's past" and discourage the growth of any national sentiment on the peasant's part. Rather than challenging the image of a nation led by a guiltless aristocracy, the council cautioned,

---

[80] Franciszek Nowicki, director of the Teachers' Seminary in Tarnów, writes that "especially keenly felt is the absence of a suitably written textbook for the study of the history of the Fatherland." Report from Franciszek Nowicki (October 16, 1891), "Documents pertaining to curriculum in crownland elementary schools" (1891–1892), TsDIAL, fond 178, op. 2, spr. 3004.

[81] Władysław Boberski, Director of the C. K. Teachers' Seminary in Tarnopol, to C. K. Presidium (October 23, 1891), TsDIAL, fond 178, op. 2, spr. 3004.

rural children should be taught "virtue and love of the fatherland." Unquestioning support of the nation, with its rigid social hierarchy, was an "elementary law of pedagogy," according to the officials on the council, and the analysis of social tensions had no place "as an academic topic in elementary schools."[82] The populist, peasantist approach to national history that rural teachers believed might attract the interest of their pupils was thus strongly discouraged by official attempts to preserve the illusion of the preemancipation leadership structure within Polish society.

More accessible than debates over history textbooks, the stories and historical anecdotes rural schoolmasters told their pupils about the national past helped to mobilize them in support of nationalist goals. Bypassing the content of officially sanctioned textbooks (of which a severe shortage existed in any case), many village teachers violated the letter of the crownland law and presented Polish history from a peasant perspective. Teachers "spoke about the Kościuszko Rising, about Bartosz Głowacki [the serf who was ennobled for his bravery during the rising], and about the scythemen at Racławice."[83] Village schoolmasters were credited with knowing "how to tell these things in a way that a peasant child could immediately understand."[84] Emphasis on the scythemen and on Głowacki meant teachers could stress both peasant sacrifices for the Polish nation and the possibility of social change (i.e., ennoblement) through national sacrifice.

Neither the Głowacki story nor information on the 1830 or 1863 insurrections appeared in the primary history texts used in grade schools. Yet these were the very stories that motivated peasant pupils to comment that they "practically swallowed all this whole, so absorbed" did they become in the nationalist cause through the lessons of the schoolhouse.[85] Schoolteachers emphasized the heroic deeds of Polish national heroes like Kościuszko, King Jan Kazimierz and national bard Adam Mickiewicz. Yet they also sought consistently to integrate a social element into their instruction about nationalist struggles. They filled their library shelves with nationalist poetry and literature and eagerly loaned these materials to

---

[82] H. Schmidt, "Report to the Galician School Council from Cracow" (May 24, 1875), TsDIAL, fond 178, op. 2, spr. 1228.

[83] Jan Madejczyk, "Dwa lata w szkółce," in Knot, *Galicyjskie wspomnienia*, 452. Village instructor Benedykt Wygoda also recalls teaching children about historical figures such as Kościuszko and Polish cultural leaders like Adam Mickiewicz. "Instruktor Benedykt Wygoda przez Zofię Mańkowską-Wygodzina." *Wiejscy działacze społeczni*, 2: 8–12.

[84] Madejczyk, "Dwa lata w szkółce," 452.

[85] Ibid.

villagers. They subscribed to nationalist newspapers and shared their contents with local peasants. And they sought to establish libraries "to promote patriotism . . . among the rural population . . . to awaken the spirit of nationalism among the peasantry."[86]

Beyond encouraging patriotic sentiment within the schoolhouse, village schoolmasters were also increasingly active in social reform efforts outside their normal duties. Teachers were the most frequent nonpeasant initiators of agricultural circles, often facilitating the formation of circles by holding meetings and inviting circle representatives to speak in the schoolhouse.[87] Teachers promoted the construction of community buildings to house reading rooms. They contributed books and periodicals from their own collections to newly established reading rooms. And they volunteered their time to oversee the operation of circle stores.

Rural teachers also provided the symbolic support needed for progressive educational measures to take effect in the countryside. The christening ceremony for new circles was invariably held in the schoolhouse or its courtyard as a means of lending added prestige to the new organization.[88] Indeed, so active were many rural teachers in local reform efforts that their scholarly commitments sometimes began to suffer as a result. One villager complained of his schoolteacher father's "rarely being at home" as a consequence of his attention to the community. Benedykt Wygoda's father spent his time conducting a campaign to rid the village of thieves, coordinating local and crownland elections, serving as an intermediary for a thirty-year battle between the village and the estate, and working with peasants to plant trees in the village orchard. The time spent on these community activities meant that the instructor "rarely spent more than the obligatory several hours per week in the schoolhouse."[89]

The message communicated through these public activities frequently combined social with national elements. Young teachers were often also members of radical nationalist organizations, such as Odrodzenie (revival), through which they became active promoters of Polish patriotism in the countryside. Members of this secret association

[86] "Nauczyciel z powiatu mieleckiego," in Knot, *Galicyjskie wspomnienia,* 361.
[87] Teachers were on the boards of 471 out of a total of 701 circles in 1891. Gurnicz, *Kółka rolnicze,* 106. Franciszek Kuś describes the encouragement the local teacher gave the agricultural circle in his village by inviting Professor Stefczyk to speak in the schoolhouse about his scheme for a network of credit societies. Kuś, "Z pamiętników moich," 57.
[88] *Wieniec,* October 16, 1879; J. J., Laszki, Jarosław district, to *Wieniec,* November 27, 1879, 191–92.
[89] Benedykt Wygoda describes the social activism of his schoolteacher father in "Instruktor Benedykt Wygoda," 2.

traveled about the countryside giving courses and conducting lectures. . . . [They] emphasized the concept of nationality and the feeling of civil rights, such as the right and the responsibility to vote. [They] never worked "over" the peasants or "for" the peasants, but always "with" them. [They] taught the peasants about such important historical figures as Mickiewicz and Kościuszko. . . . [and] about the goal of Polish independence and always used the term "we" with the peasants. Eventually [they] created a second Polish army, this one consisting of peasants.[90]

Members of such nationalist associations conceived of the village schoolhouse as a forum for tutoring in national identity. Benedykt Wygoda, a teacher in the village of B. and member of the Tarnopol chapter of Odrodzenie, asserted that "the concept of Poland" should be transmitted to village youth along with general education.[91] Schoolteachers were also in the forefront of organizing villagers in commemorative activities to celebrate historic events in Polish national history, often against the direct wishes of their pedagogical superiors.[92] Both in the lessons they taught in the school and in their social activism within the larger community, teachers helped introduce the idea of peasant membership and participation in Polish national struggles.

The more socially egalitarian posture many rural teachers adopted toward national goals may have been closely tied to their daily financial struggles. The low pay and difficult working conditions country teachers suffered helped them identify with the needs of the peasant families among whom they worked. The extraordinarily low wages awarded state elementary instructors in one-and two-class schools were a focus of constant complaint among teachers and peasant communities alike. The 200-zloty annual salary collected from *gmina* taxes represented a severe hardship for rural communities and yet was too little to keep teachers in a position for long. Local school councils complained about the state of village education, noting that the low salary attracted "only very young teachers" who "come and go." Moreover, it was said to be difficult to find a teacher with "good qualifications" for such a "miserable salary." The low wage meant

---

[90] Ibid., 8–13; "Nauczyciel z powiatu mieleckiego," 349–50.

[91] Wygoda, "Instruktor Benedykt Wygoda," 10–11.

[92] Czuła comments that teachers "did not have any instructions from their supervisors to conduct such social work," but were instead encouraged to devote themselves entirely to the work of the schoolhouse. Czuła, "Niedola szkolna," 467–68. Sirka notes that in predominantly Ukrainian villages, the teachers in Polish-language elementary schools tended to be more engaged in political activity. Sirka, *Nationality Question*, 81–82. Madejczyk comments specifically on the nationalist activities of his village schoolmaster, "Dwa lata w szkółce," 452. See also "Nauczyciel z powiatu mieleckiego," 351–57.

that many teachers quit when the workload grew too overwhelming, often returning to their own homes to tend ailing parents or to help on the family farm. Yet the tax structure for raising the salary, combined with the frequent opposition of a portion of the *gmina*, meant that overcrowding in the schools could not be remedied through the hiring of a second teacher. Throughout the 1880s and 1890s, complaints from pupils and teachers alike about overcrowding and low pay in the schoolhouse reached the Galician School Council.[93] Partly in response to these criticisms, the Galician School Council under the guidance of Michał Bobrzyński decreed in the 1890s that criticism and debate about the curriculum or the required textbooks were strictly forbidden among schoolteachers. Teachers who expressed their disagreement with the established curricula and who implemented changes in their own schoolhouses were to be transferred to another location immediately.[94]

And yet, it was not until elementary school teachers began to organize in associations of their own that working conditions finally began to improve for rural instructors. The birth of separate associations to recognize the needs of Galician elementary teachers marked the radicalization of rural instructors' agendas and their increased support of peasant political goals over those of the Galician conservatives. In 1891, elementary teachers founded the Society of Elementary Teachers (Towarzystwo Nauczycielstwa Ludowego) to fight for the rights of grade school instructors, most of whom served in rural areas. The society founded a journal, *Szkolnictwo Ludowe* (Peoples Education), which quickly established itself in opposition to the Galician School Council, the Pedagogical Society (Towarzystwo Pedagogiczne), and the conservative educational newspaper *Szkoła*. Originating in the traditional center of social radicalism, Nowy Sącz, the teachers' organization soon cast its net through the entire crownland, publishing its demands for improved teacher training and increased salaries in the columns of the *Szkolnictwo Ludowe*. The general criticism of the educational realities in the countryside prompted members of the School Council to accuse the organization of "antisocial agitation" and recommend that the paper's circulation be curtailed.[95]

By the early years of the twentieth century, the Society of Elementary Teachers had begun to ally with the newly founded peasant political party

---

[93] "Correspondence from Local School Councils," TsDIAL, fond 178, op. 2, spr. 5611, includes letters from villages in Myślenice, Krosno, Brody, and Lwów districts. School inspectors also complained that village teachers were violating crownland law by serving as commune scribes in order to supplement their income. TsDIAL, fond 178, op. 2, spr. 3118.

[94] Michalski, *Dzieje szkolnictwa*, 276.

[95] Ibid., 276–78.

Stronnictwo Ludowe. The two organizations cooperated in the school-teacher strike of 1902 in eastern Galicia and in general efforts to end the rural/urban differences in elementary school curricula. Overall, both the Peasant Party and the Society of Elementary Teachers saw the need for a more challenging primary curriculum that enjoyed a more "patriotic character."[96] By the 1910 conference of the National Union of Elementary Teachers (Krajowy Związek Nauczycielstwa Ludowego), the educational needs of rural youth and the needs of the nation were neatly combined in the celebration of the five-hundred-year anniversary of the victory of Grunwald over the Teutonic Knights. Speakers at the conference in Rzeszów marked the occasion by stressing the need to reform elementary education to help develop national and social consciousness among rural children. "Elementary education must develop in connection with the life of the nation," commented activist and pedagogical theoretician Henryk Kanark-Rowid at the conference.[97]

The Demographics of Activism:
Priests and Teachers as Transitional Figures

The advent of the dual curriculum in Galician primary schools during the 1880s and 1890s succeeded in limiting secondary and tertiary educational opportunities for most peasants. Only a minority of village children ever stepped inside a rural schoolhouse in nineteenth-century Poland. As late as 1900, barely half of all school-aged children (age 6–12) in Galicia were enrolled in school, fewer than half of whom appeared on any given day, and those who did attend did so for only a year or two.[98] Since one- and two-class village schools did not allow pupils to transfer directly to town schools or gymnasia without passing a formal exam, it was rare for peasant families to aspire to more than a basic education for their children.[99] Of those who attended a country school, only a fraction possessed the resources and familial support to transfer to an urban school and then on to gymnasium.

Yet even in the period of increasingly restricted elementary education during the Bobrzyński reforms, a steady trickle left the countryside and

---

[96] Ibid., 276–78.
[97] Ibid., 278–79.
[98] Ibid., 276–78; school inspector reports, TsDIAL, fond 178, op. 2; Sirka, *Nationality Question,* 74, 78.
[99] On the types of education available to peasants in late-nineteenth-century Galicia, see Sirka, *Nationality Question,* 77–78.

made their way to educational centers beyond the village. Those who left to attend classes in the regional capital and even to enroll in universities tended to aspire to one of two professions: educator or cleric. Village notables such as priests and schoolteachers thus served a dual function in pulling peasants into the wider world of social and political institutions beyond the village. They helped train a new generation of village activists by working with them on reform projects, and, at the same time, they functioned as the physical manifestation of the blending of social classes after emancipation.[100] Clerics and schoolmasters became icons for social mobility in a heavily peasant society, forming a core of the rural intelligentsia that shaped the early leadership of the populist movement.

Clerical and pedagogical training in the late nineteenth century pulled hundreds of peasants into these two fields, creating a stratum of village intellectuals that would serve as the adhesive binding national and local concerns. The dramatic expansion of the network of primary schools in the crownland along with a sharp rise in rural population created a need for increased numbers of trained clerics and elementary teachers. Peasant families took advantage of this demand and, despite the official restrictions on rural education, found ways of sending their children to secondary schools and institutions of higher learning. By 1900 some 16 percent of the students studying at Jagiellonian University in Cracow were peasants.[101] Among these, the largest portion consistently matriculated into the theological faculty. Indeed, so many peasants matriculated into clerical training programs in the 1880s that the Theology Department was characterized colloquially as the "peasant department." Beginning in 1880, students of peasant background made up over half of the total theology matriculates who declared their social background on admission forms.[102] For Jagiellonian University, theology enjoyed far larger peasant enrollments than any single department anywhere in the university.[103] Indeed, so

---

[100] Wiącek, "Wiejska szkoła zimowa," 396–98, and Madejczyk, "Dwa lata w szkółce," 452. Michał Sała, the organist and schoolmaster in Izdebnik, was addressed with the informal *ty* by most villagers because he was a godfather to so many of them. "Chłop-Nauczyciel," *Piast,* June 25, 1947, 3.

[101] Michalski, *Dzieje szkolnictwa,* 288. Podraza, "Kształtowanie się elity," 65–66. See also Józef Mężyk, "Młodzież chłopska na Uniwersytecie Jagiellońskim i jej udział w ruchu ludowym (od powstania styczniowego do 1923 r.)," *Roczniki Dziejów Ruchu Ludowego,* no. 7 (1965): 17–50.

[102] After emancipation, the total number of students matriculating into the Theological Faculty of Jagiellonian University shot up sharply, as did the percentage of matriculates of peasant background. "Matriculation Records of the Theological Faculty," Jagiellonian University Archive, WTII 86–116.

[103] On the breakdown of students matriculating into Jagiellonian University, see Zbigniew Tabaka, *Analiza zbiorowości studenckiej Uniwersytetu Jagiellońskiego w latach, 1850–1918 (studium statystyczne)* (Cracow, 1970), tables 43–51. Of those who noted their social origin

heavily influenced was the Theology Department by this influx of village matriculates that even the highest-ranking professors in this field were from the village. During the period 1860–1920, seven of thirteen docents of the department were peasant born.[104]

Similar proportions were reflected in the entrance of students into teacher-training seminars throughout the crownland. The sharp increase in the number of primary schools prompted the seven teacher seminaries in western Galicia that trained Polish-speaking instructors to expand the number of applicants they accepted. A Galician School Council report from 1890 notes that the dramatic increase in elementary schools from 427 in 1867 to 3,692 in 1890 prompted a severe shortage of qualified teachers.[105] Throughout the 1880s, the School Council reported, "the majority of communes . . . [had] no elementary school, and in almost half the children [did] not even have access to a neighboring school." The council judged primary schooling to be "adequate" in only four of thirty-five Galician school districts, while twenty districts (including most of western Galicia) were judged "inadequate" for the needs of the population.[106] To respond to the severe shortage of primary schoolteachers, the School Council allocated increasing funds for stipends to seminary students without means. Some 58 percent of the male seminary matriculates in Galicia were granted stipends to help with tuition in 1907, making it more possible for peasant applicants to train as school instructors.[107]

The rise in the number of elementary school positions and the upswing in stipends available to train poorer students offered new channels for social mobility among peasant pupils. Completing the teacher-training seminar and passing the qualifying exam represented a significant elevation in status for those who hailed from the village. Because the exam involved testing the applicant's German-language proficiency, passing it "represented in the eyes of the country people . . . a sort of patent as a member of the intelligentsia and gave the individual a certain vital importance as one who is able to speak the language of the authorities."[108] This

---

on admissions documents, 21 (46 percent) were peasant born in 1880, 33 (57 percent) in 1885, 34 (51 percent) in 1890, 36 (68 percent) in 1895, and 27 (55 percent) in 1900.

[104] Urszula Perkowska, *Kształtowanie się zespołu naukowego w Uniwersytecie Jagiellońskim (1860–1920)* (Wrocław, 1975), 137.

[105] "Report by Galician School Commission for School Year 1889–1890," TsDIAL, fond 178, op. 2, spr. 2988. This was the first report of its kind comparing the educational situation in the period before the School Council came into existence with conditions under mandatory education.

[106] "Report on the Condition of Teachers in Galician Elementary Schools in 1883" (February 11, 1884), TsDIAL, fond 178, op. 2, spr. 5546.

[107] Michalski, *Dzieje szkolnictwa*, 275.

[108] Wygoda, "Instruktor Benedykt Wygoda," 1–5.

jump in social stature could be obtained without long years of education by simply enrolling in a brief pedagogy course prior even to finishing gymnasium.[109]

Yet the individuals who broke with family tradition and chose career paths that took them beyond the village also experienced a sense of dislocation from their social origins, placing them in an in-between position on a continuum from peasant to intellectual. This sense of social dislocation often began with the psychological transition involved in leaving the village to pursue education in an urban center. Moving to the district capital meant a difficult and alienating adjustment for peasant youth and their families. Parents experienced a period of "mourning" preceding the child's departure for the city. "My mother would no longer be able to bring food and I could not return on weekends," wrote one migrant of his impending journey to a gymnasium in Wadowice.[110] Students from the village felt their peers' resentment of their peasantness and confessed to symbolically "looking in the mirror" for the first time upon arrival in the city. Embarrassed at their status as "peasants in sackcloth clothing," village students quickly donned urban clothes despite objections from the village community.[111]

Part of the process of adjusting to town life involved coming to terms with the "special" role peasants played in rebuilding the Polish nation. Indeed, exposure to the "foreign" (mostly German-speaking) cultures of the city prompted a solidification of many peasants' identity as Poles. In the four-grade schools, "History of the Native Land" had a mandatory place in the curriculum, and it was only in these schools that peasant pupils received regular formal exposure to Polish history, literary figures, patriotic songs, and the politics of the partitioned state.[112] Peasants who came to the city to study for their teaching certificate also came into direct personal contact with leading intellectuals, many of whom were involved actively in nationalist struggles. It was as a guest in the home of a Polish officer that Benedykt Wygoda first learned of the 1863 January Rising and

---

[109] One teacher in the Mielec district explained that he could not complete high school because of a lack of funds and so enrolled in a pedagogy course in Tarnopol. "Nauczyciel z powiatu mieleckiego," 349–50.

[110] Jakóbiec, "Szkolna droga," 420–22.

[111] In one case, the parish priest sought to maintain social distinctions between peasant students and their urban classmates by forbidding parents to outfit their children in urban attire when they went off to high school. Madejczyk, "Dwa lata w szkółce," 454–55; Jakóbiec, "Szkolna droga," 408–11, 420–22; Michalski, *Dzieje szkolnictwa*, 288.

[112] Jakóbiec discusses his first exposure to Mickiewicz and Sienkiewicz, his first singing of patriotic songs, his first "Polish" history lesson in a gymnasium in Biała. Jakóbiec, "Szkolna droga," 408–11.

realized for the first time that "he [himself] was a Pole."[113] Yet the populism of the village schoolhouse tainted the nationalist lessons peasant children received in urban schools. Rather than accepting a hierarchical image of Polish social organization, with the nobility standing in a permanent leadership position, students from the village came to advocate a leading role for the peasantry—especially educated peasant activists. As one young scholar recalls realizing, "it would again be necessary to fight for Poland," but this time "the peasants had to be won over to the fight."[114]

Although many educated peasant sons and daughters undoubtedly remained in urban centers after completing their professional training, hundreds returned to their native villages or, in the case of priests and teachers, to settlements they were assigned to serve. Even more than their initial arrival in town, the educated peasants' reentry into the village community prompted tensions and a sense of separation between the educated migrant (typically of a younger generation) and the traditionally schooled old guard. Educated villagers took on positions as village mayors, commune secretaries, or heads of agricultural circles. And yet, even as these literate peasants served to link urban centers with village traditions, to bring the village closer to national culture, they were forever separated from the origins to which they sought to return. More than one returning villager noted the social distance separating him from his closest family members and friends after his time away from the village:

> After this, in my family or village environment, among the ignorant people of the countryside, I felt myself to be somewhat superior, for that which I know they do not know. Even my father, although I was intensely afraid of him, I politely wondered how it was that he knew nothing of Poland, that he couldn't read, and hence that he was somehow disabled, as though he was not quite a whole person.[115]

The individuals who were trained in the thousands of one-room schoolhouses in the Galician countryside and who were able to leave the countryside for even a short sojourn in an urban center found themselves caught between two worlds. The two-way tension that pulled them simultaneously toward and away from the village of their birth is the same tension that pulled peasant society as a whole closer to national political struggles. These peasant leaders and village notables would prove to be

---

[113] Wygoda, "Instruktor Benedykt Wygoda," 4–8.
[114] Jakóbiec, "Szkolna droga," 408–11.
[115] Madejczyk, "Dwa lata w szkółce," 452.

the instruments through which the village and the nation, the little and the great communities would find common ground for cooperation.

The Process of Mediation

As villagers became increasingly interested in local activism, they began to link up with nonpeasant notables (or educated villagers of peasant birth), forming alliance systems that would help further rural reform agendas. The increasing availability of an educated and somewhat worldly peasant cadre helped facilitate sustained political and social activity in many areas by the 1890s. Peasant "leaders" engaged in local activism by quietly creating coalitions of support among villagers, while maintaining a patron-type relationship with local notables such as priests and schoolteachers. Eventually, however, peasant leaders began to break away from their upper-class patrons and instead pursue initiatives for rural improvement on their own.

Peasant leaders such as Franciszek Magryś, a minimally educated weaver and commune secretary, worked intimately with nonpeasant figures to bring about social reform on a local scale. Magryś, who spent his whole life in his native village of Handzlówka, teamed up with the reforming parish priest, Father Krakowski, after the prelate's arrival in the commune in 1889. Well before this, however, Magryś had established an aggressive agenda of political and ethical activism in his village. After his election as commune secretary in 1874, he led a vicious temperance campaign, instigating the village council to pass legislation allowing local crime enforcers to patrol community watering holes and take down the names of those inside. In an early effort at clerical alliance, he also convinced Father Krakowski's predecessor to read out the names of those drinking on the Sabbath from the pulpit.[116]

Using his own literacy as a bargaining chip, Magryś managed to build a tentative coalition among village councillors, announcing he would serve as commune secretary only on the condition that council meetings were transferred from the tavern to the home of the organist.[117] The council passed this and other Magryś proposals "somewhat reluctantly," but nonetheless the changes were made. In small personal ways, such as giving evening reading lessons to village youth, Magryś was able to encourage the spread of literacy in his native village.[118] Yet he remained frustrated at

[116] Magryś, *Żywot chłopa*, 62–63, 75.
[117] Ibid., 58–59.
[118] Ibid., 50.

the lack of support in the community for more ambitious projects, such as the establishment of a permanent schoolhouse and the repair of the parish church. Relying only on his personal influence and the prestige he derived from his status as a literate farmer, Magryś was unable to raise the commune funding necessary to enact these more far-reaching programs.

These difficulties with rallying communal support diminished when in 1889 "help came . . . in the form of a young priest, full of enthusiasm for social work, Father Władysław Krakowski."[119] For most of the next two decades Magryś would work closely with the prelate on projects of mutual interest. The priest and the *pisarz* agreed, for example, to team up in the founding of a permanent school. Ignoring all imperial and crownland legislation restricting the participation of clergy in primary education, Krakowski advised Magryś to "try and get a schoolhouse and I will teach the children." With this endorsement, Magryś turned to the village council to try and obtain funds for building the school.

In a debate that pitted preemancipation attitudes against the "progressive" ideas of the younger generation, the council was torn between those who argued that their own fathers "could neither read nor write" but "managed [and] hence [their] own children will also survive without a school" and Magryś's growing reformist coalition. The secretary himself presented the schoolhouse as a partial remedy to the village's poverty, the decline of agriculture, the problem of drunkenness, and the perceived control of Jews in the village. The council eventually reached a compromise, agreeing to the creation of a permanent school but placing it in the home of the organist in order to avoid levying new taxes to build a schoolhouse. A combination of Magryś's compelling speeches throughout the village and the priest's "appeals from the pulpit" prompted some forty village children to study at the organist's the following year. Three years later, the priest assisted the villagers in obtaining a "government school" in the village.[120]

Over the next two decades, Magryś worked closely with Father Krakowski to raise funds for a new church (1899–1901), a lending society (1901), a community building (1905), and a village orchestra.[121] The cleric used Magryś as a conduit to the village council (of which he was not a member), persuading councillors to release funds for his projects. At the same time, Magryś was able to marshal Krakowski's support for his desire to found an agricultural circle. Krakowski promoted the plan from the

[119] Ibid., 76–78.
[120] Ibid., 76–77.
[121] Ibid., 78–85.

pulpit so convincingly that some sixty-three villagers signed up on the spot.[122] The alliance that developed between peasant leaders such as Magryś and rural notables helped to mold a cadre of villagers devoted to a reformist agenda.

Working relationships arose in other villages with activist clerics, including the strong ties established between Father Tyczyński and the educated villagers of Albigowa and between Father Stojałowski and newspaper correspondents such as Maciej Szarek. Father Radzecki, who served in the village of Wróblowa from 1883 until his death in 1894, linked up with Jan Madejczyk's grandfather to found a school. Radzecki too focused his reform efforts on ethical issues such as abolishing drunkenness and "immorality," insisting that couples he married refrain from holding their reception in the tavern, investigating whether christening parties turned up at the bar, and encouraging farmers to take oaths of abstinence from vodka.[123]

Similarly, rural teachers worked closely with their pupils to bring about improvements to their adopted villages. In contrast to the temperance campaigns and other locally based projects supported by rural clergy, however, the projects schoolteachers introduced tended to strengthen links to communities beyond the village. Pedagogues placed particular emphasis on communication between their home village and the wider world, promoting road construction and networks of village stores and agricultural cooperatives linked with those in neighboring villages. One teacher in the district of Mielec focused his early efforts on "the completely destroyed village road, and especially the road connecting the countryside with the school and with the high road." Using his knowledge of the crownland bureaucracy, the teacher managed to obtain state funds to repair the road.[124]

Elsewhere economic and social networks passed through the schoolhouse, placing the schoolmaster at the center of a complex web of connections between village and surrounding centers of authority. Jakub Salek, the teacher in the village of Machów, assisted the village council, read and interpreted official documents that arrived in the village, and wrote purchase orders for commune land sales. "Everything that was important in the village" was the business of this rural teacher, without whom villagers believed "nothing could get done."[125]

---

[122] Ibid., 80–81.
[123] Some farmers managed to follow the letter of the law by drinking rum instead of vodka! Madejczyk, "Dwa lata w szkółce," 450–51.
[124] "Nauczyciel z powiatu mieleckiego," 355–57.
[125] Wiącek, "Wiejska szkoła zimowa," 396–98.

Pedagogical activism frequently relied on formal political channels, including the commune council, district officials, and members of the Galician diet, to raise funds and gain permission for village improvements. Teachers often dealt with opposition to their projects via formal political activism, working to replace intransigent commune councillors and appealing directly to Sejm delegates for assistance.[126] These ties to larger centers of political authority helped expand the intellectual horizons of villagers themselves.

Decades of mentoring by rural notables helped provide their peasant allies with models for activism on a small scale. Clerical and pedagogical activists offered examples of personal persuasion, coalition building, the use of formal political alliances and elections as means to bring about changes in the conditions of country life. Taking a page from their educated associates, peasant leaders soon began to inaugurate reform measures on their own, establishing vital links beyond the village. Franciszek Magryś, for example, was active in local reform efforts after the death of Father Krakowski in 1906, as he had been before the latter's arrival in the village. His duties as village mayor brought him into contact with district council members in Łańcut, who helped him gain funding for a government road through his village. Magryś also developed a close relationship with Sejm deputy Żardecki, a peasant advocate, who offered ongoing support and advice to the village mayor.[127]

Another rural mayor with an unusually long tenure in office developed connections with the district school council that helped provide funds for the renovation of the village schoolhouse, and with the Galician Governing Board (Wydział Krajowy), for the building and repair of roads through his village. Close ties to urban intellectuals, especially in the district capital of Tarnobrzeg, brought this mayor (anonymous in his memoir) the influence and support necessary to launch an agricultural circle, found a village store, establish a fire department, and inaugurate a school for housewives. Intellectual liaisons helped the mayor convince villagers to purchase estate land for the use of the villagers and to authorize the funds to rebuild the rectory and the organist's house. "I grew accustomed to their habits and made use of many of their suggestions," he commented about his relationship to nonpeasants in urban centers.[128]

By far the most important ties peasant leaders developed with urban

---

[126] "Nauczyciel z powiatu mieleckiego," 350–51.

[127] Magryś, *Żywot chłopa*, 78–79.

[128] The author of "Gospodarz na 8 mg." served as mayor of his village from 1881 to 1912, following a short tenure as commune secretary. See *Galicyskie wspomnienia*, 227–38.

intellectuals were the close relationships they established with newspaper editors. Peasant leaders served as correspondents, reporters, distributors, and eventually full-time staff members of a series of periodicals intended for peasant readership, including Stojałowski's *Wieniec i Pszczółka* (The Wreath and The Bee), Bolesław Wysłouch's more progressive *Przyjaciel Ludu* (People's Friend), and the organ of the first short-lived peasant political party, *Związek Chłopski* (The Peasant Union). Wysłouch, the editor of *Przyjaciel Ludu*, intentionally sought out a cohort of educated villagers whom he trained at his newspaper offices in Lwów to help guide the peasant movement.[129] Indeed, future leaders of the Peasant Party, Jakub Bojko and Jan Stapiński, were first mobilized into the crownland-wide peasant movement by serving as subscribers and writers for Wysłouch's paper. Bojko would later testify that it was in the offices of *Przyjaciel Ludu* that he met the democratic activists, writers, and publicists who helped propel him into wider leadership positions outside his own village. Bojko acquired a number of new subscribers and correspondents for the paper in his native village, and his own articles appeared regularly in the columns of this and other peasant papers.[130] By the time the Stronnictwo Ludowe was founded in 1895, only six years after *Przyjaciel Ludu*'s first appearance, young Bojko had a strong enough reputation as a peasant activist to be selected as vice-president of the new party. He was elected to the Galician Sejm the same year and served as a representative to the Viennese Reichsrat from 1897 to 1918, often sending reports from Lwów and Vienna to be published in the columns of the paper.[131]

The somewhat more radical Jan Stapiński used his connections with Wysłouch to promote the mobilization of wider communities of peasants behind Peasant Party and Polish nationalist activities alike. Stapiński reportedly "came to the village [of Kombornia] with several copies of the paper [*Przyjaciel Ludu*] and circulated them widely." Schooled in political activism through his links with urban intellectuals, Stapiński sought to gain the political support of local peasants by "intervening with the authorities on [their] behalf."[132] Wysłouch probably stood behind some of the more conspiratorial activities in which Stapiński reportedly engaged, such as his efforts to organize outdoor meetings of peasants in the Bochnia and Tarnów districts. Circulating issues of the newspapers and a pamphlet about Kościuszko among gymnasium students, Stapiński's goals for these

---

[129] Kieniewicz, *Galicja*, xxxv–xxxvi.
[130] Albin and Szaflik, "Listy Jakuba Bojki," 59–60.
[131] Ibid., 60–61.
[132] Reported by longtime resident of Kombornia Stanisław Pigoń, in *Z Komborni*, 60–61.

rallies reportedly included encouraging the election of more peasants to the Sejm, promoting membership in the illegal Liga Narodowa (National League), and attracting subscribers to *Przyjaciel Ludu*.[133]

The development of working relationships with urban intellectuals and the formation of extravillage clubs and political bodies to represent peasant interests marked a transition away from local alliances between educated and less educated villagers as the primary pattern of peasant activism. Links with nonpeasant mentors outside the village and with a wider peasant community represented an important break with alliances based on traditional centers of authority. Once Galician peasants began to move beyond the guidance of rural notables, calling into question the monopoly of village clergy over political and social organization in the countryside, they were increasingly available for mobilization by regional and even crownland-wide movements. The peasant leaders who were trained by nonpeasant notables and urban intellectuals, and who eventually developed independent agendas for rural reform, constituted the founding cadre of the peasant movement. This stratum of educated rural intellectuals, who made up an important component of the late-nineteenth-century village elite, maintained firm attachments to both the rural world and larger centers of power and influence. These peasant go-betweens would make up the first generation of leaders in the peasant movement.

In the process of developing liaisons with influential intellectuals and upper-class politicians, peasant leaders, including rural intellectuals and other local activists, began to constitute a substratum within their villages with complex and often ambivalent relationships to other small farmers.[134] In time, a separate moral code evolved among peasant leaders, a code of sobriety, industriousness, religious piety, and patriotic sacrifice, which separated peasant leaders from their nonactivist village neighbors. Such a set of shared ethical prescriptions offered the possibility of links

---

[133] "Report of activities of Jan Stapiński in Bochnia and Tarnów gymnasia by school inspector Dr. Samolewicz" (1890), TsDIAL, fond 178, op. 3, spr. 703, 1–9.

[134] Regarding the similarly ambivalent relationship that developed among "vanguard workers" and the majority of other industrial workers in nineteenth century Russia, see Mark Steinberg, "Vanguard Workers and the Morality of Class," in *Making Workers Soviet*, ed. Lewis Siegelbaum and Ronald G. Suny (Ithaca, 1994), 66–67. Steinberg argues that this substratum of industrial workers stood out in front of their fellow workers and also apart from and above them. In some cases this meant that these workers had strong sympathies with employers and other social elites, while in other cases vanguard workers were conscious of their membership in a separate working class. This tendency to blur class lines and to establish positive and ongoing psychological ties with nonpeasants was also reflected among peasant leaders.

joining the village elite with sympathetic intellectuals. By pursuing alliances across social lines, peasant leaders helped bring about the construction of a new cadre of small farmers committed to the transformation of peasant and upper-class behavior alike. This new circle of village leaders would help in the regenerative work of the Polish nation, forming the first step in making peasants into self-conscious Poles. The linkage across social lines represented by joint projects, alliances, and collaboration played a vital role in shaping this first generation of peasant Poles.

Chapter Eight

The Nation in the Village:
Competing Images of Poland in Popular Culture

Each of us already knows that we are of Polish nationality. Several years ago, we peasants did not know what sort of nationality we were. We spoke among ourselves, that we were "imperial," as if we were his cattle and not a nationality. . . . Now . . . although we are not very well-educated, we know well that we are the Polish nation and what our country . . . used to be and what it is today.

Letter to Wieniec, 1878

The legend circulated throughout the villages of Galicia among the people . . . that [peasant deputy] Jakub Bojko possessed tremendous powers over the gentry in the Sejm. . . . This Bojko "cult" grew out of a feeling that Bojko presents us with a symbol—a symbol of the peasantry won for the nation—a symbol of the peasantry who are becoming Polish from having been "imperial," [a peasantry] that is providing the Fatherland with new members.

Monokl, pseudonym of Stanisław Rossowski, 1903

By the latter years of the nineteenth century, Polish peasants had begun to adopt national symbols from outside the village and incorporate them into public interactions in rural communities. They used national imagery to promote a variety of agendas, including local reform projects, electoral choices, and parliamentary strategies. From the moment patriotic symbols and ideas arrived in the village, Galician peasants interacted with them and adapted them to local conditions. They shaped their own images of the nation, combining rural cultural practices with narratives and icons from outside the village. The outcome of this negotiation process was the formulation of new national meanings among Polish peasants.

At the turn of the twentieth century, several understandings of the Polish nation coexisted in village public life. One conception of peasant nationalism, an idea promoted among the peasant "elite," was that of a morally defined community, consisting of ethical, sober, pious, and industrious smallholders who stood apart from and above the corrupt, urbane, disloyal nobility and clergy.[1] This elite community of peasant nationalists evolved among literate, activist peasant leaders who carefully separated themselves from the "dark masses" of uneducated rural laborers and smallholders. Rejecting many romantic notions of simple villagers as a symbol of the nation, peasant activists sought to shape a new Poland consisting of these "moral" residents of the countryside and excluding those who indulged in "primitive" uneducated behavior. Rural leaders would make use of the negative stereotypes of village society produced among upper-class scholars and literati as tools for reforming the behavior of their fellow villagers. In this way, outsiders' characterizations of the peasantry helped form a new dynamic that put identity formation back into the hands of the peasantry, allowing them to select, construct, and adapt the qualities essential for a modern "moral" Polish nation.

At the same time that this package of national mores was being promoted among village leaders, an equally powerful conception of the nation grew up in wider quarters of the rural population. This version of peasant nationalism was an outgrowth of the folk nationalism examined in chapter 2. It freely employed supernatural forces and divine intervention to account for past national glories, and it incorporated harvest rituals and pre-Christian rites into the celebration of important moments in the history of the nation. Folk nationalism and the nation as moral community coexisted within Galician peasant communities in the years before the founding of the Second Polish Republic. Individual peasant spokespeople even promoted versions of both approaches to national renewal. An examination of the typologies of nation forming within Galician villages thus helps remind us that many national identities shared space within the single discursive field of the term "Poland" or "Polish."

---

[1] The concept of "moral community" has been used in the work of E. P. Thompson and James Scott to discuss precapitalist forms of subaltern rebellion against outsiders threatening a community's economic security. The term is associated with the idea of "moral economy," a system of subsistence maintainance for the poorest members of a community. Although still referring to the power of the powerless, "morally defined community" is employed here in a much more literal sense, referring to a new cadre of elite villagers and upper-class intellectuals who shaped a public agenda that separated them from other community members based on moral criteria. For the origins of the terminology, see E. P. Thompson, *Customs in Common: Studies in Traditional Popular Culture* (New York, 1993), chaps. 5 and 6; and James Scott, "Everyday Forms of Resistance," in *Everyday Forms of Peasant Resistance*, ed. Forrest Colburn (Armonk, N.Y., 1989), 3–33. Mark D. Steinberg has adapted the moral community idea to discuss fissures within classes. See his *Moral Communities: The Culture of Class Relations in the Russian Printing Industry, 1867–1907* (Berkeley, 1992); and "Vanguard Workers and the Morality of Class."

Peasant visions of the nation were hammered out through a variety of media. One of the most important instruments, especially among the village elite, was the rural press. Exchanges of opinion and information in country journals allowed literate peasants to define themselves both against the rural rank and file and against allegedly disloyal priests and gentry landholders.

A second and much more accessible forum for national expression among the wider masses of small farmers was the series of historical commemorations celebrated throughout the Galician crownland from the 1880s to the 1910s. Beginning with the bicentennial of King Jan Sobieski's defeat of the Turks at Vienna (1883) and ending with the five hundredth anniversary of the victory over the Teutonic Knights at Grunwald (1910), anniversary activities allowed large numbers of villagers to learn about and participate in reshaping the Polish national past.[2] It was in these more popularly based celebrations and in the integration of patriotic content into folktales that village culture and "premodern" rural beliefs found their way into expressions of national interest.

As villagers debated national symbols, participated in historic celebrations, and retold their legends to incorporate new national imagery, a paradigm of national participation emerged that took the form of a social contract between peasants and the gentry controlling crownland political life. This implied "contract" committed the peasants to support national regeneration by protecting and defending Polish land (both militarily and through cultivation), preserving the nation's culture and folkways, and upholding an ethical code perceived as superior to that of the traditional leadership classes.

In exchange for the promotion of this moral-national vision, peasant spokespeople sought a package of concessions from the Galician social elite. This public agenda, articulated most clearly through debate in the Reichsrat and in the provincial diet (see chapter 9), included demands for increased legal and social equality, and for economic reforms to protect and preserve the family farm. This rural reform agenda, promoting close linkages between building the fatherland and improving cultural and economic conditions in the countryside, became the key manifestation of peasant nationalism and was positioned at the very crux of the social contract between peasants and the nation they sought to join.

---

[2] See Patrice Dabrowski, "Celebrating the Past, Creating the Future: Commemorations and the Making of a Modern Polish Nation, 1879–1914," Ph.D. diss., Harvard University, 1999.

Procession commemorating the Grunwald anniversary, village of Wampierzów, district of Mielec, 1910. Courtesy of the Ethnographic Museum, Cracow. Inventory number III/17647/F. Reproduction by Jacek Kubiena.

The Construction of Peasant Nationalism through the Rural Press

The most articulate version of peasant national identity came from the elite cadre of well-educated, activist small farmers that had been exposed to upper-class images of the nation through periodical literature, agricultural circles, reading rooms, and penny novels. This subgroup of literate villagers adopted the discourse of enlightenment and self-improvement communicated through these media, and internalized the ethical standards proposed by reforming gentry and intelligentsia who worked in the villages. Armed with these principles, village activists set out to construct for the countryside a new morally based national community, in which they themselves would serve as guiding members.[3]

This community of peasant nationalists was necessarily "imagined" since its membership consisted of unseen residents of villages throughout Galicia and beyond, as well as members of the educated classes who

---

[3] Jeffrey Brooks looks closely at a similar phenomenon in assessing the interactions between reader and publisher in Russia. See *When Russia Learned to Read: Literacy and Popular Literature, 1861–1917* (Princeton, 1985).

shared a set of ethical norms.[4] One of the key vehicles for imagining a Polish national identity among the peasant elite was the rural press. For peasant activists, who were relatively isolated in their villages and enjoyed little day-to-day contact with one another, rural periodicals acted as a symbolic public sphere through which collective opinions could be formed and new interest groups shaped. Newspaper readership and correspondence served as alternatives to meeting and discussing strategies and goals with other activists. Interacting with the press became an extension of, or a substitute for, mass peasant meetings, campaign rallies, and strategy sessions. Engagement with periodic literature helped to forge an elite stratum of Polish farmers who perceived themselves and their social mission as standing apart from the activities of the rural masses.

Newspapers intended for the peasantry first circulated in Galicia following the 1848 revolution.[5] Early rural periodicals were driven by noble worries about peasant violence during the revolutionary fervor of the Springtime of Nations. Though their concerns were mostly unfounded, clerical and noble writers continued to use the press as a forum to promote the cause of the Polish nation according to a conservative social model. It was not until the founding of Father Stojałowski's papers in 1875 that the rural press was transformed into a medium for social reform. The inauguration of Stojałowski's biweeklies, *Wieniec* (The Wreath) and *Pszczółka* (The Bee), along with the arrival in 1889 of Bolesław Wysłouch's *Przyjaciel Ludu* (The People's Friend), helped usher in a new trend in rural reporting.[6]

---

[4] The concept of bringing together unseen "imagined" communities in the construction of national identity is, of course, Benedict Anderson's. See his *Imagined Communities*.

[5] Information on the Galician rural press can be found in Irena Homola, "Prasa galicyjska w latach 1831–1864," in *Prasa polska w latach 1661–1864* (Warsaw, 1976); Irena Turowska-Bar, *Polskie czasopisma o wsi i dla wsi od XVII w. do r.1960* (Warsaw, 1963); Jerzy Myśliński, "Prasa polska w Galicji w dobie autonomicznej (1867–1918)," in *Prasa polska w latach 1864–1918*, ed. Jerzy Łojek (Warsaw, 1976); Henryk Syska, *Od "Kmiotka" do "Zarania": z historii prasy ludowej* (Warsaw, 1949); Stanisław Stępien, *Prasa ludowa w Polsce: Zarys historyczny* (Warsaw, 1984); and Krzysztof Dunin-Wąsowicz, *Czasopiśmiennictwo w Galicji* (Wrocław, 1952).

[6] Stojałowski alternated his two biweekly papers, with *Wieniec* covering political developments and *Pszczółka* focusing primarily on religious issues, probably to avoid the higher taxes on weekly publications. Bolesław Wysłouch, founder and editor of *Przyjaciel ludu* beginning in 1889, was a dispossessed estate owner from Russian Poland. Wysłouch moved with his wife, Maria, to Lwów in 1887, establishing the short-lived socialist-nationalist journal *Przegląd społeczny*. Wysłouch was more ideologue than agitator, but circulated his ideas in the countryside through a loyal cadre of educated villagers associated with his publishing office in Lwów. See Peter Brock, "Bolesław Wysłouch, Founder of the Polish Peasant Party," *Slavonic and East European Review* 30, no. 74 (December 1951): 139–63; and Brock,

Stojałowski's and Wysłouch's publications encouraged village readers to challenge their social position and to demand greater political rights in the name of a stronger Polish nation. As literacy rates in the countryside climbed, the number of peasant subscribers and the circle of regular correspondents to these papers expanded.[7] Having opened a space for debate on the public role of the peasantry, editors of rural papers found themselves adjudicating in a discussion over the appropriate position for smallholders in postemancipation Polish life.

A battle over the image and future of the Polish nation was waged in the pages of these papers, as symbols of gentry nationalism converged with the peasantry's budding vision of Polishness. The papers, all of them edited initially by members of the gentry or clergymen, offered examples of upper-class national ideology and the historical and cultural references that served as its symbols. Villagers were struck by "the story of the partitions of Poland" that appeared in the *Wieniec* and *Pszczółka* calendar for 1878, and at least one reader confessed that he would "hold [the tale] in [his] heart until death."[8] Peasant subscribers were encouraged to associate religious imagery with national development. They read about and saw pictures of "the Virgin of Częstochowa, the Queen of Poland and the Polish eagle with one beak that eats little," reporting these as among the "wonders in the . . . issues of [rural] papers."[9]

Villagers often encountered for the first time in these publications historical figures such as Queen Jadwiga and King Jagiełło, founders of the Jagiellonian dynasty and authors of the historic union between the Kingdom of Poland and the Grand Duchy of Lithuania.[10] They learned of King Jan Sobieski (defender of Vienna) and his beautiful wife Maria, and saw pictures of their palace at Wilanów outside Warsaw.[11] They found informa-

---

"Maria Wysłouchowa (1858–1905) and the Polish Peasant Movement in Galicia," *Canadian Slavonic Papers* 3 (1959): 89–102.

[7] The subscription base for Stojałowski's papers peaked in 1897 at 4,500, declining to some 3,000 just after the turn of the century. Wysłouch's *Przyjaciel Ludu*, on the other hand, was published in lots of 3,000 three times per month in 1897, and by 1907 was printing and distributing 10,000 copies of the paper each week. Memoir evidence indicates that each of these issues was shared among readers of a single village and even read aloud at agricultural circle meetings and other informal gatherings. The rise in the popularity of *Przyjaciel Ludu* as subscriptions to *Wieniec* and *Pszczółka* dropped reflects the relative following among peasants of the political organizations both editors led. On circulation figures for rural papers, see Stanisław Łato, "Galicyjska prasa 'dla ludu' 1848–1913," *Rocznik historii czasopiśmiennictwa polskiego* 2 (1963): 57–74.

[8] Jan Deren, Chodaczków Wielki, to *Wieniec*, September 18, 1879, 150–51.

[9] Mayor of Tyniec, near Cracow, to *Wieniec*, July 24, 1879, 118–19.

[10] "Jadwiga and Jagiełło," *Wieniec*, January 12, 1882, 10.

[11] *Wieniec*, January 1, 1882, 7–8; and January 12, 1882, 15.

tion on the anti-Russian insurrections of 1830 and 1863.[12] One of the first numbers of the journal *Związek Chłopski* (The Peasant Union) depicted King Jan Kazimierz's seventeenth-century defense of the Polish Republic from the Swedes.[13] More contemporarily, the papers informed Galician readers of the fate of their countrymen living under other governments, outlining especially the policies of the *Kulturkampf* in German-occupied Polish territory.[14] Clearly one important raison d'être of these papers was the depiction of a historic and often embattled Polish state, a nation that had survived the collapse of independent state structures. The papers presented an image of a besieged society, under constant attack from the west (Germany), the south (Turkey), and the east (Russia), which needed the help of its peasant classes in order to regain its lost independence.

Rural editors also used the press to transmit Polish cultural symbols and introduce peasant readers to the linguistic and literary past villagers supposedly shared with upper-class Polish speakers. *Wieniec* marked the birthday of Józef Ignacy Kraszewski in October 1879 by publishing selections from his works and ran a yearlong series on Adam Mickiewicz, "the greatest Polish poet," in 1881. The literary output of these writers was presented as "nourishment for the entire Polish nation," so important to what it meant to be Polish that there was "almost no literate [Polish] person who has not read some of them—even those abroad."[15] By acquainting their readers with historical and cultural symbols, rural newspaper editors aimed to teach peasants "how to be good citizens of the country and sons of Poland, [their] Fatherland," and to cooperate with their former landlords for the future of a united Polish state.[16]

In the first flush of discovery, peasant readers passively accepted many of the symbols of gentry nationalism as their own. Village subscribers confessed to reading "with rapt attention . . . about Kościuszko, Sobieski, the battles with the Germans, the Turks, and finally with the Russians." They pronounced themselves enchanted with "the heroism of the nation and its leaders."[17] Editors like Father Stojałowski, Wysłouch, and others were

---

[12] *Wieniec* took the occasion of the anniversary of the November Uprising in 1879 to publish a review of Polish history since the eighteenth century. Similar pieces appeared on the occasion of other national anniversaries, including in January 1882 the January 1863 Rising. *Wieniec*, November 27, 1879; *Wieniec*, January 26, 1882, 21.

[13] *Związek Chłopski*, March 15, 1894, 11.

[14] One article in *Wieniec* carefully explained the impact of the 1873 laws limiting the activities of the Catholic Church in the German Empire on Polish residents of the German state. *Wieniec* September 7, 1881, 133.

[15] *Wieniec*, October 2, 1879, 153–54.

[16] *Wieniec*, July 7, 1889, 200–201.

[17] Ibid.

successful in demonstrating to a new generation of literate peasants that "each of us already knows . . . we are the Polish nation."[18] Disseminating information about Polish culture through rural newspapers helped Galician smallholders identify with the traditions they had previously viewed as exclusively upper class. Yet on a deeper level, the expression of this national identity in an existential form—"we are the Polish nation"—suggests peasant readers were internalizing and personalizing upper-class tropes, reinterpreting Polish nationalism for use in the peasant context.

As symbols of gentry nationalism circulated in the countryside, Galician smallholders offered their own contributions to the national imagery. One component of the patriotic vision peasant readers promoted was the notion that the village's supposedly superior ethical standards would contribute to the national revival. Rural correspondents critiqued the behavior of the aristocratic leaders of old Poland, seeking to eliminate the terms and conditions that kept the lower classes socially inferior and replace a morally bankrupt social system with a new standard of ethics rooted in village life.

The moral code that would form the basis of this reformed nation was limited to a select subgroup of villagers. Only "enlightened," temperate villagers, who worked hard and lived in accordance with the church's teachings, were believed to be capable of leading the movement for national renascence. Villagers who continued to cling to traditions of tavern socializing and political corruption, who opposed formal education, were the focus of derision from rural reformers. As peasant leaders redoubled their efforts to bring about local improvements, the rift between the educated and ambitious village "elite" and the peasant rank and file widened.

The moral vanguard that defined itself against such "immoral" and retrograde actions was initially defined through the rural press. The sense of belonging to an elite club is reflected in the rhetoric peasant correspondents used as they delimited the boundaries of the circle of contributors to the newspapers. Writers proclaimed their affection for their unseen editors and readers, confessing a love for "our honest papers and their editor" and a "love [for] each of you dear readers." This select group portrayed itself as "a camp" separated from the majority of Polish villagers.[19] Village correspondents responded directly to one another in their letters to the press, essentially engaging in a dialogue with one another using the pages

---

[18] Letter to *Wieniec*, no. 25 (1878), as cited in Kącki, *Ks. Stanisław Stojałowski*, 43–44.
[19] From a poem by Waleryan Pelc, Jankowice, *Pszczółka*, second Sunday in November, 1895, 235–37.

of the press as a vehicle for their activism.[20] The act of writing to a newspaper in many instances became a moment of self-definition for correspondents, broadening their horizons to extend across village lines and eventually to include the possibility of alliances with nonpeasants.

This subset of morally acceptable individuals was both larger and more limited than the actual pool of subscribers to rural newspapers. Clearly excluded were the "immoral" villagers who remained uninterested in many of the reform projects promoted through the press and who ridiculed those who subscribed to and read rural newspapers. Yet villagers who enjoyed listening to and discussing the contents of the papers were counted as part of the rural elite's national "community," even if they were illiterate.[21] At the same time, certain groups of peasants who undoubtedly read the papers became the focus of sharp attacks from peasant correspondents. Included among these were the so-called aristocratic peasants, those who had "turned their backs" on fellow smallholders after achieving personal success. Longtime peasant activist and correspondent Jan Myjak complained, for example, in 1893 that "[w]e are embarrassed that . . . unfortunately these [wealthy peasants] no sooner feel a penny in their pockets than they puff up with genteel or even almost princely pride—and suddenly neglect to pay attention to the peasant interests—because things are good for them."[22]

Among the peasant "aristocrats" who came in for harsh criticism were those who feigned interest in the peasant cause but who supposedly used their rural supporters for personal gain. These opportunists were attacked as "imposters" who "care[d] more about [their] swine than about [the peasants]!" The Potoczek brothers, Jan and Stanisław, founders of the first short-lived peasant party and delegates to the Reichsrat and the Sejm, were accused of such hypocrisy. The Potoczeks owned large plots of land, yet purported to speak for the small farmer. "When I hear your prattle," attacked one writer, "something terrible stirs in my soul that such hypocrisy could exist in a Christian soul."[23] Applying a universal standard

---

[20] On the role of the printed word in the circulation of public values in late-nineteenth-century Russia, see Jeffrey Brooks, "Competing Modes of Popular Discourse: Individualism and Class Consciousness in the Russian Print Media, 1880–1928," in *Culture et Revolution*, ed. Marc Ferro and Sheila Fitzpatrick (Paris, 1989), 72.

[21] Reading newspapers aloud to groups of villagers either at formal agricultural circle meetings or at informal sessions appears to have been common practice in many communities. See, for example, Maciej Czajkowski's letter to *Związek Chłopski* telling of "reading the paper to the assembled members of the agricultural circle and to the members of the village council." Letter from Biała to *Związek Chłopski*, July 15, 1894, 85.

[22] Myjak, Zagorzyń, to *Wieniec*, February 19, 1893, 60–61.

[23] Maciej Fijak, Pietrzykowice, to *Pszczółka*, fourth Sunday in January, 1895, 57–58.

of ethics, writers appealed to a set of shared Christian values to promote one view of peasant priorities above another.

One of the first instances when the rural press was employed as a tool for identifying and castigating "immoral" peasant behavior was during rural election campaigns. In the early years of Galician autonomy, elections were occasions of drunken feasts rewarding peasant supporters, widespread intimidation of electors, and ballot falsification. Newspaper editorials and letters from peasant reformers sought to rein in the bacchanalian activities of electors and candidates alike, arguing that vote selling sacrificed one of the most cherished rights of peasant citizens. Though voting for electors was the privilege of only an elite group of male property owners paying above a minimum tax level, even these relatively well-off voters satiated themselves on kielbasa, vodka, beer, wine, and cigars.

Peasant writers attacked their gullible compatriots in scorching tones. Józef Przyborowski emphasized the moral line he believed village revelers crossed by engaging in such election-day antics:

> I left that tavern-like place with sorrow and pity, wondering how our peasant could still be so greedy and hungry for beer, wine, and kielbasa. I would have been less surprised had these been poor people, but they were village mayors and well-off people who eat and drink very well every day, and many of them were knowledgeable people who well understand our needs. To sell such an important right [the right to vote] for a lousy mess of pottage is a shame, a horrible embarrassment.[24]

Correspondents carefully separated villagers bound by an ethical code from those who engaged in such frivolous activity, portraying the latter as culpable according to a higher ethic. Those who succumbed to election bribery were criticized for being "negligent of [their] rights" and failing to "demand justice" through the legitimate use of the ballot box.[25] Contributing to electoral corruption was tantamount to "treason" to the peasant cause in the eyes of peasant reformers.[26] Seeing the electoral process as a legitimate and effective avenue for social reform, peasant leadership distinguished its own behavior from that of villagers who were more concerned with short-term material gain or whose behavior remained rooted in earlier social norms.

---

[24] Józef Przyborowski to *Pszczółka*, second Sunday in March, 1895, 104–5.
[25] Village of Wietrzychowice to *Wieniec*, February 19, 1893, 61–62; poem by Piotr Furte and Franciszek Libucha, Kalembina, *Pszczółka*, fourth Sunday in February, 1895, 83.
[26] Waleryan Pelc, "Those Whom I Love and That Which I Do Not Love," Jankowice, *Pszczółka*, second Sunday in November, 1895, 235–37.

Delimiting the Moral Community:
Anticlericalism and Hostility toward the Gentry

Village subscribers also used the press to draw distinctions among members of the upper classes. They sought to contrast their own behavior with that of the selfish, impious, and arrogant members of the clergy and the landed gentry, while reaching out to establish links with more virtuous members of nonpeasant classes. These linkages, often founded on the basis of shared values, had the effect of expanding the boundaries of the imagined community of rural reformers and increasing the possibility of membership in a multiclass "national" entity. Just as the relationship between peasant leaders and the rural masses was cast in moral terms, so too were the actions of the upper classes. Those who sought to serve as the peasantry's false protector, to guide the lower classes in a paternalistic manner, or to prevent them from challenging the established social order came in for harsh criticism.

In a continued reflection of growing anticlericalism, for example, peasant writers criticized parish clergy who "acted with a cold heart" toward peasants and landed gentry who were guilty of religious improprieties. Such transgressions contributed to an impression among peasant readers that certain members of the nobility occupied a lower moral plane than did peasants. Village correspondents communicated with barely veiled condescension that "there are a lot of [gentry] who don't even know where the church is" and that local lords "lately seem to forget about the Lord God." One newspaper epistle opined that "more than one [gentlemen] has boasted in front of a peasant: I was only in church to get married." Such insights led peasant readers to conclude, "the younger generation [of nobles] carries on without piety."[27] Polish intellectuals also came in for harsh criticism when their "immoral atheism" and "wild anarchy" were contrasted unfavorably with the peasantry's efforts "to lift [themselves] up through work and education." In these comparisons, peasants appeared as the greater patriots, "continuing to love [their] fatherland, [their] land, and [their] cottages" despite the negative example their "social superiors" set for them.[28]

By contrast, peasant activists depicted village life as boasting higher moral standards than towns or estates. One peasant deputy to the Galician diet noted that if there was a problem with the moral fiber of Polish

---

[27] Ibid.
[28] Ibid.

society, it was much more pronounced in urban areas where "at eleven or twelve o'clock at night the streets are full of people singing." Meanwhile, "among us in the village," orderliness and industry were so prevalent that "no one ventures to walk about without need." Indeed, submitted this deputy, the Galician leadership classes might learn something from the example of village communal life since "these days there is more peace in the villages than in the towns."[29] Holding up rural society as a standard against which others could measure the morality of their own behavior, peasant activists proposed the reform and regeneration of Poland based on values that had been preserved and protected within rural communities.

At the same time that the moral elite in the countryside was seeking to establish boundaries between its own public behavior and that of the supposedly "immoral" upper classes, village leaders tried to reach out to other nonpeasants as potential allies in the campaign for social reform. Reports of early political meetings among peasants indicate that the rural intelligentsia, including "poor teachers and good priests," were well represented at the sessions.[30] One poem submitted to *Pszczółka* ranks the village school and its energetic teacher at the top of the author's hierarchy of affection, followed by the church and the priest. The gentry stood at the bottom of this ranking because the *szlachta* had reportedly "done nothing for this Polish land."[31] This growing in-between stratum in Polish society, consisting of rural priests and schoolteachers and others with connections outside the village, functioned as a constant source of alliances for peasants leaders, helping to link them to larger organizations and encouraging them to expand their perceptions of community identity. Whereas the pre-emancipation peasant community was bounded by both geography (the village limits) and class or estate (the enserfed peasants), this new moral group extended across social lines to include unseen actors engaged in enlightening activities outside the village.

Peasant writers also made use of history to sharpen the differences between their contribution to national causes and the historic behavior of the nobility. Village poets and correspondents contrasted the peasantry's historical sacrifice in national battles to the supposedly abusive and treasonous behavior of the gentry. As one village poet put it, applying the old metaphor of Poland as the wall of Christendom to the peasants, "it was the peasants who made up the armies that "held back the Tatars and the

---

[29] *SsSk* (1890), 383–84.
[30] Tomasz Kłoda to *Wieniec*, February 19, 1893, 53–54.
[31] Pelc, "Those Whom I Love," 235–37.

Turkish invasions, / In order that the entire Christian nation was not done away with."[32]

Drawing on upper-class and external accounts of key national battles, village writers stressed peasant participation in the last battle to keep the Polish state alive—the Kościuszko Rising of 1794. More than the mere presence of Polish serfs at these battles, authors emphasized the forward-looking thrust of their participation. Kościuszko himself was recast as a peasant liberator who took his bread with the infantry and promised his serf soldiers land and freedom at the conclusion of the war. While enserfed peasants had borne the brunt of the fighting with Poland's historic enemies, Polish gentry and aristocrats continued to "inflict ever new [economic] burdens" on the rural classes in order to "maintain the privileges of their so-called caste." The gentry's harsh treatment of their serfs accounted, in the eyes of peasant analysts, for Poland's having "degenerated into a sort of a plague." The internal weaknesses brought about by serfdom, they argued, contributed to the country's eighteenth-century loss of freedom.[33]

The Polish nobility's moral infractions were repeatedly cited as evidence of the upper classes' unfitness to rule on their own. Peasant writers argued that the gentry alone did not possess the moral competence to bring about the regeneration of the Polish nation. Only by including the lower classes in the struggle for political redemption could the Polish nation hope to be reborn. According to peasant authors, the continued exclusion of Polish villagers from political struggles threatened to weaken the battle for national unity and independence. Rural activists complained repeatedly that "there is not unity in the nation because, although the gentry themselves want Poland to be rebuilt, they are not attracting peasants . . . to the task." Using a particularly vivid peasant simile, they argued that just as "a fish begins to rot from its head and then is completely spoiled, so it is with the Polish nation."[34] Social unity was, in the minds of peasant activists, vital to political salvation. In a very real sense, village leaders argued, the continued oppression of the peasantry was keeping the entire country backward. Only through economic and cultural reform would this situation change, they proposed. The only hope that Poland would not find itself "standing among the most backward of nations until the

---

[32] Poem by Franciszek Magryś on the occasion of the centennial of the Kościuszko Rising, *Związek Chłopski*, April 1, 1894, 17–19.

[33] Poems by Franciszek Magryś in *Związek Chłopski*, April 15, 1894, 26–27, and April 1, 1894, 17–19.

[34] Prawdzicki to *Wieniec*, January 9, 1887, 5–6.

end of time" was for the lower classes to "think for ourselves" and take part in a reform movement.[35]

The Moral Agenda of Peasant Nationalism

The agenda of the peasantry's imagined community was presented in dozens of letters, poems, and short stories written to newspapers circulating throughout the Galician countryside as well as in the speeches of peasant deputies in local and imperial diets. As peasant writers and spokesmen began to articulate the values of country life and distinguish them from the ostensibly corrupt, foreign, and immoral influences they saw in towns and on estates, a clearer image of the contribution they hoped to make to the national revival emerged. The supposedly superior peasant "values" that had been protected and insulated in rural communities during centuries of foreign rule rested on four main principles: sobriety, industriousness, piety, and protection of the native land. Peasant leaders portrayed village society as contributing strength and vitality to national struggles in each of these spheres.

Probably the most often promoted tenet of peasant national reform was the emphasis on sobriety and personal enlightenment, both of which challenged depictions of rural ignorance and passivity found in nineteenth-century realist novels. Everywhere education was put forth as the panacea for ills besetting the countryside. Peasant writers depicted school attendance as the most direct path to personal success, to "getting ahead" within rural society and beyond. "Study and education are what we need aplenty," one village poet advocated, "in order to bring us success and enough bread."[36] Unforgiving of their less enlightened fellows, peasant writers publicly chastised villagers who were unreceptive to education. "No one in our village ever thinks about any enlightenment," wrote one frustrated villager, carefully naming his native community.[37] Village poets decried the fact that "there is still much of the nation that remains dark [ignorant] and can't even give a measly penny [*grosz*] to buy a paper."[38]

Demonstrating the fate of those who did not accept the road to self-improvement, peasant poets took up their pens to warn of the early effects

---

[35] Maciej Szarek, Brzegi, to *Związek Chłopski*, April 15, 1894, 29.

[36] Poem by Franciszek Magryś, *Związek Chłopski*, April 15, 1894, 26–27.

[37] P. Stadnik, Łaszki, to *Wieniec*, May 6, 1893, 149–50. See also "Reader of *Nowa Pszczółka* from Bielsko," *Nowa Pszczółka*, fourth Sunday in February, 1895, 89–90.

[38] Poem by Waleryan Pelc, Jankowice, *Pszczółka*, second Sunday in November, 1895, 235–37.

and divine punishments accorded those who indulged in unseemly drinking bouts or who spent leisure time sitting in the village inn. One cautionary tale records the fate of a farmer named Franciszek who spent the Sabbath drinking in a village tavern, collapsed on his way to church, and froze to death in a snowbank:

> On a Sunday in the morning:
> "Give it to me, give it to me!
> Cried Franciszek.
> "Jew, give me a shot!"
>
> A second, a third, a fourth,
> Drinking is no joke;
> Finally from a shot,
> Shmul distilled Franciszek.
>
> "Go to hear the sermon,
> Since you've drunk the spirits, your Lordship;
> You don't have a cent," he yells,
> "So go from here to the church!"
>
> Franek walks along the road;
> His legs no longer can carry him,
> So soon like a burden,
> He falls on his face on the ground.
> . . . .
>
> Along came a wagon with a peasant in it,
> He lifted Franek with difficulty,
> But soon he shrank back,
> Because Franek was without a soul,
> More he would not stir.[39]

Whereas socializing in the village inn had been the primary form of rural entertainment under serfdom and in the immediate postemancipation period, by the last decades of the nineteenth century rural writers began to discourage this form of socializing. Peasant correspondents to village papers warn in no uncertain terms of the dangers of alcoholism and the effects of long drinking bouts. "It is well known," a writer called Prawdzicki commented flatly, "that drunkenness leads to murder, arson, robbery, and theft."[40]

---

[39] Józef from Bochnia, *Wieniec*, February 6, 1887, 20.
[40] Letter from Prawdzicki, "a simple peasant but a sincere Pole," to *Wieniec*, January 9, 1887, 5–6.

Not only were sobriety and industriousness stressed as values indispensable for saving rural society, piety and church attendance also received the attention of peasant authors. In the case of poor Franek, the preemancipation tavern as social institution (run by the "foreign," non-Christian Jew) was contrasted to the village church and the ethic it represented. In an only slightly veiled rejection of romantic images of pre-Christian pagan rituals, Józef from Bochnia warned that the real lesson of this tragic incident was that

> He who breaks the Sabbath,
> And indulges in such celebrations,
> Will receive a similar reward,
> The one reserved for drunks.

Elsewhere, peasant writers presented villagers as loving their "little church" and "attending it regularly."[41] Notwithstanding the rising anticlericalism among literate farmers, rural piety continued to be stressed as an essential element in the salvation of the nation.

The fourth component in the peasant elite's vision of the role of the village in national regeneration was the protection of national landholdings. Peasant writers portrayed the defense of Polish soil and native culture from foreign incursions as a fundamental responsibility borne by the rural classes throughout Polish history. Peasant poets' understanding of the nation was deeply intertwined with images of the soil. Going beyond romantic depictions of fields of grain glistening in the sunlight and colorfully dressed peasant laborers, the images drawn by peasant writers emphasized the productivity of the land, the sweat and toil farmers contributed to its successful cultivation, and the dedication they felt toward their responsibilities. The land was an active trope in peasant literature, one with which farmers engaged. Out of the land they constructed not only a rudimentary living for themselves but also food for the cities and the estates. The close connection between cultivation and the nation emerged in the work of village poet Wincenty Pol, especially in his piece entitled "Four Things":

> Four things in Poland are known:
> The plow and the scythe on the fallow land.
> .   .   .   .
>
> Four things represent Poland:
> The dark forest, the fields of rye,

[41] Ibid.

> The peasantry who toil by the sweat of their brows,
> And also the love, which flows like blood.[42]

Even the love of Poland was portrayed as an active symbol. Like blood, peasant patriotism was viewed as vital to the health of the nation.

Cultivation and rural custom took on a more dynamic quality in peasant composition than in the romantic literary and ethnographic representation of exotic crafts and rhythmic folk tunes supposedly preserving a distant Slavic past. The healthy and vital rural landscape was depicted as containing seeds for national regeneration through the social integration of the peasants. Echoing ethnographic and literary sentiment that linked peasant traditions with the essence of Polish culture, rural writers sought to impress upon their audience the need to return to core village values. Just as Kolberg, Kartowicz, and Kalina had argued, peasant authors stressed that the fundamental tenets of Polishness—the land, village traditions, and the native tongue—had been protected from foreign incursions in rural communities throughout Polish territory. It was to these supposedly unsullied origins that Polish nationalists ought to return, rural leaders argued. And so they pledged:

> How could I not love you, my beloved Fatherland?
> In you I was born, you fed me,
> Here mother rocked me to sleep, and taught me my prayers,
> Here I spent my youth, my childhood years,
> Here there is a country garden and a peasant hut,
> There I pastured cattle, in among the meadows and flowers,
> Humming country songs, not knowing abundance,
> Here clear water runs and a healthy wind blows,
> Here are forests and mountains and a pair of sheep,
>
> . . . .
>
> Here the priest taught me,
>
> . . . .
>
> To love one's Fatherland and respect the land,
> Here are one's traditions and one's mother tongue.

In poems such as this, the "here" of the fatherland was intimately intertwined—almost interchangeable with—depictions of the native village. Images of peasant huts and country gardens, meadows, flowers, and respect for the land were used to evoke feelings of romantic attachment to historic Polish territory among Polish speakers of all social groups. References to humming folk tunes, cultivating native traditions and preserving

---

[42] Wincenty Pol, "Cztery rzeczy," *Wieniec*, October 30, 1879, 171.

the mother tongue—all elements of the new cultural nationalism introduced by ethnographers and other intellectuals—drove home the point that rural customs could now function as core elements of a revived national spirit.

On one level, the link peasant writers drew between their attachment to the soil and their commitment to Poland can be viewed as an effort to make the abstract notion of "the nation" familiar and accessible to rural readers. The most important symbols of peasant community life were easily broadened to denote devotion to the nation. Everywhere peasant authors refer to their "beloved land [*ziemia*]" as synonymous with their "beloved Fatherland . . . Poland."[43] Nostalgia for the native village among Polish émigrés living abroad was expressed in terms of a longing for the "Fatherland." Émigré depictions of the nation focused on "the beautiful west Galician villages." Indeed, the family farm became a substitute in much peasant literature for the nation itself, as in the nostalgia one émigré in Herzegovina experienced for the Polish "Fatherland," expressed in a longing for his "native plot . . . [his] beloved family and the hut under whose roof [he] was born."[44]

Taken together, these individual descriptions of rural communities in the peasant press produced a picture of a peasant nation, accessible to villagers throughout the Polish lands and even abroad. Peasant authors portrayed the unseen entity of "Poland" as sharing many of the specific characteristics found in the villages of readers everywhere. Local patriotism, in the promotion of the virtues of particular villages, in the emphasis on their orderliness and their "industrious, God-fearing, honest, and sober" inhabitants, helped to build an image of Poland in which small farmers found a reflection of themselves, of their interests and their values. The abstract notion of an unseen nation was made concrete through the promotion of local attachments.

Images of the land and the village were also central to depictions of the peasantry as defenders of Polish culture from foreign aggression. The "national" folk costumes many peasants wore to church became emblematic of the ways in which Polish traditional culture was protected in the countryside while townspeople adopted the dress and habits of foreign occupiers.[45] Elements of the Galician rural landscape became personified

[43] Franciszek Magryś to *Ziemia* (The Land) (1892): 2, as reprinted in Magryś, *Żywot chłopa*, 101–3.

[44] Jozef Domin, Mokra, Herzegovina, to *Wieniec*, December 11, 1879, 198–99.

[45] The residents of Albigowa, Łancut district, pointed to their donning of "national" attire (i.e., regional folk costumes) each Sunday as sign of their patriotic commitment. Franciszek Magryś to *Niedziela* (1893): 875, as reprinted in Magryś, *Żywot chłopa*, 113–15.

in peasant poetry, helping to protect inhabitants from external attacks. Peasant writer Maciej Szarek emphasized the power of the Vistula River as he sought to communicate the connection between his self-perception as a "Cracovian" peasant (i.e., living in a village in the Cracow district) and his identity as a Pole:

> The Vistula flows, it flows
> Through the Polish Land.
> Our dear Poland
> Will never perish.
>
> On the left side of the Vistula
> Lovely Cracow stands.
> It did not fear the Swedes,
> And is not afraid of the Russians.
>
> To the east from Cracow
> Lies the grave of Wanda.
> She did not want the Germans,
> And rightly so . . . [46]

The Vistula River that was so important to Galician peasants in providing transportation to markets and off-season rafting work, and whose tributaries irrigated their crops, was transformed in this poem to serve as a key means for connecting Galician villages to the larger concept of Poland. Szarek, who worked as a raftsman for years and who first encountered information about the November and January Risings in Russian Poland on a rafting trip, came to see Poland's largest river as a symbol of national unity and strength. Bisecting the Polish lands on a north-south trajectory, the Vistula was presented as representing Poland's ability to maintain her cultural and political independence from her neighbors. Indeed, the seventeenth-century Swedish invasion was turned back beginning in Częstochowa, north of Cracow, and the legendary figure of Wanda reputedly threw herself into the waters of the Vistula in order to avoid betrothal to a foreign (German) prince. Poland's topography and the peasants who interacted most closely with the land are thus presented as the constant source of the salvation of the nation against foreign enemies.

In a much more literal sense, peasant spokesmen also insisted that the physical defense of Polish territory from foreign aggressors depended primarily on them. Vividly aware of Poland's "occupation" by outside powers, village authors bid their readers,

---

[46] Maciaj Szarek, "Krakowiak," *Wieniec*, January 29, 1880, 19.

Don't trust the Russians . . .
Because Russia is treacherous . . .
Nor will the heretic Bismarck [Protestant] ever be a brother to Poles,
Always looking out for his own interests,
He would like to maintain Poland for himself.[47]

Extricating Polish territory from the control of its aggressive neighbors would require peasant soldiers who were "hardened in fire" from previous battles and who were prepared "with weapon[s] by [their] side" to defend their fatherland once again. One such call to arms ends with the plea to fellow smallholders:

> With all our strength, my brothers,
> Let us preserve this inheritance,
> Because each and every one of us
> Should be advised to die for our Fatherland.[48]

The Social Contract

The rural contribution to rejuvenating society was strongly predicated on assumptions of moral equality among the postemancipation Polish social strata. The social contract implied by the village elite's agenda involved a strong commitment to serve the fatherland in exchange for legal and political concessions from the Polish upper classes. If the Polish gentry would concede to sharing political power and eliminating the most onerous of social inequalities suffered by peasants, the possibility for renewed national independence would be dramatically increased, peasant writers suggested. Without social unity based on equality, however, Poland's future existence as a state was in doubt.

Within the moral universe constructed by peasant activists and their upper-class allies, members were assumed to be equal in their value to society. All were expected to approach one another on a horizontal rather than a vertical plane. Enlightened peasants sought to be treated as the "brothers" of their former landlords in a fraternal social order that replaced the preemancipation patriarchal arrangement. They appealed to the upper classes to cease acting as the peasants' protectors and instead

[47] Maciej Szarek, "Krakowiak," *Wieniec*, December 24, 1879, 203.
[48] Wincenty Pol, "Cztery rzeczy," *Wieniec*, October 30, 1879, 171.

permit smallholders to defend their own interests.[49] Peasant writers believed that "equal are the peasant son and the country squire" and that this rough equality was a "God-given right."[50] By fashioning an imagined community made up of equal members who shared certain moral perceptions and goals, peasants found a means by which to declare the ethical validity of their membership in the historic Polish nation.

This supposition of equality in the eyes of God was soon translated into a political principle. Peasant activists argued in political bodies during the 1890s that the contribution smallholders could make to the national corpus entitled them to a more or less equal social and legal position within representative institutions. Taking into account the changes to rural society in the previous generation, peasant activists made clear to their former overlords that "the peasantry is not what it was twenty or thirty years ago. Today . . . it feels its own strength, its rights, and you wish to treat it as if it was a tool of yours as in bygone days! . . . Your house built on sand is crumbling."[51] Instead of continuing to function as the clients of their former lords, the "working people" were bid to "demand equality, which you deserve."

Closely associated with demands for a more equitable role in Galician public life was the peasant argument that historical inequity had contributed to the social discord that was responsible for the collapse of the eighteenth-century Polish state. Without equality across social classes, rural spokesmen argued, disunity would continue to plague the body politic.

> The land was without unity, like a nation diseased.
> Making use of this quarrel were our nearest neighbors,
> Especially that neighbor who lies to the north.[52]

This very "absence of brotherly love" was held up as the cause of Poland's continued political misfortunes. Predicating national revival on the promotion of legal equality across social classes, activists argued that "until we . . . treat one another with sincere brotherly love, Poland will not be returned to us."[53]

---

[49] As in the plea made by Maciej Szarek in a letter to *Wieniec*, September 16, 1893, 100–101, in which "brother gentry" are politely asked to cease their "protection" of the rural classes.

[50] Franciszek Magryś to *Związek Chłopski*, April 15, 1894, 26–27.

[51] Maciej Szarek, Brzegi, *Wieniec*, September 16, 1893, 100–101.

[52] Franciszek Magryś, *Związek Chłopski*, April 1, 1894, 17–19.

[53] Prawdzicki to *Wieniec*, January 9, 1887, 5–6.

Among the peasants' formal political demands was equality of political access, which they portrayed as a source of national strength. Activists demanded direct elections, rather than two-stage elections through electors and class-based curia, as a means of introducing new blood into political assemblies. They sought through open elections to have the diversity of Polish society reflected in and thereby to strengthen elective institutions.

> Only through direct elections will it be possible to beautify the group in the Reichsrat and in the Sejm because a wreath adorned with flowers of one and the same color is not as attractive as flowers of varied colors. Similarly the Reichsrat and the Sejm look uniform and colorless when they possess only people who have not seen any poverty.[54]

Through this kind of fraternal exchange among all social groups, peasant leaders hoped to encourage "a new [Polish] phoenix to rise from the dust," bringing about a return of the Polish state.[55]

Peasant newspapers played an important symbolic role for literate villagers in offering them a medium to break through the invisible social barriers separating Polish social classes and to demonstrate their preparation for assuming the full responsibilities of citizenship. In the early years of peasant subscription to rural papers, the road to an elevated sense of social status remained rocky for peasant readers. Young Maciej Szarek was forced to defend his interest in rural newspapers in the mid-1880s during an interrogation by Galician police. Asked about his need to read such material, Szarek explained to the officer,

> I read them because I want to keep informed about what is happening in the world. "And what does the world have to do with you?" [asked the police officer]. "You are a peasant, so pay attention to the plow, the scythe, the pitchfork, and not to newspapers or the world." This made me boiling mad . . . but I answered politely, "Mr. Governor, we peasants are free, just as the lords are to [read papers]."[56]

In time, rural newspapers were able to offer their readers a glimpse into a world with fewer social barriers. The simple process of contributing to rural papers helped initiate a shift toward a greater sense of personal dignity among peasant readers. Seeing their poetry and prose published

---

[54] Jędrzej Pacuła, Ostrów, to *Wieniec*, April 1, 1893, 108–9.
[55] From a poem by peasant activist Ferdynand Kuraś, Wielowieś, to commemorate the death of peasant leader Father Wojciech Michna, *Wieniec*, April 1, 1893, 103.
[56] Albin and Szaflik, "Listy Macieja Szarka," 72–73.

alongside articles by gentry writers prompted literate peasant readers to question certain elements of the preemancipation social structure. One subscriber depicted the revolutionary reaction he had to peasant and noble writing sharing space in the columns of a single newspaper:

> Reading these newspapers, I discovered something new. I noticed that peasants . . . took up their pens and wrote letters, which the editor then published. . . . I changed my impression, because writing and publishing a newspaper or book was something only the educated did—such as priests, teachers, etc. Thus here peasants . . . were also equal to the gentleman and the priest. I myself wanted to try it and was beside myself with joy when I saw my own letter published.
>
> Thus was broken that humiliation of feudal labor, which despite the elimination of serfdom reigned among the people, who showed their respect by means of a deep bow to the ground with cap in hand, or going down on their knees if they wished to request something and kissing the hand of a young official by a [peasant elder]. This made a revolutionary impression in my head.[57]

In a symbolic but visually significant way, peasant newspapers offered readers the opportunity to boost their social status vis-à-vis members of the Galician gentry and intelligentsia.

Peasant writers highlighted the social tensions that would materialize if inequality amongst Poles were not overcome. Franciszek Magryś argued that a society such as old Poland's, divided as it was into rigid social classes, would not be supported by new peasant citizens. A return to the prepartition social code was not possible, Magryś insisted, because "our Fatherland was lost by those large families for lack of faith and unity among the people." Only a revision of the unequal social code would bring about the alliance among Polish classes that was necessary for resurrecting the state. The internal weaknesses stemming from social disunity would, Magryś suggested, thwart any efforts to regain national independence for the Polish lands. Instead, he concluded, appealing to the higher authority of common religious belief, "only when there is national unity" would "God take pity on [the Poles] and grant [them] victory." Social reform, allowing the previously disenfranchised peasantry to share the rights and privileges of other classes, was necessary, according to Magryś, if the "nation torn apart" was to heal.[58] This social reform agenda would

[57] Nocek, "Wspomnienia," 8–9.
[58] Franciszek Magryś, "W smutną stuletnią rocznicę rozbioru drogiej ojczyzny," *Związek Chłopski* (1895): 118–19, as reprinted in Magryś, *Żywot chłopa*, 104–7.

take center stage once peasant representatives returned to formal political bodies.

Popular Images of the Peasant Nation

The agenda peasant activists put forward for strengthening Polish society in preparation for independence was but one manifestation of national sentiment in the countryside. One of the most important losses in the joining of peasant iconography with the imagery of upper-class writers and reforms was the support of many illiterate, uneducated, and impoverished rural residents, a high proportion of whom worked as landless laborers. The melding of intellectual images with peasant self-representation reveals the limited applicability of many nationalist tropes. The very rural images that were eventually infused with nationalist meaning—including that of the small farmer tilling his own plot—served to alienate subcultures that felt unrepresented in the new imagery.

Those who did not find themselves reflected in the new national discourse were effectively hidden by much of the new national symbolism, seeing in it little reflection of their own interests. The expanding and increasingly militant stratum of rural proletarians would find itself excluded both from literary and ethical tropes circulating in the countryside and from the economic and political efforts to galvanize rural resources. This differentiation of village society would be one of the most significant and far-reaching developments in the late-nineteenth-century transformation of the Polish countryside. In conjunction with the evolution of a self-appointed moral elite in the village, the displacement of the peasant masses from the larger populist movement in the early stages of mobilization would profoundly influence the character of rural political engagement in succeeding decades and beyond.

In contrast to the discourse of enlightenment and moral renewal flowing from the pens of peasant leaders, images of the nation among the rural masses permitted a more prominent role for village folk culture. Myth and magic, along with fantastical reinterpretations of national history, were central to the understanding of the nation found in popular songs, legends, public performances, and holiday rituals in Galician villages. Since these mass celebrations and orally communicated tales did not depend upon literacy or access to the printed word, larger numbers of Polish-speaking peasants were able to take part in these types of "nation-forming" activities.

Events and historical figures in Polish history may not have had the same meaning for the rural masses as they did for members of the peasant elite or their upper-class and urban allies. The quarter century preceding the outbreak of World War I witnessed a series of opportunities for peasants to express their national sentiment in popular ceremonies and demonstrations commemorating important occasions in the nation's collective past.

Beginning with the bicentennial of Jan Sobieski's victory at Vienna, celebrated in 1883, Galician peasants participated in planning and celebrating "national" Polish anniversaries at regular intervals until the collapse of the Habsburg state. In 1890, a peasant committee was formed in Wadowice to determine the part the masses would play in the celebrations honoring the return of Adam Mickiewicz's remains to the Wawel castle. The following year, village councils began raising money and establishing local committees to organize festivities for the centennial of the May 3 constitution. Villagers flocked to Cracow and other crownland cities to take part in demonstrations marking the anniversary of the second and third partitions of the Polish state in 1892 and 1895. Rural residents staged massive reenactments of battles during the 1894 commemoration of the Kościuszko Rising.

In each case, the initiative for the style and content of peasant celebrations came from the village. Rural symbols and rituals were merged with patriotic images and processes coming from the Polish upper classes. New meaning was added to nationalist celebrations to underline the significance of particular historical moments for peasant citizens. By integrating rural symbols into commemorative events and suffusing historic moments with elements of a peasant reform agenda, village actors managed to transform Polish nationalism into a vehicle for peasant expression about public affairs. The merging of nationalism and rural politics would create a populist base for nationalism in the Polish lands.

From the first organizational efforts in the countryside, Galician political leaders stonewalled peasant efforts to write themselves into national history by publicly participating in commemorative celebrations. The Crownland Governing Board refused to grant peasant participants reduced train fare or assistance with lodging during the Sobieski centennial or the transfer of Mickiewicz's remains to Cracow.[59] Moreover, the date of Mickiewicz's funeral ceremony was changed at the last minute,

---

[59] Father Stojałowski believed that the government's refusal to help peasant visitors to Cracow during the celebrations indicated that conservatives viewed "with disfavor . . . a peasant meeting and . . . [thus] hindered them and presented dishonest difficulties." *Wieniec*, June 1, 1890, 187–88.

arguably to discourage peasant participation.[60] Local police denied permission for a peasant meeting following the Mickiewicz procession, claiming it would threaten the town's peace and public security. Stojałowski himself was put under arrest to keep him from participating. And the organizing committee in Cracow, led by a deputy of the Galician viceroy, limited the number of villagers who were permitted to participate in the funeral procession.[61] Clearly both Galician and Austrian authorities were apprehensive about the participation of large numbers of peasants in these public events, even forbidding a contingent of smallholders from Poznań to take part at all.[62]

Through their attempts to reinterpret Mickiewicz's political philosophy, Galician villagers sought to coopt Mickiewicz and other national symbols and infuse them with peasant meanings. Emphasizing the poet's supposed concern for the common people and his support for their liberation from serfdom, the peasant coordinating committee (the Wadowice Society for the Defense of the Land and the People) circulated an appeal to Polish peasants in all lands, portraying Mickiewicz as a poet of their beloved land, its fields and woods. As a physical manifestation of the poet's links to the soil, the committee proposed to make a "gigantic wreath, as great, long, and wide as our land, and cover the mortal remains of this immortal father of the nation in the royal tombs in the Wawel."[63] Villagers throughout all regions of Poland responded to this announcement by sending packages of local grain, branches, and grasses from which some forty-four wreaths were braided by hundreds of local volunteers. The procession in Cracow represented a concrete effort by Galician peasants to link this greatest of Polish national symbols with the farming population and the products of their labor, at the same time symbolically uniting the lands of the old commonwealth in a visual display of unity. The message was clear: through the work of Polish-speaking peasants, the nation will be united again.

Participation in other ceremonies honoring icons of Polish national history provided peasants with further opportunities to revise the symbols

[60] So argues Dunin-Wąsowicz in *Dzieje Stronnictwa Ludowego*, 94–95.

[61] APKr, DPKr 37 L. 427//pr/90. I am grateful to Patrice Dabrowski of Harvard University's Department of History for this information.

[62] After learning of the intent of a Poznań group to march in the procession, the Austrian Ministry of the Interior secretly forbade the Cracow organizing committee to allow foreign associations and institutions to participate. APKr, IT 876, 359.

[63] The text of the appeal was reprinted in *Złożenie zwłok Adama Mickiewicza na Wawelu dnia 4-go lipca 1890 roku. Książka pamiątkowa z 22 ilustracyami* (Cracow, 1890), 46.

and myths of Poland's greatness.[64] During centennial celebrations honoring the May 3 (1791) constitution, peasant ceremonies highlighted the interrupted legacy of social reform initiated by the aborted document. Again, although upper-class scholars and statesmen focused on the state-strengthening measures introduced in the constitution, and the injustice of the Russian invasion following its proclamation, peasants highlighted the protections for the lower classes the constitution's framers envisioned. In a wildly optimistic understanding of the mandate with which the constitution's "special commissions" were charged, peasant leaders argued that

> [r]egional commissions . . . were to watch over each individual in their district so that no harm or injustice would come to the poor and hardworking. [These commissions] would prevent new taxes from being assessed on the peasantry; [and] they would help establish hospitals and nursing facilities on estates, and encourage the church to maintain teachers to educate the peasantry.[65]

News of the constitution's passage and its ostensible reform of perfdom was, according to this nostalgic view, "greeted . . . with great joy" by contemporary serfs. For peasant celebrants one hundred years later, the constitution had come to represent "the clear and just idea . . . that one class ought not to be exploited by another, that all people have the right to exercise their freedom and happiness."[66]

This peasant conception of Poland differed markedly from that of the gentry and magnates—differences that were revealed in the manner in which the social groups chose to celebrate national holidays. During May 3 centennial celebrations, peasant festivities reflected a deep desire for access, opportunity, and the incorporation of rural symbols into the iconography of the nation. Although Father Stojałowski announced the founding of a fund for joint celebration of the anniversary of the constitution already a year before the event, individual village councils chose to coordinate commemorative activities in their own communities as well.[67]

---

[64] The speeches given during the Mickiewicz funeral are summarized in *Wieniec*, July 20, 1890, 209–16. A revisionist interpretation of the bard's significance to peasants was printed in *Wieniec*, June 1, 1890, 187–88.

[65] *Przyjaciel Ludu* May 1, 1891, 129–31. The significance of the constitution for Polish peasants is also discussed in the previous issue of *Przyjaciel Ludu*, April 15, 1891, 113–14.

[66] *Przyjaciel Ludu*, May 1, 1891, 130.

[67] Stojałowski announced the establishment of the May 3 fund in *Wieniec*, June 15, 1890, 202. In each succeeding issue for the entire year preceding the celebration, the paper announced the names and villages of those contributing and the plans of village councils for local commemorative ceremonies.

Indeed, the May 3 ceremonies in Cracow were dwarfed by the dozens of provincial celebrations staged throughout the Galician countryside.[68]

Rather than mimicking official celebrations in large cities, these rural commemorations witnessed a complex blending of folk culture, Catholic ritual, and modern political representation. May 3 festivities in the village of Zawadka, for example, merged traditional May Day celebrations with that of the constitution. Agrarian ritual and political agendas were united behind an overarching application of Catholic symbolism. The insignia "Maria" was inscribed at the top of the may pole with the notation "Queen of Poland," and participants "kneeled and said the litany to Maria . . . and the head of the agricultural circle read a mass."

In this and other such rural celebrations, the mass was followed by a speech detailing the contents of the historic constitution, at the conclusion of which the peasants cheered, "Long live Poland!"[69] In an echo of annual celebrations honoring local patron saints, the festivities following the formal part of the program involved beer drinking, singing, storytelling, and dancing. By participating in their own fashion in the celebration of solemn national occasions, peasants were able to bring together images of enlightenment (the reading room as locus of celebration), piety (the holy mass and prayer to Mary), patriotism (the speech and cheer), and traditional peasant culture (stories and songs). Taking part in these historic events made it possible for them to integrate new national content into time-honored rural rituals.

Peasant adaptation of national meaning was perhaps most dramatically represented in events surrounding the centennial of Tadeusz Kościuszko's radical 1794 attempt to save Poland by mobilizing an army of serfs against the tsarist invasion. Customary ritual was integrated with commemorative activities in these festivities, including the use in several locations of "pitch barrels" that "smoked on all the high peaks the day of the celebration" in order to drive away malevolent spirits.[70] Catholic rituals, such as the traditional June Corpus Christi procession, were used as models for processions honoring Kościuszko. Parades began and ended with prayer; outdoor masses were held en route, and the village church formed the end point for the "parade." Rather than religious icons or effigies from folk culture, however, busts of the great general were carried and monuments erected to him on village squares. Secular figures displaced church

---

[68] Józef Ryszard Szaflik discusses the rural celebrations of the May 3 centennial in "Czynniki kształtujące świadomość narodową chłopa polskiego w końcu XIX i w początkach XX wieku," *Przegląd humanistyczny* 27, no. 4 (1983): 43–82.

[69] J. S., Zawadka, near Wadowice, to *Wieniec*, September 22, 1891, 225.

[70] *Przyjaciel Ludu*, May 1, 1894, 140.

Scene from the play *Kościuszko at Racławice* performed at the Town Theater, Cracow, 1916. Courtesy of the Ethnographic Museum, Cracow. Inventory number III/79803/F. Reproduction by Jacek Kubiena.

officials during these parades as members of the local fire department in uniform served as the military brigade leading the procession, followed by representatives of the district and town councils and school officials. Besides celebrating mass along the parade route, stops were often made at the building of the Sokół national club or the schoolhouse for speeches dedicated to the fallen hero.[71]

Rural celebrations of the Kościuszko rising managed deftly to switch the focus of commemorative events away from the noble leader, turning village attention instead on the peasant soldiers who fought in the general's army. The famous battle involving peasant scythemen, *"pod Racławicami,"* was remembered in dramatic reenactments in which local residents competed to represent Polish pikemen rather than the hated Russian soldiers.

Perhaps the most important symbol of the Kościuszko Rising for peasants was Bartosz Głowacki, the serf who was ennobled for his heroism in the battle. Bartosz would become a symbol of the sacrifices peasants could make for the Polish nation as well as for the compensation they hoped to gain for their efforts. One peasant poet was carried about the meeting hall

---

[71] Local celebrations of the Kościuszko holiday are summarized in *Związek Chłopski*, May 1, 1894, 35–36; and in *Przyjaciel Ludu*, May 1, 1894, 150, and July 15, 1894, 213.

on the shoulders of his comrades after reading a poem dedicated to the constitution to the shouts of "Bartoszu, Bartoszu!" Many years after the centennial celebrations for the Kościuszko Rising had been completed, peasants were still erecting busts of Bartosz throughout the Galician countryside using funds from the local community councils.[72]

Participation in commemorative ceremonies permitted activists from the countryside to voice their goals for a more egalitarian reborn Polish nation. A less programmatic means of articulating a peasant vision of the nation were the legends and songs performed by peasants. Nationalist tropes were incorporated into peasant mythology or music, sometimes as decorations adorning preexisting cultural forms. Schoolgirls in Dobczyce, for example, set Mickiewicz ballads to music yet were unable to explain the meaning behind the words they had selected from the bard.[73]

By the late nineteenth century, rural legends incorporated Polish historical figures into their largely mythological or miraculous story lines. One tale, perhaps invented to explain the existence of a statue of King Zygmunt standing in the village square, portrayed the curious king's efforts to get to the bottom of the ocean. Wholly unrelated to any documented event in the king's life, the legend depicts the king being swallowed up by a whale but managing to kill his captor. The ocean casts the beast up on the shore and a peasant discovers the king within its belly while he is hacking up the dead whale. King Zygmunt then resolves never again to think about reaching the bottom of the ocean.[74]

Such a tale—an obvious adaptation of the biblical Jonah story—could simply be interpreted as an attempt by rural society to discourage curiosity and the questioning of natural phenomena. It could also be viewed as the incorporation of the Polish king into a tale in which a peasant is cast in the position of a hero rescuing the monarch—and by extension the nation as a whole. Regardless of which interpretation is most compelling, the composition of this tale suggests that Polish folk culture had transformed a seventeenth-century historic figure into a mythological personality capable of performing superhuman miracles.

The intervention of God, the Virgin Mary, or any number of holy figures also figures frequently as an explanation for heroic moments in Polish history—moments that appear in formal history texts as testimony to the earthly strength of the old Polish state. Divine intervention in these historical moments effectively reduced the power of Polish noblemen, who are portrayed as willing pawns of the almighty. One recurring example was

---

[72] Stauter-Halsted, "Peasant Patriotic Celebrations," 93–94.
[73] H. Windakiewiczowa, "Ballady Mickiewicza wśród ludu," *Lud* 8 (1902): 1–4.
[74] Wanda Pławińska, "Jak Król Zygmunt spenetrował morze," *Wisła* 2 (1888): 603–4.

that of the famous defense of Vienna from the Ottoman armies by the seventeenth-century Polish king Jan Sobieski. At least two musical renditions of this heroic deed drastically deemphasized the influence of Sobieski himself, in one case failing to mention him until the ninth stanza, and attributed the military victory instead to the aid of seventy Viennese nuns and the intervention of the Virgin Mary herself.[75] Admittedly the use of biblical imagery to portray Poland's destiny is not foreign to a nationalist movement that has long portrayed Poland as the Christ among nations and the Virgin Mary as the Queen of Poland. However, the complete reinterpretation of national historical moments to correspond with the mythology of the village represents an important component in recasting the meaning of Poland for the uneducated masses of villagers.

Within two generations after peasant emancipation, nationalism had begun to find some resonance in the Polish village. However, in cases where peasants were not yet prepared to engage with the upper classes in formal public negotiations, the nation had to be made familiar to them on their own terms. The inclusion of national symbols, metaphors, heroes, and moments into peasant rhetoric was a first step in the expansion of the nation to include all social classes. Yet it was only a first step. On the eve of the reemergence of an independent Polish state, there were at least two sets of national meanings in existence just among the peasantry. One view of the future of the nation embodied a social revolution in which peasants would be drawn into a multiclass political arena, offering their support to the state in exchange for a program of increased equality and economic reform in the countryside. This conception of peasant nationalism was based on a contractual understanding of negotiated exchanges. It was the basis for most of the political goals articulated by the Peasant Party (Stronnictwo Ludowe) after its 1895 founding.

Another less programmatic conception of the nation shared space with the first. This alternative understanding of Poland came about through the absorption of national and historical symbolism into rural folk culture. Whereas the formal conception of the nation among the village elite had elements of modern political interaction, this more popular understanding of Poland still contained elements of the premodern. Both of these conceptions existed simultaneously, and each referred to a single entity called "Poland." The divisive structure of peasant nationalism reflected many of the preemancipation rifts within rural society. It also demonstrates the varied routes available for peasant mobilization into the public sphere in turn-of-the-century Poland.

[75] Bronisław Grabowski, "Pieśń dziadowska o bitwie pod Wiedniem r. 1683," *Wisła* 4 (1890): 426–29.

Chapter Nine

The Village in the Nation:
Polish Peasants as a Political Force

These recent elections show us that Galicia is in a state of social transformation. This battle before us may be a good and necessary thing, but the way in which it is being conducted makes me fear that our society will come out of this transformation not more vigorous and more unified, but weaker and more divided than it now is.

Count Stanisław Tarnowski, July 8, 1889

We all, poor farmer-peasants and craftsmen, led through a variety of unfavorable circumstances to our ultimate misery, want to govern ourselves, want to give a mandate to the kind of person whom we know and who knows us, and who will try to relieve our poverty.

Appeal signed by 500 peasants of Turka district
to the Kurier Lwowski, March 1, 1891

Beginning with the "return" of Polish peasants to the Galician Sejm in 1889 and the founding of a formal party apparatus thereafter, smallholders have made a consistent mark on the political fortunes of modern Poland. Peasant politicians offered compromise in periods of turmoil, as during Wincenty Witos's premiership in the 1920s. They served as bastions of opposition to unpopular regimes, as with Stanisław Mikołajczyk's determined stance against Communist domination in the 1940s. One of the fundamental premises of peasant political contributions (a priority admittedly shared by other major Polish parties) has been a moral commitment to the welfare of the "nation." Much of the legitimacy rural representatives have been accorded stems from the symbolic position of the peasantry as an icon of national vitality and continuity. The power and influence of this rural force grew out of decades of links uniting the village with "national" centers in hundreds of discrete ways. The agenda peasants presented in the Sejm and the Reichsrat in the months and years before the collapse of the three partitioning powers

216

provides one of the clearest reflections of village aspirations for Polish society.

By the last decade of the nineteenth century, peasants had emerged as a potent force in Galician public life. After 1889, when they returned four delegates to the Galician Sejm Krajowy, smallholders sent representatives to every session of the provincial diet and the imperial Reichsrat until the outbreak of the Great War. The 1891 elections to the Viennese Parliament were hard fought in the countryside, and by 1894 several independent groups began working toward the formation of a unified peasant party, the Stronnictwo Ludowe. Founded in Rzeszów in July of 1895, the new party comprised bourgeois members of the newly established Polish Democratic Society (Polskie Towarzystwo Demokratyczne), along with non-peasant newspaper editors and representatives from the village elite.[1]

The party's diverse social origins were reflected in the broad range of programs and goals to which it aspired. The loose coalition of interests would prove difficult to sustain, first as intellectuals withdrew from leadership positions and later as the more socially radical peasants drew closer to the Polish Socialists. Party leaders veered between charting an independent course, allying with conservative gentry and clergy, and negotiations with the Socialists. By 1913, the Stronnictwo had fractured into a left and right wing, one loosely tied with Józef Pilsudski's Polska Partia Socjalistyczna (PPS), and the other working closely with Roman Dmowski's National Democrats. Notwithstanding its internal divisions, many of which grew out of the factions existing in rural society, the Polish Peasant Party (the name was changed to Polskie Stronnictwo Ludowe in 1903) and its successor organizations managed to represent peasant interests into the interwar Second Republic and beyond.[2]

Peasant representatives in parliamentary bodies pursued an ambitious agenda of political reform that was closely related to the responsibility many of them felt to introduce elements of a rural-based morality into public life. Specifically, village deputies helped further the long-term trends of declining gentry paternalism, increased lower-class access to power, and

---

[1] Since only about two-thirds of adult male rural taxpayers were entitled to vote (about 10 percent of the total rural population), the interests of landless laborers, dwarf farmers, and, of course, women were not directly represented in political parties and agendas. See Kieniewicz, *Emancipation*, 205–6.

[2] The tumultuous history of the Peasant Party can be accessed through Kieniewicz, *Emancipation*; Narkiewicz, *Green Flag*. In Polish, the classic study is Dunin-Wąsowicz, *Dzieje Stronnictwa Ludowego*. On the link between nationalism and peasant politics in Poland, see Tadeusz Kisielewski, *Ojczyzna, chłopi, ludowcy* (Warsaw, 1987), and Barbara Jakubowska, *Ruch ludowy wobec przeszłości narodowej (do 1939)* (Warsaw, 1995).

the democratization of the electorate. They sought to make politics relevant to their constituents and to increase the level of civic dignity accorded officeholders from the village. They challenged long-standing assumptions concerning delegate selection, accountability to voters, and the rules of debate on the floor of parliamentary assemblies. They fought for the reform of electoral laws to make rural elections general, secret, and direct. Peasant leaders, along with other political reformers, succeeded in gaining universal manhood suffrage to the Austrian Parliament in 1907, though elections to the Galician diet remained limited and based on the curia system. In the Sejm and Reichsrat alike, populist representatives introduced a far-reaching reform agenda calling for the reevaluation of crownland fiscal priorities, including the elimination of the gentry alcohol monopoly, increased funds for rural education, and financial assistance for small farmers. They also fought for the eradication of unequal social burdens among gentry and peasant residents of the countryside.

This reform program was closely tied to conceptions about the Polish nation and the patriotic perspective peasant deputies brought with them from the village. Convinced that the *stańczyk*-led Galician government was destroying the vitality of the nation through its economic and cultural neglect of the countryside, peasant politicians set out to "save" the nation by promoting measures to strengthen and preserve traditional village life. Like members of populist movements elsewhere,[3] Galician peasants sought a seemingly inconsistent combination of economic protectionism and laissez-faire capitalism, support for the family farm and incentives to leave it, staunch opposition to industry and efforts to attract factories to the countryside. These counterintuitive combinations can be reconciled partly by understanding the passionate belief many peasants held in rural society as a reservoir of moral strength and in the consequent need they felt to preserve and protect the key components of peasant culture, even while encouraging temporary migration to cities and abroad.

The variety of village conceptions about the ways in which peasants could contribute to the national project also reflected multiple and even conflicting images of the nation's trajectory. As the public sphere expanded to include peasant participants, the extent to which peasants shared commitment to a particular patriotic notion declined. Instead, the idea of Poland came to be associated with a host of different reform programs, and reference to the national cause became code for a range of visions of the future. Still, the impulse to reform Galician politics, to reduce political

---

[3] See Ghita Ionescu and Ernest Gellner, eds., *Populism: Its Meanings and National Characteristics* (London, 1969).

corruption and increase access for peasant citizens, was driven by a general desire among peasant politicians to bring village values and national priorities into closer alignment.

Of all the territories of partitioned Poland, only Galicia, with its relative political openness and Polish control over local government, witnessed the clear and direct reflection of village interests in public sphere interactions. In the Prussian partition, German efforts to colonize Polish farmlands after 1885 prompted small farmers to ally with the Polish bourgeoisie and landed gentry in a unified effort to prevent the transfer of Polish holdings into German hands.[4] The economic and cultural activities organized to promote improvements in the Poznanian and West Prussian countryside paralleled those in Galicia, sometimes even predating them, and allowed a certain degree of smallholder initiative. The network of agricultural circles, farming cooperatives, reading societies, and parceling banks allowed peasants to strengthen the rural economy, working in concert with gentry patrons. Restricted political conditions prevented this grassroots economic and cultural movement from taking on explicitly political forms. Only in 1912 did this loose coalition come together into a peasant party, the Catholic Polish Peasant Party (Katolicko-Polska Partia Ludowa), which helped organize strikes on German-language schools and coordinated agricultural circle activities and credit cooperatives.

In the Congress Kingdom of Poland, the complete prohibition on political organizations of any type severely inhibited social activity in the countryside until the revolutions of 1905. The postemancipation peasant "movement" in Russian Poland was limited in the 1880s to the circulation of newspapers for the peasantry and the founding of agricultural circles and agronomic schools. Periodicals such as *Gazeta Świąteczna, Zorza,* and others helped encourage literacy and basic economic improvements in the countryside. Not until the eve of the 1905 revolution was the peasantry's long-suppressed frustration with tsarist rule manifested in the founding of a peasant political organization, the Polish Peasant Union (Polski Związek Ludowy) and later in a series of widespread strikes of farmworkers and boycotts of Russian-language schools. The press organs of the new party were suppressed after the revolution was quelled, however, and the peasantry had no representation in any of the four Dumas erected in the aftermath of the unrest, since peasant leaders boycotted elections to the first Duma and later assemblies returned predominantly National Democrats. The mass agitation in the countryside was effective,

---

[4] Zakrzewski, *Od Stojałowskiego do Witosa,* 45–50, 57–59; Kieniewicz, *Emancipation* 190–202.

however, in galvanizing support for clandestine Polish-language schools, including agricultural schools for both men and women. Moreover, the revolutionary activities in the Congress Kingdom encouraged educational activism and school boycotts in Prussian Poland and increased pressure for widening suffrage in Galicia.

In each of the three Polish partitions, smallholders engaged in a wide variety of forms of social activism, each with a nationalist agenda. In both the Prussian and Russian cases, illegal associations and educational establishments were explicitly organized in opposition to imperial rule. In Galicia, the national agenda of peasant groups could be openly debated in legitimate political institutions. The similarities in cultural and economic organization across all sectors of old Poland make Austrian Poland representative of a process that was proceeding apace in each of the lands of the old republic.

The 1889 Sejm Elections and the Erosion of Galician Paternalism

The Sejm elections of 1889 helped usher in a new era in Galician peasant politics. For the first time since the conservatives took over the crownland government, peasants energetically challenged parliamentary mandates from the seventy-four rural curia. The campaign for peasant delegates was played out in the pages of Father Stojałowski's journals and in Bolesław Wysłouch's new periodical, *The People's Friend (Przyjaciel Ludu)*, as well as in dozens of village meetings staged across the crownland. Despite Governor Badeni's arrest of both newspaper editors in the days preceding the voting, smallholders won mandates to the provincial diet for the first time in twelve years, displacing noble representatives in four districts.[5] Once in Lwów, the handful of peasant deputies teamed up with Bolesław Żardecki, a member of the Cracow intelligentsia, to found the Catholic Peasant Club, the first formal parliamentary caucus in the Polish lands devoted to rural reform.[6]

The significance of the peasants' "return" to the Sejm was reflected in a parallel increase in the level of confidence with which peasant deputies approached their work and in the erosion of the politics of deference that had previously characterized Galician public life. Fin de siècle Galicia saw

---

[5] The Polish peasant deputies were Stanisław Potoczek from Nowy Sącz district, Franciszek Kramarczek from Biała, Walenty Jachym from Nisko, and Wojciech Stręk from Ropczyce.

[6] Significantly, the two Ruthenian peasant deputies elected to the 1889 Sejm, Olexy Barabasz of Bohorodczany district and Józef Huryk from Stanisławów, did not join the Catholic Peasant Club, allying themselves instead with the Ukrainian radicals in the eastern part of the province.

a general rise in the levels of political engagement in the countryside, challenging the paternalistic notions of Polish noblemen who sought to represent smallholders. No longer could aristocrats assume success when standing for a seat in the peasant curia. Thanks partly to the encouragement of the rural press, smallholders were increasingly eager to "vote for one of their own." And yet social stratum alone did not determine voting patterns in the countryside. Noble and village candidates alike found themselves exposed to sharp commentary from voters.

The Sejm elections of 1889 saw clear manifestations of the changing social makeup of the political nation. Meeting in Cracow a few days after the elections to discuss their results, members of the conservative Central Election Committee acknowledged with some discomfort that their monopoly on Galician political life was disintegrating and that undercurrents of social tension were appearing in public affairs. Aristocrats foresaw a general popularization of Galician politics and an evolution of democratic traditions beginning with these elections, all at the expense of domestic tranquillity.[7] Indeed, the three decades since the advent of Galician autonomy and the return of representative institutions to the crownland had witnessed the steady erosion of the conservative power monopoly. The return of peasant deputies to the Sejm was accompanied by electoral victories for the Socialists, the crystallization of the urban-based Polish Democratic Society, and an increase in the clandestine agitation of the Polish League, a precursor to the National Democrats.[8] The 1889 elections also brought the election of two Ruthenian deputies in smallholders' curia, presaging the use of the Galician provincial diet as a forum for promoting Ukrainian nationalist goals.

Along with the introduction of more voices into Polish representative bodies after 1889 came a parallel shift in the political culture of the countryside. Rural voters took an interest in the ongoing workings of the Lwów diet and expected more accountability from their representatives. Village activists wrote letters to their representatives as never before. They applied the lessons they had learned about political reform within their communes to practices and strategies in national assemblies. They attended *sejmiki* held by deputies, followed their activities in newspapers, and participated actively in electoral campaigns. Peasant deputies provided the personal link, uniting village activism with national political priorities. After 1889, rural reform was no longer limited to a small handful of

---

[7] "Cztery przemówienia na zebraniu wyborców obszarów dworskich w Krakowie d. 8 lipca," *Wieniec*, July 21, 1889, 209–11.

[8] Jacek Jędruch provides a neat overview of the activities of the Galician Sejm during its half century of existence from 1861 to 1913 in *Constitutions*, 249–65.

activists, isolated from one another in scattered settlements. Instead, through local election committees, district-wide meetings, and a rural press with widening circulation, the seeds of a genuine movement were thriving. Still, as peasant leader Jakub Bojko would later complain, thousands of unlettered villagers undoubtedly remained "cold" to a movement in which they failed to see their own interests reflected.[9] Momentary rural electoral enthusiasm notwithstanding, a socially diverse Galician countryside found political expression in an increasingly factionalized and stratified political scene.

The election campaign that brought peasants back to the Galician diet represented a transitional moment for civic consciousness in rural Poland reflected in the heightened levels of critical judgment peasant electors exhibited. The predominant pattern in these and later electoral competitions was for peasant electors to shrug off the advice of upper-class advisors and base their votes instead on village-level priorities. Peasant electors and rural election committees uniformly rejected the candidates recommended by Father Stojałowski's newspapers, preferring to emphasize a candidate's record at home rather than the closeness of his ties to the editor. Of the four peasants and one nonpeasant who would make up the Peasant Club, Stojałowski opposed two (Potoczek and Żardecki), made no mention of two, and offered lukewarm support of one (Kramarczyk). In the special election of 1890, Stojałowski heartily endorsed two peasant candidates who were rejected by their local election committees. Stojałowski's nominees were rejected by peasant voters in the districts of Krosno, Brzesko, Mielec, Wadowice, and Tarnów. In Myślenice, Łańcut, and elsewhere the editor's longtime supporters did not even receive the nomination from peasant election committees.[10] This tendency to reject Stojałowski's endorsements anticipated the next stage of the movement when, after the Peasant Party's initial founding, leaders having gentry or intellectual background were replaced with peasant-born agitators.

Closely associated with an increased critical approach to electoral choices was the peasantry's intensified effort to clean up political corruption at all levels. Turning against the short-term gain associated with vote buying in earlier times, rural voters shifted to a new calculation of local benefit in these elections. The more educated and politically active small farmers of the 1880s and 1890s focused on bringing about long-term vil-

---

[9] Jakub Bojko, *Przyjaciel Ludu*, no. 13 (1905): 2, as quoted in Michał Heller, *Ruch ludowy w Małopolsce zachodnej i na Śląsku Cieszyńskim (1890–1908)* (Katowice, 1988), 71–72.
[10] Suchonek, "Działalność polityczna," 129; *Pszczółka*, June 9, 1889, and June 23, 1889, 181, 194; *Wieniec*, June 16, 1889.

lage-wide improvements through their political representatives. Peasant electors formally challenged incidents of election bribery and vote changing beginning in the 1880s. Rural activists submitted a formal charge of fraud in the Nowy Sącz district already after the Sejm elections of 1883 in which Stanisław Potoczek's father-in-law lost out to the gentry candidate.[11] Later, in the weeks preceding the 1889 Sejm elections, another group of electors telegraphed a complaint directly to Governor General Badeni in Lwów and to Prime Minister Taaffe in Vienna describing the district head's coercion.[12] Increasingly, peasant electors refused the generous bribes offered them. Stojałowski's papers carried information from twelve election districts in 1889 where groups of peasant electors refrained from accepting "presents and treats" from "the princes."[13] Even more threatening to the conservative project, on at least one occasion a farmer collected his fifty zlotys only to support the smallholder candidate. In a new assessment of collective welfare, Farmer Fryc reportedly "used the money for the common good—he bought beer for the village."[14]

Turning away both from Father Stojałowski's nominations and from the well-established practice of accepting bribes, peasant voters increasingly stressed candidates' local reputations and record of activism in making electoral choices. Yet in contrast to the choices made in the 1848 and 1861 elections, the peasant victors in these elections were more than mere agitators. Many of them had long-standing records of local achievements and had developed strong connections to centers of power outside the village.

The extent to which rural elections served to link local agendas and the "national" political situation is exhibited in the electoral practices of the Nowy Sącz district. Lying in the foothills of the Polish Carpathian Mountains (the Beskids), the district of Nowy Sącz had a long tradition of peasant activism.[15] Over two hundred of these upland farmers were arrested

---

[11] In the complaint, Adam Sikorski's supporters attributed the victory of the gentry candidate Żuk-Skarszewski, solely to the "abuses of the administration." Kącki, *Ks. Stanisław Stojałowski*, 112.

[12] *Pszczółka*, June 23, 1889, 189.

[13] In Nowy Targ, seventeen peasant voters abstained from voting after their candidate dropped out, despite the generous incentives the opposition offered them. Fifty-five peasants in Wadowice turned down offers from conservatives and supported the unsuccessful peasant candidate. *Pszczółka*, July 14, 1889, 199–201; *Wieniec*, July 7, 1889, 194.

[14] *Wieniec*, July 21, 1889, 219.

[15] Regarding this unusually active election district, see Stanisław Antoń, "Dzieje ruchu ludowego Sądeczczyzny w latach 1870–1919," *Rocznik Sądecki* 8 (1967): 65–113; Jerzy Potoczek, "Chłopi sądeccy a reprezentacja powiatowa (1890–1914)," *Rocznik Sądecki* 10/11 (1969–70): 313–48; Jan Konefał, "Parlamentarna działalność posłów chłopskich Jana i Stanisława Potoczków (1889–1922)," *Roczniki Humanistyczne* 29, no. 2 (1981): 223–43;

for their participation in the Galician jacquerie of February 1846.[16] The national committee formed here in 1848 sent three peasants to the Constituent Assembly in Vienna.[17] Later, a Nowy Sącz peasant was among the first group of smallholders to sit in the Galician Sejm in 1861.[18] Beginning in 1868, peasant councilmen filled one-quarter of the seats in the Nowy Sącz district council.[19] Partly as a result of this consistent representation, issues of concern to smallholders were tackled here earlier than in other districts.

Organized agitation for peasant candidates to larger assemblies began in Nowy Sącz with the Sejm elections of 1876 when Adam Sikorski (Stanisław Potoczek's father-in-law) ran in the peasant curia. Sikorski lost, but these elections appear to have awakened the ambition of local organizers.[20] Sikorski was nominated again in 1883 and again defeated, but this time the election fraud was calculable. Sikorski himself recounted his disillusionment upon discovering the vote tampering:

> Everyone was at the elections [listening as the votes were cast]. At the end we tallied up the results: Adam Sikorski was elected. The commission counted: Żuk-Skarszewski elected. Something had been swindled. Ah! I think to myself, that is too much! Get on your horse! I get on, another does the same, then a third. We traveled throughout the hills, through all the holes, and found all the votes. The majority was for me. But what was funniest was that they had written the ballot of my own son-in-law Stanisław Potoczek for Skarszewski.[21]

Although Sikorski's supporters were unable to get the vote changed, they vowed never to be tricked again by the local gentry administrators.[22]

Soon after the elections, a handful of influential peasants gathered in a

---

and Potoczek, "Kalendarium historii ruchu chłopskiego sądeczczyzny w latach 1848–1918," *Rocznik Sądecki* 12 (1971): 165–219.

[16] Imperial police arrested 233 serfs for their violent opposition to the gentry national rising. Plechta, "Rada narodowa," 48–49.

[17] Ibid., 54–63.

[18] Antoń, "Dzieje ruchu ludowego," 68.

[19] "Protokoły z posiedzeń reprezentacji powiatowej od 1868–1890," Archiwum Państwowe w Nowym Sączu, zespół R. Pow. 34, as cited in Potoczek, "Chłopi sądeccy," 316.

[20] See Antoni Gurnicz, "Nowo Sądecki Z.S.Ch. [Związek Stronnictwa Chłopskiego] w opinii prasy galicyjskiej," *Rocznik Sądecki* 8 (1967), 115–16.

[21] As quoted in Antoń, "Dzieje ruchu ludowego," 69–70.

[22] The group was unable to prevent election fraud from occurring in elections to the Nowy Sącz district council the following year, however. Jan Potoczek complained that "it is our fault we did not carry all of our candidates because we did not guard the entrance of the hall where they were voting and tearing up our cards and replacing them with others." Potoczek, "Chłopi sądeccy," 316.

small house on the outskirts of Nowy Sącz to plan their election agitation for succeeding campaigns. Key figures in this movement belonged to a handful of leading smallholder families—the Sikorskis, the Potoczeks, the Ciągłos, and the Maciuszeks.[23] The relative prosperity of these families combined with their positions as village mayors and council members has prompted historians of the movement to brand it as an elitist organization with little support among the peasant masses.[24] And indeed, because of the limited suffrage in the countryside, support for peasant candidates provides a measure of the attitudes only of property-owning villagers. Nonetheless, the movement to elect a peasant was widespread enough in Nowy Sącz that the smallholders in this district fielded the largest peasant election committee in the crownland in preparation for the 1889 elections. In a reflection of the importance of familial connections in rural politics, the mantle of leadership passed from Adam Sikorski, now aged seventy-one, to his son-in-law, Stanisław Potoczek, who was nominated as the peasant candidate.

Potoczek's successful bid for the nomination, winning out over peasant competitors, was not solely the result of his kinship ties. Rather, his formal education, his thirteen years of service as village mayor, and his record of district-wide political activism seem also to have attracted voter support. His most formidable opponent for the nomination, the peasant poet Jan Myjak, was a longtime associate of Father Stojałowski, had been heartily endorsed by Stojałowski's papers, and had his own record of village organization. Myjak could boast of having led an agricultural circle and organized a reading room in his native village.[25] Yet in the end, Myjak's literary talents and his endorsement by a "national" peasant newspaper proved less attractive to peasant voters than Potoczek's regional connections. Family ties and local political experience proved more important than the advice of upper-class advisors as this district-wide peasant movement chose its representative to the provincial assembly. Potoczek won an overwhelming victory and began a long career of national and imperial political service.

---

[23] Participants included Adam Sikorski and his son Narcyz, the brothers Stanisław and Jan Potoczek and their cousin Jan, and cousins Tomasz and Wojciech Ciało. Antoń, "Dzieje ruchu ludowego," 70.

[24] Seventy of the seventy-five members of the 1889 peasant election committee in Nowy Sącz were mayors, assistant mayors, or councilmen. *Wieniec*, June 2, 1889, 167–68. On historians' interpretations of the support base of the party, see Antoni Gurnicz, O *"równą miarkę" dla chłopów. Poglądy i działalność pierwszej chłopskiej organizacji politycznej w Polsce, Związku Stronnictwa Chłopskiego (1893–1908)* (Warsaw, 1963).

[25] ZHRL, zbiór Stanisława Potoczka, sygn. 16, 6–7.

However much peasant election committees debated the relative merits of smallholder candidates, a consensus was developing that sending any peasant to the diet was markedly preferable over the candidacy of a nobleman. By the Reichsrat elections of 1891, village newspaper correspondents appealed to voters as they had during the previous electoral contest to support only small farmers rather than continuing the paternalistic tradition of choosing nominees of high social standing. Only farmers who, "like us, toil every day" were qualified to represent the Galician village, according to rural writers.[26] Smallholders sharply attacked gentry incumbents for taking their mandates for granted and "never bothering to get to know us." They expressed revulsion at the candidacy of aloof, disinterested nobles with little attachment to or concern for village problems.[27] The peasants of Turka district communicated their dismay at the candidacy of Dr. K. P. Ostaszewski-Baranski in a passionate appeal to the *Kurier Lwowski*, a journal partly owned by Wysłouch. The five hundred signatories addressed the candidate directly, imploring,

> We simply don't want to support this; such a thing simply cannot take place in the world. We simply don't know you, we have never even seen you—we are complete strangers to you. What is it you want from us? Have you simply set your mind on us? We all, poor farmer-peasants and craftsmen, led through a variety of unfavorable circumstances to our ultimate misery, want to govern ourselves, want to give a mandate to the kind of person whom we know and who knows us, and who will try to relieve our poverty.[28]

In part, villagers believed that only untitled, working farmers could adequately understand rural needs. As Jakub Ludwik, from Trzemężna, summarized plainly at a peasant election committee meeting in 1895, "we agreed we don't want any more lords, not in the district council, not in the Sejm, and not in the Reichsrat."[29] These increasingly populist sentiments also stemmed from a sense that the Polish nobility's soft lifestyle was in many ways inferior to the rough standards of the countryside. Reflecting their perceptions of a clearly circumscribed moral community, peasant leaders such as Maciej Szarek argued that "those who spend time in

---

[26] "Peasant from Besko in Sanocki district" and Antoni D. (Zabierzów) to *Przyjaciel Ludu*, March 1, 1891, 69–71, 75.

[27] Adam Grzywacz, village mayor of Gorzyce, Tarnobrzeg district, to *Przyjaciel Ludu*, March 1, 1891, 70–71.

[28] Reprinted in *Przyjaciel Ludu*, March 1, 1891, 77.

[29] *Wieniec*, third Sunday in March, 1895, 163–64.

salons, who sleep on mattresses, who do not know hunger and cold, or what it is to hurt an arm or a leg because they rarely go more than a few hundred paces by foot" should not receive the peasant mandate. Instead, during the 1895 election campaign, Szarek extolled the virtues of rural life, challenging voters to elect "one from among ourselves, who comes straight from the plow, with black hands, not wearing gloves, but educated on black bread, surviving unvaryingly on cabbage and potatoes."[30]

Such sentiments sounded the death knell of paternalistic politics in Galicia and marked the birth of a more populist conception of leadership in which only those born as peasants were perceived to be fit to represent the rural classes. More important, the emphasis on familiarity, on needing to "know" the candidate and have him "know us," points to a growing desire to have the village more closely linked to national political bodies and to have its needs more directly represented there. Leadership from outside the rural setting could not be expected to maintain this intimacy and was less able to "feel" the needs of the rural population. Even older peasant activists, such as Maciej Szarek, a longtime contributor to Stojałowski's socially conservative paper, argued that villagers had "lived to see the day" when they refused "to be led down the path to the elections." Szarek couched his assessment of the shifting crownland social relations in the language of paternalism, emphasizing the severed father-son relationship with landlords. He stressed that Galician peasants were now "adult citizens of [their] country" who were fully prepared to represent themselves rather than trusting people from "high stations" to do so. According to Szarek, the peasants had "come of age," such that the paternalistic guidance of the nobility was no longer necessary or welcome.

Recognition of the "maturity" of peasant representatives as "adult citizens" would also bring a challenge to the very language employed in political assemblies. Particularly during the 1905 revolutionary fervor in Russia, which was echoed in many ways in Galicia, village deputies complained of the continued use of informal means of address, appealing for the elimination of semantic differences in parliamentary debate. One complaint argued that such language did not adequately recognize peasants as fit to serve in public office, since

> the use of the titles *ty* or *wy* gives the impression: I am your omnipotent Lord, and you are . . . a peasant who is required to do my bidding. The most modern, practical conception, whether among higher, highest, or

---

[30] Szarek to *Wieniec*, third Sunday in March, 1895, 128–29.

lower officials, indeed even for the category of coach-driving peasants . . .
is that it is important to utter the word *pan* [sir].[31]

As social conceptions changed, *pan* could no longer maintain its original
meaning of "lord" but instead was coming to connote "citizen."

The egalitarianism and social leveling that characterized the rural electorate in the 1890s were also sometimes a barrier to the advancement of
peasant leaders. Unenthusiastic about promoting prominent peasants
regardless of their credentials, rural electors refused, for example, to nom-
inate Jakub Bojko, vice-president of the Peasant Party, in his own rural
district. Instead, Bojko was nominated and eventually elected from the
urban curia of Lwów—an indication of the support the party enjoyed
among urban intellectuals and burghers.[32] Indeed, peasant voters promoted a model of "averageness" as the ideal for peasant representatives,
sometimes overlooking well-educated or prosperous peasants in favor of
more unassuming small farmers because "in the *Sejm* every peasant will
know what to say and what to demand because he knows where and what
the problems are. Any peasant can be a good deputy for us who has a plot
of some seven and a half acres . . . some familiarity with the law, and some
experience in the world. . . . There is no shortage of such peasants among
us."[33] Elsewhere, peasant electors preferred to support village candidates
known to them rather than unite behind a single candidate, with whom
many electors might have been unfamiliar.[34] In some cases, electors arbitrarily supported the poorer of two peasant candidates on the assumption
that the smaller farmer would better understand their problems. Jan
Madejczyk complained about his father's tendency to use economic criteria when he served as an elector in 1895. "My father was unable to decide
between the two candidates, both of them peasants," he recalled. "In the
end, he decided to support [the poorer of the two] because he was . . . a
mountain man and has a miserable chunk of land. . . . On the other hand,
Czelusnica, in which Drewniak lived . . . was one of the wealthiest villages
in the Jasło district. My father only paid attention to such factors."[35]

[31] From complaint submitted by Deputies Krempa, Bojko, Kubik, and Olszewski to the head
of the Council of Ministers in Vienna, 1905. Szaflik, *O rząd, chłopskich dusz*, 17.

[32] On Bojko's election, see *Wieniec*, fourth Sunday in April, 1895, 172–74.

[33] Piotr Pacult and comrades, Stanisław Dolny, Wadowice district, to *Wieniec*, third week of
March, 1895, 129.

[34] The Sejm elections of 1895 in Gorlice district saw peasant electors supporting those "closest to them" on the first ballot and uniting only on a second ballot behind the gentry candidate (A. Skrzyński). *Wieniec*, fourth Sunday in April, 1895, 172–74.

[35] Ironically, in this case, Data, the poorer peasant, was supported by local landlords, the
church, and the somewhat elitist Peasant Union. Young Madejczyk successfully prevailed

The initial experience of peasant deputies during the Sejm session of 1889–95 helped further this increased faith in the efficacy of peasant representation. Once peasant delegates appeared in the Lwów assembly, villagers increasingly believed "in their own strength," as one peasant correspondent wrote to a village newspaper.[36] Frequent gentry opposition to peasant motions helped remind small farmers "how dangerous it is to trust these lords." Moreover, gentry deputies representing rural curia exhibited signs of disrespect for the peasants they represented. According to peasant correspondents, gentry delegates believed the villagers they represented should "die like vermin if they cannot find enough to eat," that they "wanted to eat for free," and that their station was "that of an ox" whose life should be devoted solely to work.[37] The appearance of this kind of rhetoric in the columns of rural newspapers helped shape propeasant attitudes among rural voters. Karol Lewakowski, Democratic deputy and co-founder of the Peasant Party, condemned these signs of gentry elitism and insensitivity as "eliminating any doubt about trusting large landholders with deputy mandates."[38]

Access: Peasantizing Galician Politics

The period following the 1889 Sejm elections witnessed an increased tendency for peasants to rely on crownland institutions for assistance. The accomplishments of peasant deputies in the Sejm and in the Reichsrat and the attentiveness they showed to the needs of their rural constituents established stronger psychological links between the village and national representative bodies. Village representatives instituted a series of mechanisms to keep their constituency informed of crownland and imperial political affairs. Regular reports from deputies to village newspapers and meetings of electors in their home districts strengthened links between rural communities and the national assembly. Rather than passively accepting these reports, however, peasant constituents expressed their commitment to the political process and their belief in its efficacy by challenging their representatives to work harder.

---

upon his father to vote for the candidate from the wealthier village who was the more independent of the two. Madejczyk, *Wspomnienia*, 48–49.

[36] Wincenty Smolczyński, Muszyna, Nowy Sącz, to *Wieniec*, last Sunday in March, 1895, 144–46.

[37] Szarek to *Wieniec*, third Sunday in March, 1895, 128–29.

[38] Lewakowski seemed to have excluded his own middle-class origins from the realms of suspicion in making this observation. Letter to *Nowa Reforma*, August 21, 1895, Zbiór Średniawski, Z.S./I-1, ZHRL.

Peasants complained of the lack of progress on rural reform at one of the frequent *sejmiki* organized by Deputy Stanisław Potoczek for the electors of Nowy Sącz district. Simultaneously frustrated with the seeming inefficiency of their representatives, yet confident in the potential of representative institutions, the opined that "we have had autonomy for some thirty years, and how have we used it? We've sent peasant deputies to the Sejm, but the high price of land and the lengthy court process still exist."[39] Although the present deputies may have failed to solve these problems, newly elected delegates might yet manage. Such sentiments, uttered at what appear to have been campaign rallies immediately preceding the 1895 Sejm elections, suggest that electors perceived the electoral mandate not as an entitlement of the well-connected Potoczek family but as something that had to be continually earned.

Confident of the power of their representatives to correct these problems, village electors nevertheless revealed in their comments at these meetings a vision of still greater access, and a desire for speedier reforms. They demanded a wider electoral franchise so more smallholders could participate. They sought help from the Sejm for emigrating family members. They appealed for an expansion of the educational system for rural women, for the parceling of large estates, for relief from natural disasters, and for the reduction of rural alcoholism.[40]

Even when requests from peasant voters proved to be beyond the purview of the provincial diet, the tone of rural appeals still reflected an attitude of increasing confidence in the power of political institutions to cure the ills plaguing the countryside. One village activist appealed regularly to the Sejm for help in reducing rural alcohol consumption. Frustrated with slow signs of progress, he pled in 1895 that the peasants "cry in one unified voice for the National Board and the High Government to fix what is bad, what is destroying our farms."[41] More than a reference to the ravages of rural alcoholism, such sentiment suggests an increased reliance, even dependence, on political solutions to local problems as peasant deputies drew the village closer to the nation. Once relieved to have

[39] Report on Piwniczna meeting from Wincenty Smolczyński, Muszyna, Nowy Sącz, to *Wieniec*, last Sunday in March, 1895, 144–46. Stanisław and his brother Jan, representative to the Reichsrat, made frequent use of these *sejmiki* to keep voters informed of issues in the political assemblies. See, for example, *Wieniec*, December 18, 1891; Gurnicz, O *"równą miarkę,"* 50–51.

[40] Smolczyński to *Wieniec*, last Sunday in March, 1895, 144–46; Magryś, *Żywot chłopa*, 72–73, 111; Pigoń, *Z Komborni*, 64.

[41] Magryś to *Związek Chłopski* (1895): 236–37, as reprinted in Magryś, *Żywot chłopa*, 118–20.

the village legally and socially detached from the estate and protected from the landlord's potential abuses, many peasants now saw advantages in drawing closer to gentry institutions. Smallholder attitudes toward the work of official political organs had shifted since the 1861 Sejm in which Deputy Siwiec declared crownland law "cold like you judges who are interpreting it."[42] They had created a separate and independent sphere of existence in commune councils, agricultural circles, and reading clubs. Now they sought the fulfillment of that autonomously developed agenda in higher institutions of governance.

The "public sphere" that comprised these rural *sejmiki* was characterized more by criticism of deputies than praise, especially in the case of nonpeasant representatives in rural curia. Reichsrat deputy Father Dr. Adam Kopyciński found himself backed into a corner at an 1891 meeting where his constituents criticized his record of failure to support peasant programs, finishing by accusing him of having changed his father's name from Kopyto (hoof) to the more noble-sounding Kopyciński.[43] Even more than the deputy's stance against road law reform and other populist legislation, rural voters appear to have taken offense at the candidate's efforts to hide his ostensible peasant background.

Public clashes between villagers and noble representatives ushered in a new tenor of debate across social and class lines. Comments such as those of longtime peasant activist Maciej Szarek at a 1895 meeting with Reichsrat deputy Father Chotkowski in Wieliczka that "you have done nothing for us [and] thus we testify that the trust among us for you is lost!" suggest a break with traditional patterns of deference.[44] Peasants at meetings in Jarosław district declared themselves "too worldly" to "be fooled for long" by their representative, who had opposed both changes in the hunting law and universal manhood suffrage as a "harmful distraction for small farmers."[45] Elsewhere, peasant electors refused even to engage their representatives, closing off debate instead with assertions such as "it would be a great honor if the deputy . . . could manage actually to conduct free elections" in the future.[46]

---

[42] Deputy Siwiec to Sejm, *SsSK* (1861), 198.

[43] *Przyjaciel Ludu*, April 1, 1891, 109–10.

[44] Stanisław Słowik to *Wieniec*, first week of March, 1895, 105–7.

[45] Eight peasants from Rokietnica, Tuligłowy, and Węgierka, Jarosław district, regarding the visit of Father L. Pasora to Pruchnik on January 31, 1895, *Wieniec*, last Sunday in March, 1895, 160–62.

[46] Closing comment of peasant Adam Wyciąż at a meeting of electors with Deputy Chotkowski in Cracow, March 1895. Report from Stanisław Słowik to *Wieniec*, first week of March, 1895, 105–7.

And yet activist villagers also began to see some reflection of their interests in Sejm and Reichsrat legislation. Franciszek Magryś, secretary in the village of Handzlówka, managed to convince Peasant Club member Bolesław Żardecki to fight for public funds to erect a school for peasant housewives in the 1891 Sejm session.[47] Deputies Potoczek and Kramarczyk co-sponsored a bill in 1892 to bring famine relief to ten Galician districts.[48] And Kramarczyk collected signatures from his fellow mayors in Biała district during the hoof-and-mouth epidemic to convince Sejm deputies to limit the area quarantined from meat sales.

Kramarczyk presented the task of bringing such conditions to the attention of the agricultural ministry as central to his responsibility as a village deputy. Only through the offices of deputies from among the peasant farmers could crownland officials be made familiar with "the horrible misery that exists among the agricultural population throughout the country . . . as a result of this law [since] . . . the High Ministry [of Agriculture] has no contact with agricultural people." Kramarczyk and others would allude to a stark contrast between the illusions about the countryside current among Galicia's social elite and the brutal realities of country life. "Not everything is as it is described here" in the courtly halls of the legislature, Kramarczyk insisted. "Sitting behind a beautiful desk," Sejm deputies had a tendency to lose sight of the realities of the people they governed and failed to "look around the country at what horror exists."[49] Peasant spokesmen sought to bring illusion and reality into closer alignment.

The symbiotic ties linking the village to the national assembly were strengthened through a steady pattern of Sejm funds allocated for ad hoc village projects. Each parliamentary session heard hundreds of requests for the funding of roads, bridges, schools, hospitals, community centers, and churches.[50] Crownland subsidies contributed to greater communication between city and country, bringing the villages on the national periphery closer to population centers. By making city and country more accessible to one another, activist peasants developed greater commonalties with social groups outside the village. At the same time, the fiscal assistance

---

[47] The school was part of a campaign to offer female villagers the kinds of training available to rural men through agricultural circles. The circles, for reasons of tradition, largely excluded women in their local statutes. Magryś describes his ongoing lobbying efforts for this and other rural causes in *Żywot chłopa*, 72–73.

[48] *SsSK* (March 1892), 51, 126–27.

[49] Deputy Kramarczyk to Sejm, *SsSK* (1889), 113–15.

[50] A single day in the 1894 Sejm session witnessed twenty-four petitions for school funds, four requests for roads linking villages, three for the regulation of rivers, two for new churches, and one each for flood relief and a new hospital. *SsSK* (1894), 118.

flowing from the Galician diet helped make this state institution a bearer of rural relief rather than an instrument of oppression, as the state had frequently been perceived.

The newfound trust many peasants developed in representative institutions was reflected in the Reichsrat elections of 1891, which brought an unprecedented level of activity and enthusiasm among peasant campaigners. The Galician countryside was alive with preparation and campaigning for the elections. Immediately after the election announcement in January, the coordination of peasant campaigns began. Smallholders from a three-district area assembled on the market square in Nowy Sącz to express their commitment to electing one of "their own," though increasingly no single set of qualities described the "typical peasant," so diverse had the group become.[51] Peasant poets characterized the popular agitation that gripped Galician public life. "In the villages, in the towns, and on the estates, they discuss nothing else," writers proclaimed.[52]

By early February, election committees had been established in over a dozen districts and peasant candidates nominated in each. Rural newspapers were full of campaign statements and letters of support for various peasant candidates. Debate on the campaign continued to echo in the countryside for some months after the elections. A letter from a peasant in a mixed Polish/Ukrainian village in eastern Galicia noted that even in late April, it was possible to

> go stand in front of the [Roman Catholic] church, there is a group of peasants who talk about what happened during the elections; go to a [Greek Catholic] church and one hears the same sorts of things. . . . Go to town to a fair or a tavern, or to a market and there they are still talking about the elections. Go out to the fields with a plow or a harrow, and you will see how the farmers gather together in a group in the afternoons and chat about the elections. Bah! Even women at markets argue about the elections.[53]

Derogatory comments about women and politics notwithstanding, the level of social ferment and public debate portrayed here—among all social classes and across the gender line—suggests a real transformation in civil society in the Galician countryside.

---

[51] Small farmers traveled from Limanowa and Grzybów districts as well as from throughout the Nowy Sącz area. Stanisław Potoczek to *Przyjaciel Ludu*, February 15, 1891, 50–51.
[52] *Przyjaciel Ludu*, March 1, 1891, 66.
[53] *Przyjaciel Ludu*, May 1, 1891, 131.

Populism and Political Conflict

Born in a wave of mass peasant activism during the 1895 Sejm electoral campaign, the Peasant Party (Stronnictwo Ludowe, after 1903 the Polskie Stronnictwo Ludowe) became the institutional voice for the interests and aspirations of villagers during the final two decades of Austrian rule in Galicia. Although gentry and intellectual activists, including Father Stojałowski, Wysłouch, Karol Lewakowski, and Henryk Rewakowicz, called the meeting at which the party was founded,[54] the new organization grew out of a well-established tradition of peasant participation in meetings and rallies across the crownland. Most recently, peasant gatherings in May 1894 to celebrate the Kościuszko centennial and the opening of the National Exhibit in Lwów, and in both March and April of 1895, had mobilized thousands of peasants in support of a common platform for rural reform.

Like these earlier assemblies, the momentum of the July 1895 meeting soon ran beyond the agenda of its organizers. Reflecting on the events of the previous month, Democratic Society head Karol Lewakowski acknowledged that upper-class activists had "called these meetings [them]selves, but it was not [they] who created the Stronnictwo Ludowe . . . rather [they] joined it!"[55] Soon after the mantle of power for peasant politics passed from upper-class activists to village sons, however, the underlying diversity of the interests represented in the new organization was revealed. Beginning with an inclusive and vague political program, the party narrowed its goals in its 1903 revision. Within a few years, conflicts wracked its board over issues of alliances, priorities, and leadership. Although the party was originally conceived as an umbrella organization designed to meet the interest of some five million peasants, rural society encompassed such a wide range of conflicting and competing goals that they could not always be subsumed within a single organization.

Responding to contemporary criticism of the new party as the work of nonpeasant agitators, Tadeusz Romanowicz, editor of *Nowa Reforma*, pointed out that if intellectuals and newspaper editors were the only force behind the movement, "it would be very easy to squash—simply confiscate the papers and be done with it." Yet activists had been imprisoned,

---

[54] Some two hundred representatives of district peasant election committees and a handful of Democratic Society members attended the July 28, 1895, meeting in Rzeszów. Brock, "Bolesław Wysłouch," 139–63. Minutes of the July 28 meeting were printed in *Nowa Reforma*, July 30, 1895.

[55] Lewakowski to *Nowa Reforma*, August 21, 1895, Z.S./I-1, ZHRL.

Deputies from the Polish Peasant Party (Polskie Stronnictwo Ludowe) to the Galician Sejm, 1895. Standing from left: Andrzej Średniawski, Grzegorz Milan, Antoni Styła, Franciszek Krempa. Sitting from left: Jakub Bojko, Szymon Bernadzikowski, Franciszek Wójcik. Courtesy of the Iconographic Collection of the Institute for the History of the Peasant Movement, Warsaw. Inventory number A-6682.

papers confiscated, subscription banned from the pulpit, and the growth of the movement continued unabated.[56] Peasants themselves, many of them heads of local election committees, made impassioned speeches at the founding meeting of the Stronnictwo Ludowe, stressing the dire situation many small farmers faced and appealing to the state for assistance.

The party's original platform encompassed the goals of division of gentry estates, assistance for peasant émigrés, improved rural credit facilities, and state-sponsored fire insurance for farmers.[57] It demanded a more equitable division of public burdens and the founding of more schools and teachers seminaries.[58] This diverse reform agenda circulated in campaign literature and via mass rallies, helping to "stir up the peasants of Galicia,"

[56] Tadeusz Romanowicz, *Nowa Reforma,* November 1 and 5, 1895, as reprinted in Kowalczyk et al., *Zarys historii.*

[57] Memoirist Jan Madejczyk summarized one of Stapiński's speeches during the 1895 election campaign in *Wspomnenia,* 48–49. See also, Dunin-Wąsowicz, *Dzieje Stronnictwa Ludowego,* 100–103.

[58] Report on March 10, 1895, meeting in Biała, attended by fifteen hundred local peasants. *Wieniec,* third Sunday in March, 1895, 153–57.

according to one memoirist. The party's platform spoke "to the peasant directly and openly, showing him the possibility of improving his own fate."[59]

More than simply preserving and protecting an eroding way of life, those who joined the new party sought to bring about a transition in rural society by introducing modern agricultural techniques and progressive institutions to the village. The party would become, in many ways, a symbol of the two-way link connecting rural activism with national political agendas. Through the actions of party leaders, smallholders began to see benefit in attachments to national institutions. Still, until the end of the Great War, the party's agenda spoke mostly to the ambitions of the larger peasant landholders, offering few direct benefits to dwarf farmers or the landless workers on gentry estates, to say nothing of the peasant women excluded by law and custom from many of the party's activities.

The platform of the new party, in both its 1895 and its 1903 incarnations, carefully situated the peasantry's demands in the context of the national cause. The movement's leaders boldly proclaimed the continued rule of Galician conservatives harmful for Poland. After some thirty years of autonomy, the party's founding document argues, little attention had been devoted to issues of education, credit, or the unequal division of economic burdens among the crownland's social classes. The neglect of issues that affected the economic and social welfare of the nation as a whole meant that conservative landowners were bringing about the "ruin" and "degradation" of the crownland and its political institutions. These "disloyal" gentry politicians reportedly remained "contented with their personal positions" within the empire while tax rates for the larger population continued to increase at a rate far exceeding the compensation Galicia received from Vienna. Party leaders presented peasant activism and a peasant presence in political assemblies as key to saving the crownland and reforming the nation as a whole. The party's founders echoed long-standing village conceptions about sacrifices smallholders had made for the nation, again offering the peasantry as "the fortress on which the nation can safely rely." Just as peasants had defended Poland at earlier moments in the nation's history, the party now called for a strengthening of rural society as the very heart and soul of the ailing nation.[60]

---

[59] Madejczyk, *Wspomnienia*, 48–49.

[60] The platform of the Peasant Party was devised by the governing board and presented at the July 28, 1895, founding meeting. Its authors included Karol Lewakowski, head of the Association of Democrats (president), village mayor Jakub Bojko (vice-president), and Henryk Rewakowicz, editor of *Kurier Lwowski*. The party's board members consisted of nine peasants and nine intellectuals. The program is reprinted in Stanisław Łato and Witold

The specific measures advocated in the party's campaign literature had evolved through the interaction of peasant deputies and village constituents during the course of the previous six-year Sejm and before. They grew out of the needs and concerns of an emancipated peasantry uneasy about an eroding way of life and seeking to stem the ill effects of rapid economic changes. The party's demands operated simultaneously on several levels. The most fundamental goal was the protection of the family farm from hostile interlopers, including noble landholders, Jewish moneylenders, conservative government administrators, and the benign neglect of the emperor.

Throughout the 1890s peasant deputies had worked in political assemblies to protect the traditional agrarian economy from the effects of natural disasters. They sought imperial subsidies to feed the victims of failed harvests and famine. They lobbied for legislation to regulate mountain streams that regularly flooded farmlands, ruining crops and destroying peasant cottages.[61] They fought for the creation of a fire insurance system that would help compensate small farmers for the thousands of zlotys in damage to their property they incurred each year,[62] and they worked to protect farmers from speculators who clear-cut forests leaving residents no source of firewood.[63] Attempting to combat the negative environmental effects of rural industry, peasant legislators sought to prohibit the dumping of industrial waste into crownland rivers. The appearance especially of oil from refineries reportedly turned "the surface of the water black" and rendered it unusable for "cooking or bathing" as well as "hurting the cattle" who drank it and causing the once numerous fish to "become sparse and thin."[64] Each of these goals was reflected in the new party's agenda.

On another level, the party's goals grew out of an attempt to ease the

---

Stankiewicz, eds., *Programy Stronnictwa ludowego, zbiór dokumentów* (Warsaw, 1969), 53–62.

[61] Appeals for river regulation were among the most common petitions introduced by peasant deputies in the Sejm. In a single Sejm session alone in 1890, funds were approved for the regulation of parts of nine rivers. The funding of barriers along the crownland's river system also appeared as part of the Peasant Party's official platform. *SsSK* (1890), 538–39; "Address of the Central Election Committee of the Peasant Party" (1895) in Łato and Stankiewicz, *Programy Stronnictwa Ludowego*, 55–60.

[62] "Address of the Central Election Committee," 55, 61.

[63] Stanisław Potoczek made an impassioned appeal to the Sejm in 1890 to limit the pace with which greedy landowners were bringing about the deforestation of the crownland. *SsSK* (1890), 67.

[64] The effects of industrial polution on the Galician water supply are debated in *Przyjaciel Ludu*, February 1, 1891, 39.

transition out of the realities of serfdom and into the needs of postemanci-pation life. The increased need for capital, for example, in the posteman-cipation village and the limitations of traditional moneylending prompted demands for an expansion of the crownland's credit facilities.[65] And the bid to equalize responsibility for the upkeep of rural roads, schools, churches, and community buildings was part of a perception of incom-plete economic emancipation. Estate owners received free use of the com-mune's buildings and roads while contributing a mere fraction of their cost. Finally, the continued right of gentry landowners to hunt and fish on peasant land, and to ban peasant use of weapons even to defend their crops from wild animals, was a continued reminder of the legal and social inequalities between peasant and lord remaining from serfdom times. The Game Law, along with the Road Law, was among the most detested sym-bols of gentry privilege, and their elimination was a prominent demand in the party platform.[66]

Even as populist legislation sought to protect peasants from the worst effects of a disappearing way of life, however, competing elements of the party's agenda worked against the goal of preserving village tradition. Prominent in the party's platform, for example, was the demand for an expanded educational system that accommodated peasant pupils at the primary, secondary, and trade school levels.[67] This kind of training was necessary, peasant leaders argued, to prepare peasants to take up trades other than that of a small farmer. Activists from Father Stojałowski to agricultural circle leaders to village mayors emphasized that nonfarming sources of income were necessary to help bring more capital to the coun-tryside. Father Stojałowski argued in 1889 that the countryside required "new sources of income" to help "defray new needs." The governing board of the Tarnobrzeg Agricultural Circles noted in 1891 that the Gali-cian rural population had "outgrown" farming and required "other meth-ods" for earning a living. And the election committee of Rzeszów announced in 1891 that it would support candidates to the Reichsrat who encouraged the expansion of industry in the crownland to help farmers sell their prod-ucts more readily.[68]

Peasant leaders were proactive in their efforts to modernize the country-side by introducing new industrial enterprises. Village secretary Franciszek

[65] "Address of the Central Election Committee," 60.
[66] Ibid., 60.
[67] Ibid., 54, 59–60.
[68] *Wieniec*, May 5, 1889, 132; *Przyjaciel Ludu*, April 1, 1891, 100–101; Strzyzów to *Przy-jaciel Ludu*, March 1, 1891, 72.

Magryś argued, for example, in 1897 that one of the greatest problems in the Galician countryside was "the absence of factories, handicrafts, and all branches of industry" and a lack of professional or occupational schools to train villagers in these occupations.[69] Magryś worked closely with Sejm delegate Żardecki to bring improved educational opportunities for women and men to his region of the countryside.

And yet the education of small farmers in trade and secondary schools would clearly encourage peasants to leave the countryside and abandon farming as their primary occupation. In the short run, peasant deputies were able to ease the transition to handicrafts and small industry by seeking tax breaks for the workshops and cottage industries that dotted the Galician countryside by the late nineteenth century.[70] These attempts to garner tax relief for part-time rural workers and even to introduce factories and railroads to the countryside were clearly part of an effort to preserve elements of peasant culture while expanding the sources of rural incomes. Yet the Peasant Party also acknowledged the flood of peasants leaving their farms either temporarily or permanently for new homes in Western Europe and North America. Populist legislation sought to facilitate the emigration process by pushing to expedite the release of passports.

The combination of progressive economic reforms intended to draw elements of the rural population off the land, on the one hand, and an ongoing "faith" or "belief" in the virtues of rural life, on the other, helps explain the complex pattern of peasant alliances in the years after the founding of the Stronnictwo Ludowe. The formation of the Stronnictwo Ludowe itself was the source of conflict among peasant leaders. Stanisław and Jan Potoczek, who founded and led the less popular Związek Stronnictwa Chłopskiego after 1893, refused to join.[71] Father Stojałowski

---

[69] Franciszek Magryś to *Związek Chłopski* (1897): 133.

[70] Peasant Club member Deputy Żardecki articulated the problems encountered by peasant-workers and petitioned for tax relief for them during the 1894 Sejm. *SsSK* (1894), 101–2, 165.

[71] The Związek Stronnictwa Chłopskiego seems to have been founded at Stojałowski's encouragement, though the priest was not included on its board so as to sidestep the papal ban on his newspapers and agitation. Polish scholarship suggests the Związek was unpopular outside its native Nowy Sącz district, since it represented mostly the interests of larger farmers. The party's compromising stance toward the church hierarchy and the conservative Galician administration probably hurt its credibility among peasant voters as well. For a refreshing assessment of the Związek's fortunes, see Henryk Wereszycki, *Historia polityczna Polski, 1864–1918* (Wrocław, 1990), 148–49; and Zygmunt Hemmerling, *Ruch ludowy w Polsce, Bułgarii, i Czechosłowacji* (Warsaw, 1987), 55–56.

turned down a position on the board of the new party, instead founding his own Christian Peasant Party (Stronnictwo Chrześcijańsko-Ludowe). Within the new party, the patriotic socialist program of Bolesław Wysłouch coexisted with the less radical program of the Democratic Society and the stylistically more aggressive vision of Jan Stapiński, the peasant agitator who would take over the publication of Wysłouch's *Przyjaciel Ludu* after 1902.

The party's decision, reflected in its revised program of 1903, to focus its efforts on parceling large gentry estates among peasant farmers effectively alienated the rural voters who lacked the means to buy these often exorbitantly priced plots of land. With the passage of universal manhood suffrage for imperial elections, these dispossessed villagers had voting rights to the Reichsrat, though the conservative stranglehold on Galician politics prevented the passage of electoral reform within the crownland. The twenty populist deputies sent to Vienna after the elections of 1908 quickly fell to feuding among themselves. Deputies disagreed first about Jan Stapiński's decision to join the conservative loyalist Polish Circle (Koło Polskie) in the Reichsrat and then disagreed about his decision a year later to break off relations with the circle and begin negotiations with the Socialists. Stapiński would later argue that he received valuable assistance from the conservatives in mobilizing rural voters, as well as a substantial donation that would help him found a new journal. Still, much of the unprepared rural population was left confused and abandoned as Stapiński negotiated away pieces of the Stronnictwo's cherished program.

The party's ultimate split in 1913 between a right wing (PSL-Piast) and the more radical left wing (PSL-Lewica) came about partly as a result of differences in style and personality among the party's peasant leaders. Stapiński's volatile style of agitation conflicted with the more subdued approach of Jakub Bojko and Wincenty Witos, leaders of the Piast camp. Yet differences on programmatic and alliance questions also contributed to the severing of relations among the party's top leaders. Ultimately, Stapiński's leftist party would represent the interests of dwarf farmers and the landless rural proletariat, working for higher agricultural wages, help with emigration, and the attraction of industry to the countryside. Bojko and, later, Witos served as spokesmen for the more educated and prosperous peasant landholders. This fracturing of the peasant movement was the reality of a new rural presence in public life and was accompanied by a set of conflicting conceptions about the Polish nation.

By the outbreak of World War I and the dawning of a social and political situation characterized by the political enfranchisement of millions of villagers, the real battles in the Polish countryside were no longer between

Jan Stapiński, leader of the Polish Peasant Party-Left (Polskie Stronnictwo Ludowe-Lewica). Archive of the Institute for the History of the Peasant Movement. Courtesy of the Ethnographic Museum, Cracow. Inventory number III/7123/F. Reproduction by Jacek Kubiena.

the village and the manor, but among peasants themselves. Distinctions separating groups of peasants threatened the unity of the peasant movement as it took on a more public role.[72] The Peasant Party's shifting alliances and increasingly differentiated agendas are all evidence, however, of an active, effective, and adaptable public sphere, which included, in the Second Polish Republic, equal input from all adult citizens, male and female, urban and rural, gentry and peasants.

The peasantry's demands were made with the increasing self-confidence of leaders who believed they had something to offer an ailing Polish society. A century after the partitions of the Polish state, a half century after peasant emancipation, and thirty years after the introduction of Galician autonomy, village representatives presented their agenda for helping the rural masses as part of a contribution to the moral regeneration of Poland itself. The promotion of the small farmer to a position of increased equality and the expansion of his ability to earn a livelihood would, they hoped, introduce more elements of village culture into national life. Peasant representatives had every confidence that the nation as they understood it would benefit from such increased social contact and cooperation.

---

[72] On the splits and alliances within the Peasant Party, see Kisielewski, *Ojczyzna*, 169–97.

Conclusion:
The Main Currents of Peasant Nationalism

National consciousness . . . matured slowly, and up to our own day there were still those who only got angry and cursed when the name of Poland was mentioned. . . . The number of these people has shrunk; and that of the intelligent people has grown, who have been true to their nation, and have been ready to defend her. They see why Poland should be reunited, and should be free to run her own house.

Jan Słomka, mayor of the village of Dzików, 1912

By the early years of the twentieth century, at least two streams of peasant nationalism coexisted in Galician villages. One was the nationalist sentiment of the broad masses of Polish-speaking small farmers who conceived of ethnic and religious boundaries in terms of folk cultural motifs. This version of nationalism was reflected in the imagery and patterns of village celebrations, legends, songs, and aphorisms. Its oblique references to Poland or to Polish heroes portrayed the nation as savior, as miracle worker, as rooted in the land and the rhythms of the agricultural calendar. Non-Poles appeared as otherworldly characters in this perspective, and the mental boundaries separating the Polish peasant "us" from the foreign "them" were rigid and unnegotiable. This more plebeian vision of the nation rooted in popular culture stood in marked contrast to the discourse of patriotism found in the atmosphere of formal political debate in the crownland and the empire.

A second current of peasant national sentiment was associated with the social reform agenda reflected in Słomka's reference in the epigraph to the "intelligent people" in his village who had been "true to the nation."[1] This approach was closely tied to the project of modernizing the countryside, making economic improvements available to small farmers, and educating

---

[1] Słomka, *From Serfdom to Self-Government*, 172–73.

243

peasants to take part in public life within and beyond the village. Nation forming as social reform was most clearly articulated by the village "elite," those peasants who were minimally educated or who held leadership positions in village government and associational life. The agenda of this rural leadership cadre connected most easily with the message brought to the village by agents of the liberal intelligentsia beginning in the 1870s. Educated and increasingly activist peasants saw benefit in allying with gentry and intellectual reformers on common projects for local improvement. They learned to couch their demands for socioeconomic progress in the nationalist language of their visitors, portraying their own desire for political access, expanded opportunities, and the greater integration of country with city in terms of building the Polish nation. By employing key national symbols in the representation of their aspirations for the village, reforming peasants offered a long-term justification for directing Galician resources and public attention to the countryside.

This second variety of rural national expression should not be taken as a purely instrumental usage of national symbolism in the service of economic and cultural goals. Rather, peasant activists managed to suffuse preexisting folk symbols with national meaning and to project a populist agenda onto the upper-class images of historic national heroes. They succeeded in melding rural customary beliefs with a vision of the future partially created outside the village. The writings and local activities of peasant leaders suggest that they passionately believed in working toward the strengthening and eventual reunification of their newly "discovered" nation. Part of the reason for the deep commitment they felt, however, was that they were not only "discovering" the Polish nation, but also "inventing" a new understanding of that national idea—an understanding that included representation of specific peasant aspirations. Rural reform and images of the nation formed symbiotic ties in this strain of peasant nationalism.

At the same time that these uses of nationalism, social reform, and folk imagery interacted in the village public sphere, a substratum of peasants continued to oppose any mention of alliances with the social elite in a resurrected Polish state. Sharing the retrograde sentiment to which Jan Słomka alludes, a significant but dwindling minority of Polish-speaking villagers at the turn of the twentieth century remained fearful of a return to serfdom and saw little common cause with their former lords. To the extent that "Poland" represented the resumption of feudal relations, this substratum of villagers refused to contemplate reunification as a desirable goal. Perceptions of the inspirational value and programmatic uses of the nation thus varied widely throughout the Galician countryside. Some small farmers remained uninterested in or unmotivated by national ideas. Others were swept up in the emotional appeal of national miracles and folk imagery. Still others formed a commitment to the nation through the socioeconomic programs they constructed.

In the years prior to the founding of the Second Republic, the most successful approach to nation forming among peasants was the program circulated in rural newspapers, in broad-based political assemblies, and among activists of the Peasant Party. This program for national regeneration resulted from an amalgam of pious efforts at rural reform among the village elite and their linkage with the ideas of village outsiders. The "premodern" conceptualization of national boundaries undoubtedly overlapped with the vision of a morally based community of Polish speakers that was promoted among many activist peasants. Yet it was the activists, with their language of local reform and self-improvement, who were able to form a common bond with nonpeasants and ultimately make their way into positions of administrative, economic, and cultural power. Only by finding a shared language—the language of a community of nation builders—could village leaders hope to promote village affairs at the crownland and imperial level. Those who were unable or unwilling to present village needs in terms understandable to upper-class administrators, educators, and philanthropists found themselves and their visions cut out of the interactions of formal public life.

These two ways of understanding and employing the idea of the Polish nation grew out of a set of social dynamics rooted in the preemancipation village. Social divisions based on patterns of landholding, access to local power, gender, and generational differences had created a peasantry that, even at the moment of emancipation, was differentially capable of taking advantage of the opportunities emancipation offered and of handling the new problems that emancipation imposed. Villagers varied widely in the benefits they were able to accrue from the appearance in the village of new institutions such as agricultural circles, credit cooperatives, Christian stores, and vernacular language elementary schools. The growth of such reforming institutions helped create a critical mass of villagers interested in promoting social and economic change in the countryside. At the same time, interactions within these same bodies—especially agricultural circles and reading clubs—alienated and distanced certain subgroups within the village. Landless laborers, farmwives, and the majority of illiterate smallholders remained less attracted to the agenda introduced through agricultural circles and reading clubs. Indeed, the activities of these organizations drove a new wedge through village society, both replicating preexisting divisions within the community and producing new social stratification.

The moral community that formed the basis for "elite" peasant nationalism effectively cut out at least two social groups: the conservative *stańczycy* who were accused of having collaborated with Austrian authorities to the detriment of the peasantry, and the immoral, backward, lazy, or intemperate village "rabble" uninterested in rural improvements. The latter group of "underdeveloped" villagers was placed on a moral continuum and encouraged to attain membership in the club of rural reformers once they learned "proper" public behavior. Socially conservative aristocrats and church officials, however, were the focus of unrelenting hostility for their unwillingness to take seriously the peasants as public actors who could be responsible for their own fate and that of their larger community.

With the advent in the 1890s of formal political institutions representing peasant interests, the rural "masses" found it increasingly difficult to see themselves reflected in the agenda of associations claiming to speak for them. Indeed, the first peasant parties concerned themselves above all with the needs of rural property owners—those who were legally entitled to vote in crownland elections—and neglected the interests of landless laborers in many of their deliberations. Unable to truly represent all Galician peasants or to express a universal smallholder sense of national priorities, organizations such as the Stronnictwo Ludowe spoke only for a subset of Galician villagers. Increasingly, then, political factions in the countryside became formalized. By the early years of the twentieth century, much of the rural proletariat was drawn to socialist parties, Ruthenian peasants joined separate nationalist organizations, and peasant women chafed at the virtual absence of institutions representing their interests. Nation forming in the Polish countryside involved a constant process of social stratification as new divisions and fresh alliances formed and reformed. Political mobilization and nation forming in the Galician countryside both reflected and precipitated the sociological realignment of the Polish-speaking population.

The rural public sphere was the forum in which the components of peasant nationalism and rural reform were shaped and molded, at times uniting villagers in mass celebrations and at times dividing them in closely fought electoral contests. Parades and public spectacles, as much as debate at village council meetings and in the columns of the peasant press, helped communicate ideas and negotiate shared senses of local priorities. While the entire village community could participate in popular cultural events, the reformist national agenda was hammered out before a more self-selected audience. The concentric circles of public sphere activity in Austrian Poland remind us of the premodern sources of political behavior even in "modern" public interactions. Public debate in the countryside continued to rely heavily on folk images and traditional practices even as peasant activists were introducing these practices into fora outside the village. Far from being a field for "logical" discussion based on shared assumptions, debate about the future of "Poland" brought forth multiple meanings and conflicting assumptions about the future. The shifting sense of national meaning and consequent process of public accommodation depicted here reflect the fluidity involved in the formation and reformulation of modern nations.

Bibliography

Archival Sources

APKr   Archiwum Państwowe Miasta Krakowa i Województwa Krakowskiego
       (State Archives for the City and District of Cracow)
AUJ   Archiwum Uniwersytetu Jagiellońskiego (Jagiellonian University Archive)
DPKr   Dyrekcja Policji w Krakowie (Director of Police in the Cracow District)
ME   Muzeum Etnograficzne im. Seweryna Udzieli, Cracow
SKKKr Sąd Krajowy Karny w Krakowie (Provincial Criminal Court in Cracow)
St.B   Starostwo Bielskie w Krakowie (Biała Township in the Cracow District)
ST.NT Starostwo Nowotarskie w Krakowie (Nowy Targ Township in the Cra-
       cow District
TsDIAL Tsentralnyi Derzhavnyi Istorychnyi Arkhiv u m. Lvovi, L'viv (Central
       State Historical Archives in L'viv)
       Fond 146: Dyrekcji Policji we Lwowie
       Fond 178: Rada Szkolna w Galicji
Oss   Ossolineum, Wrocław
       Papiery Jakuba Bojki
       Papiery Bolesława i Marii Wysłouchów
ZHRL   Zakład Historii Ruchu Ludowego, Warsaw (Department of the History
       of the Peasant Movement)
       Papiery Stanisława Potoczka
       Papiery Karola Lewakowskiego (ZL)
       Papiery Andrzeja Średniawskiego (ZŚ)
       Papiery Stanisława Stojałowskiego

Unpublished Manuscripts in ZHRL

Kozicki, Stanisław. "Pamiętnik" (P-127/I).
Kurczak, Teofil. "Pamiętnik, 1877–1939" (P-56a).
Kuś, Franciszek. "Z pamiętników moich" (P-64a).
Nocek, Jozef. "Wspomnienia, 1880–" (P-17).
Noczniki, Tomasz. "Moje wspomnienia z ubiegłego życia" (P-18).
Rymar, Stanisław. "Chłopi polscy w Parlamentach i Sejmach, 1848–1939" (O-158).
——. "Pamiętniki z lat życia, 1880–1962" (P-183/I).
Słomba, Franciszek. "Początki ruchu ludowego w Galicji" (O-12).
Wiatr, Władysław. "Ruch ludowy w powiecie ropczyckim dawniej i dzisiaj" (P-43).

Contemporary Press and Serials

Czasopismo dla spółek rolniczych. 1909.
Lud. Lwów, 1895–1913.
Przyjaciel Ludu. Lwów, 1881–1910.
Pszczółka. Lwów, 1876–1910.
Stenograficzne sprawozdania Sejmu Krajowego (*SsSK*). Lwów, 1861, 1889–95.
Ster. Warsaw, 1907–14.
Świat. 1888.
Szkoła. Lwów, 1893–95.
Szkolnictwo Ludowe. Nowy Sącz, 1891–92.
Wieniec Polski. Lwów, 1876–1910.
Wisła. Warsaw, 1887–1913.
Zorza. Lwów, 1904–5.
Związek Chłopski. Nowy Sącz, 1894–95.

Published Documents

Albin, Janusz, and Józef Ryszard Szaflik. "Listy Jakuba Bojki z lat 1891–1916." *Ze skarbca kultury* 27 (1976).
——. "Listy Macieja Szarka z lat 1861–1904." *Ze skarbca kultury* 39 (1984).
Bojko, Jakub. *Dwie dusze.* Warsaw, 1949.
Instrukcja dla kółek rolniczych. Lwów, 1883.
Kieniewicz, Stefan. "Obrazki wiejskie 1847–1849. Z korespondencji Wodzickich." *Ze Skarbca Kultury* 2, no. 1 (1952).
Knot, Antoni, ed. *Galicyjskie wspomnienia szkolne.* Cracow: Wydawnictwo literackie, 1955.
Kolberg, Oskar. *Lud. Dzieła wszystkie.* 75 vols. Wrocław, 1961.
Kolberg, Oskar. *Lud, jego zwyczaje, sposób życia, mowa, podania, przyslowia,*

obrzedy, gusla, zabawy, pieśni, muzyka i tańce. Warsaw and Cracow, 1860–1910.

Konopka, Józef. *Pieśni ludu krakowskiego*. Cracow: Nakładem i drukiem Józefa Czecha, 1840.

Konopnicka, Maria. *Poezje*. Warsaw: Czytelnik, 1969.

"Listy Jana Stapińskiego do Karola Lewakowskiego." *Roczniki Dziejów Ruchu Ludowego* 18 (1976).

Madejczyk, Jan. *Wspomnienia*. Warsaw, 1965.

Magryś, Franciszek. *Żywot chłopa działacza*. Warsaw, 1987.

Pigoń, Stanisław. *Z Komborni w świat. Wspomnienia młodości*. Cracow, 1957.

Wiejscy działacze społeczni. Vol. 1: *Życiorysy włościan*. Warsaw, 1937.

Wiejscy działacze społeczni. Vol. 2: *Życiorysy inteligentów*. Warsaw, 1938.

Witos, Wincenty. *Moje wspomnienia*. Warsaw: Ludowa Spółdzielnia Wydawnicza, 1978.

Złożenie zwłok Adama Mickiewicza na Wawelu dnia 4-go lipca 1890 roku. Książka pamiątkowa z 22 ilustracyami. Cracow, 1890.

Secondary Literature

Agulhon, Maurice. *The Republic in the Village: The People of the Var from the French Revolution to the Second Republic*. Cambridge: Cambridge University Press, 1982.

Albin, Janusz. "Z działalności bibliotek ludowych w Galicji." *Biuletyn Biblioteki Jagiellońskiej* 32, nos. 1–2 (1982): 77–102.

Anderson, Benedict. *Imagined Communities: Reflections on the Origins and Spread of Nationalism*. London: Verso, 1991.

Antoń, Stanisław. "Dzieje ruchu ludowego sądeczczyzny w latach 1870–1919." *Rocznik Sądecki* 8 (1967): 65–113.

Arato, Andrew. *Civil Society, Constitution, and Legitimacy*. Lanham, Md.: Rowman & Littlefield, 2000.

Bałaban, Majer. *Dzieje Żydów w Galicji i Rzeczpospolitej Krakowskiej 1772–1868*. Lwów, 1914.

Balakrishnan, Gopal, ed. *Mapping the Nation*. London: Verso, 1996.

Bartal, Israel, and Antony Polonsky, eds. *Polin: Studies in Polish Jewry*, vol. 12: *Focusing on Galicia: Jews, Poles, and Ukrainians, 1772–1918*. London: Littman Library of Jewish Civilization for the Institute for Polish-Jewish Studies, 1999.

Bhabha, Homi K. "Introduction: Narrating the Nation." In *Nation and Narration*, ed. Homi K. Bhabha. London: Routledge, 1990, 1–7.

——, ed. *Nation and Narration*. London: Routledge, 1990.

Blackbourn, David. *Class, Religion, and Local Politics in Wilhelmine Germany*. New Haven: Yale University Press, 1980.

Blank, Inge. "From Serfdom to Citizenship: Polish Folk Culture from the Era of the Partitions to World War I." In *Roots of the Transplanted*, ed. Dirk

Hoerder and Inge Blank. Boulder: East European Monographs, 1994. 111–73.

Blanke, Richard. *Prussian Poland in the German Empire, 1871–1900*. Boulder: East European Monographs, 1981.

Blejwas, Stanislaus A. *Realism in Polish Politics: Warsaw Positivism and National Survival in Nineteenth Century Poland*. New Haven: Yale University Press, 1984.

Blobaum, Robert. *Rewolucja: Russian Poland, 1904–1907*. Ithaca: Cornell University Press, 1995.

Blum, Jerome. *The End of the Old Order in Rural Europe*. Princeton: Princeton University Press, 1978.

——. *Noble Landowners and Agriculture in Austria, 1815–1848: A Study in the Origins of the Peasant Emancipation of 1848*. Baltimore: Johns Hopkins Press, 1948.

Boryś, Włodzimierz. "Wybory w Galicji i debaty nad zniesieniem pańszczyzny w parlamencie wiedeńskim w 1848." *Przegląd Historyczny* 58, no. 1 (1967): 28–45.

Brock, Peter. "Bolesław Wysłouch, Founder of the Polish Peasant Party." *Slavonic and East European Review* 30, no. 74 (December 1951): 139–63.

——. "The Early Years of the Polish Peasant Party, 1895–1907." *Journal of Central European Affairs* 14, no. 3 (October 1954): 219–35.

——. "Maria Wysłouchowa (1858–1905) and the Polish Peasant Movement in Galicia." *Canadian Slavonic Papers* 3 (1959): 89–102.

——. "The Polish 'Movement to the People': An Early Chapter in the History of East European Populism." *Slavonic and East European Review* 40, no. 94 (December 1961): 99–122.

——. *Polish Revolutionary Populism: A Study in Agrarian Socialist Thought from the 1830s to the 1850s*. Toronto: University of Toronto Press, 1977.

Brodowska, Helena. *Chłopi o sobie i Polsce: rozwój wsiadomości społeczno-narodowej*. Warsaw: Ludowa Spóldzielnia Wydawnicza, 1984.

——. "Koła Oświaty Ludowej. Przyczynek do badań nad rozwojem świadomości chłopów." In *Stowarzyszenie społeczne jako środowisko wychowawcze*, ed. Irena Łepalczyk, Warsaw, 1974.

——. *Ruch chłopski po uwłaszczeniu w Królestwie Polskim, 1864–1904*. Warsaw: Państwowe Wydawnictwo Naukowe, 1967.

Brooks, Jeffrey. "Competing Modes of Popular Discourse: Individualism and Class Consciousness in the Russian Print Media, 1880–1928." In *Culture et Revolution*, ed. Marc Ferro and Sheila Fitzpatrick. Paris: Ecole des hautes études en sciences sociales, 1989.

——. *When Russia Learned to Read: Literacy and Popular Literature, 1861–1917*. Princeton: Princeton University Press, 1985.

Brzozowka-Komorowska, Teresa. "Zygmunt Gloger i popularyzacja folkloru." In *Dzieje folklorystyki polskiej 1864–1918*, ed. Helena Kapeluś and Julian Krzyżanowski. Warsaw: Państwowe Wydawnictwo Naukowe, 1982. 104–9.

Bujak, Franciszek. *Galicja*. 2 vols. Lwów, 1908.

——. "Wieś zachodnio-galicyjska u schyłku XIX wieku." In *Wybór pism*, vol. 2: z *dziejów społecznych i gospodarczych Polski x–xx w.*, ed. Helena Madurowicz-Urbańska. Warsaw: Państwowe Wydawnictwo Naukowe, 1976.

——. *Żmiąca: Wieś powiatu Limanowskiego. Stosunki gospodarcze i społeczne.* Cracow: G. Gebethner i Spolka, 1903.

Burke, Peter. *Popular Culture in Early Modern Europe.* London: Temple Smith, 1978.

Burszta, Józef. "Kultura chłopsko-ludowa a kultura narodowa." *Etnografia Polska* 2 (1959): 391–415.

——. *Społeczeństwo i karczma. Propinacja, karczma i sprawa alkoholizmu w społeczeństwie polskim XIX wieku.* Warsaw, 1951.

Bystroń, Jan. *Pieśni ludu polskiego.* Cracow: Orbis, 1924.

Caro, Leopold. *Lichwa na wsi w latach 1875–1891.* Lwów, 1893.

"Chłop-Nauczyciel." *Piast*, June 25, 1947, 3.

Ciupak, Edward. *Katolicyzm ludowy w Polsce. Studia socjologiczne.* Warsaw: Wiedza Powszechna, 1972.

Clark Samuel, and James S. Donnelly Jr., eds. *Irish Peasants: Violence and Political Unrest, 1780–1914.* Madison: University of Wisconsin Press, 1983.

Cohen, Jean L., and Andrew Arato. *Civil Society and Political Theory.* Cambridge, Mass.: MIT Press, 1992.

Czap, Peter, Jr., "Peasant-Class Courts and Peasant Customary Justice in Russia, 1861–1912." *Journal of Social History* 1, no. 2 (winter 1967): 149–78.

Dabrowski, Patrice. "Celebrating the Past, Creating the Future: Commemorations and the Making of a Modern Polish Nation, 1879–1914." Ph.D. diss., Harvard University, 1999.

Davies, Norman. *God's Playground: A History of Poland*, vol. 2: *1795 to the Present.* New York: Columbia University Press, 1982.

Dawidowa, Jadwiga. *Kółka rolnicze w Galicyi.* Warsaw, 1890.

Desan, Suzanne. "Crowds, Community, and Ritual in the Work of E. P. Thompson and Natalie Davis." In *The New Cultural History*, ed. Lynn Hunt. Berkeley: University of California Press, 1989. 47–71.

Deutsch, Karl. *Nationalism and Social Communication: An Inquiry into the Foundations of Nationality.* Cambridge, Mass.: MIT Press, 1953.

Dobrowolski, Kazimierz. "Peasant Traditional Culture." *Etnografia Polska* 1 (1958): 19–56. Reprinted in part in *Peasants and Peasant Societies*, ed. Teodor Shanin. Oxford: Oxford University Press, 1987. 261–77.

Duara, Prasenjit. *Culture, Power, and the State: Rural North China, 1900–1942.* Stanford: Stanford University Press, 1988.

——. *Rescuing History from the Nation: Questioning Narratives of Modern China.* Chicago: University of Chicago Press, 1995.

Dubnov, Simon. *History of the Jews*, vol. 5: *From the Congress of Vienna to the Emergence of Hitler.* Cranbury, N.J.: Thomas Yoseloff, 1973.

Dulczewski, Zygmunt. *Walka o szkołę na wsi galicyjskiej w świetle stenogramów Sejmu Krajowego, 1861–1914.* Warsaw: Ludowa Spółdzielnia Wydawnicza, 1953.

Dunin-Wąsowicz, Krzysztof. *Czasopiśmiennictwo w Galicji.* Wrocław: Wydawnictwo Zakładu Narodowego im. Ossolińskich, 1952.

——. *Dzieje Stronnictwa Ludowego w Galicji*. Warsaw: Ludowa Spółdzielnia Wydawnicza, 1956.

Dylągowa, Hanna. *Duchowieństwo katolickie wobec sprawy narodowej (1764–1864)*. Lublin: Wydawnictwo Towarzystwa Naukowego KUL, 1983.

Eisenbach, Artur. *The Emancipation of the Jews in Poland, 1780–1870*. Oxford: Basil Blackwell, 1991.

Eley, Geoff. "Nations, Publics, and Political Cultures: Placing Habermas in the Nineteenth Century." In *Culture/Power/History: A Reader in Contemporary Social Theory*, ed. Nicholas B. Dirks, Geoff Eley, and Sherry B. Ortner. Princeton: Princeton University Press, 1994. 297–335.

——. *Reshaping the German Right: Radical Nationalism and Political Change after Bismarck*. Ann Arbor: University of Michigan Press, 1991.

Eley, Geoff, and Ronald Grigor Suny, eds. *Becoming National: A Reader*. Oxford University Press, 1996.

Frierson, Cathy A. *Peasant Icons: Representations of Rural People in Late Nineteenth-Century Russia*. New York: Oxford University Press, 1993.

Garbaczowski, Janina. "Krakowska prasa dla wsi w r. 1848." *Polska Akademia Umiejętności: Sprawozdania z czynności i posiedzeń*, 1949.

Gellner, Ernest. *Nations and Nationalism*. Ithaca: Cornell University Press, 1983.

Gerber, Rafal, ed. *Powstanie chochołowskie 1846 roku: Dokumenty i materiały*. Wrocław, 1960.

Grudziński, Tadeusz. *Boleslaus the Bold, called also the Bountiful, and Bishop Stanislaus: The Story of a Conflict*. Trans. Lech Petrowicz. Warsaw: Interpress Publishers, 1985.

Grzybowski, Konstanty. *Galicja, 1848–1914: Historia ustroju politycznego na tle historii ustroju Austrii*. Cracow, 1959.

Gurnicz, Antoni. "Ideologia i program pracy organicznej na wsi galicyjskiej (na przykładzie kółek rolniczych)." *Międzyuczelniane zeszyty ekonomiczne*, no. 11 (1966): 71–99.

——. "Kółka rolnicze na ziemiach polskich w okresie zaborów. Geneza i kierunki rozwoju." *Roczniki Dziejów Ruchu Ludowego*, no. 8 (1966): 3–46.

——. *Kółka rolnicze w Galicji*. Warsaw: Ludowa Spółdzielnia Wydawnicza, 1967.

——. "Ks. Stanisław Stojałowski a rozwój myśli chrześcijańsko-społecznej w Galicji." *Międzyuczelniane zeszyty naukowe: Studia z historii myśli społeczno-ekonomicznej*, no. 4 (1964): 127–35.

——. "Nowosądecki Z.S.Ch. [Związek Stronnictwa Chłopskiego] w opinii prasy galicyjskiej." *Rocznik Sądecki* 8 (1967).

——. *O "równą miarkę" dla chłopów. Poglądy i działalność pierwszej chłopskiej organizacji politycznej w Polsce, Związku Stronnictwa Chłopskiego (1893–1908)*. Warsaw: Ludowa Spółdzielnia Wydawnicza, 1963.

——. "System Społdzielczy F. W. Raiffeisena i galicyjska adaptacja F. Stefczyka." *Spółdzielczy kwartalnik naukowy* 1, no. 4 (1967): 129–64

Habermas, Jürgen. "The European Nation-State—Its Achievements and Its Limits." In *Mapping the Nation*, ed. Gopal Balakrishnan. London: Verso, 1996. 284–93.

——. *Structural Transformation of the Public Sphere: An Inquiry into a Category of Bourgeois Society.* Cambridge, Mass.: MIT Press, 1990.

Hagen, William W. *Germans, Poles, and Jews: The Nationality Conflict in the Prussian East, 1771–1914.* Chicago: University of Chicago Press, 1980.

Heller, Michał. *Ruch ludowy w Małopolsce zachodnej i na Śląsku cieszyńskim (1890–1908).* Katowice: Prace Naukowe Uniwersytetu Śląskiego w Katowicach, no. 990, 1988.

Hemmerling, Zygmunt. *Ruch ludowy w Polsce, Bułgarii, i Czechosłowacji.* Warsaw: Ludowa Spółdzielnia Wydawnicza, 1987.

——. "Stronnictwa ludowe wobec Żydów i kwestii żydowskiej." *Kwartalnik historyczny* 96, nos. 1–2 (1989): 155–81.

Himka, John-Paul. *Galician Villagers and the Ukrainian National Movement in the Nineteenth Century.* New York: St. Martin's Press, 1988.

——. "Ukrainian-Jewish Antagonism in the Galician Countryside during the Late Nineteenth Century." In *Ukrainian-Jewish Relations in Historical Perspective,* ed. Peter J. Potichnyj and Howard Aster. Edmonton: Canadian Institute of Ukrainian Studies, 1988. 111–58.

Hobsbawm, Eric. *Primitive Rebels: Studies in Archaic Forms of Social Movement in the Nineteenth and Twentieth Centuries.* New York: W. W. Norton and Co., 1959.

Hoerder, Dirk, and Inge Blank. "Ethnic and National Consciousness from the Enlightenment to the 1880s." In *Roots of the Transplanted,* vol. 1: *Late Nineteenth-Century East Central and Southeastern Europe,* ed. Hoerder and Blank. Boulder: East European Monographs, 1994. 37–109.

Hofer, Tamas. "The Construction of 'Folk Cultural Heritage' in Hungary and Rival Versions of National Identity." *Hungarians between "East" and "West": National Myths and Symbols.* Budapest, 1994. 27–52.

——. "The Creation of Ethnic Symbols from the Elements of Peasant Culture." In *Ethnic Diversity and Conflict in Eastern Europe,* ed. Peter F. Sugar. Santa Barbara, 1980. 101–145.

——. "The Perception of Tradition in European Ethnology." *Journal of Folklore Research* 21, no. 1 (April 1984).

Hoffmann, David L. *Peasant Metropolis: Social Identities in Moscow, 1929–1941.* Ithaca: Cornell University Press, 1994.

Homola, Irena. "Prasa galicyjska w latach 1831–1864." *Prasa Polska w latach 1661–1864.* Warsaw: Państwowe Wydawnictwo Naukowe, 1976.

Hroch, Miroslav. *Social Preconditions of National Revival in Europe: A Comparative Analysis of the Social Composition of Patriotic Groups among the Smaller European Nations.* Cambridge: Cambridge University Press, 1985.

Hryniuk, Stella. *Peasants with Promise: Ukrainians in Southeastern Galicia, 1880–1900.* Edmonton, Alberta: Canadian Institute of Ukrainian Studies Press, 1991.

Inglot, Stefan, ed. *Historia chłopów polskich.* 3 vols. Warsaw: Ludowa Spółdzielnia Wydawnicza, 1972.

Ionescu, Ghita, and Ernest Gellner, eds. *Populism: Its Meanings and National Characteristics*. London: Weidenfeld & Nicolson, 1969.

Jakubowska, Barbara. *Ruch ludowy wobec przeszłości narodowej (do 1939)*. Warsaw: Wydawnictwo Trio, 1995.

Jabłońska-Deptuła, Ewa. "Patriotyczne treści kultu św. Stanisława Biskupa w okresie rozbiorów i niewoli narodowej." *Zeszyty Naukowe Katolickiego Uniwersytetu Lubelskiego* 22, nos. 1–3 (1979).

Jaworski, Rudolf, and Bianka Pietrów-Ennker, eds. *Women in Polish Society*. Boulder: East European Monographs, 1992.

Jedlicki, Jerzy. *A Suburb of Europe: Nineteenth-Century Polish Approaches to Western Civilization*. Budapest: Central European University Press, 1999.

Jędruch, Jacek. *Constitutions, Elections, and Legislatures of Poland, 1493–1993: A Guide to Their History*. New York: Hippocrene Books, 1998.

Jersild, Austin Lee. "Ethnic Modernity and the Russian Empire: Russian Ethnographers and the Caucasian Mountaineers." *Nationalities Papers* 24, no. 4 (1996): 641–48.

Jones, P. M. *Politics and Rural Society: The Southern Massif Central, c. 1750–1880*. London: Cambridge University Press, 1985.

Judt, Tony. *Socialism in Provence, 1871–1914: A Study in the Origins of the Modern French Left*. Cambridge: Cambridge University Press, 1979.

Kącki, Franciszek. *Ks. Stanisław Stojałowski i jego działalność społeczno-polityczna*. Lwów, 1937.

Kann, Robert A. *A History of the Habsburg Empire, 1526–1918*. Berkeley: University of California Press, 1974.

Kapeluś, Helena, and Julian Krzyżanowski, eds. *Dzieje folklorystyki polskiej 1864–1918*. Warsaw: Państwowe Wydawnictwo Naukowe, 1982.

Keane, John, ed. *Civil Society and the State: New European Perspectives* London: Verso, 1988.

——. *Democracy and Civil Society: On the Predicaments of European Socialism, the Prospects for Democracy, and the Problem of Controlling Social and Political Power*. London: Verso, 1988.

Kieniewicz, Stefan. *The Emancipation of the Polish Peasantry*. Chicago: University of Chicago Press, 1969.

——. *Galicja w dobie autonomicznej*. Wrocław: Wydawnictwo Zakładu Narodowego im. Ossolińskich, 1952.

——. *Konspiracje galicyjskie, 1831–1845*. Warsaw: Książka i Wiedza, 1950.

——. *Pomiędzy Stadionem a Goslarem: Sprawa włościańska w Galicji w 1848 r.* Wrocław: Zakład Narodowy im. Ossolińskich, 1980.

——. *Ruch chłopski w Galicji w 1846 roku*. Wrocław: Wydawnictwo Zakładu Narodowego im. Ossolińskich, 1951.

Kiryk, Feliks, ed. *Żydzi w Małopolsce. Studia z dziejów osadnictwa i życia społecznego*. Przemyśl, 1991.

Kisielewski, Tadeusz. *Ojczyzna, chłopi, ludowcy*. Warsaw: Ludowa Spółdzielnia Wydawnicza, 1987.

——. "Początki ruchu ludowego. Dwaj działacze i dwa programy." *Wieś współczesna* 19, no. 7 (1975): 87–96.

Kleczyński, Józef. *Propinacja i szynkarstwo*. Cracow, 1888.

——. *Życie gminne w Galicji*. Lwów, 1878.

Kłoczowski, Jerzy, Lidia Müllerowa, and Jan Skarbek. *Zarys dziejów kościoła katolickiego w Polsce*. Cracow: Spółdzielnia Wydawnicza Znak, 1986.

Knight, Nathaniel. "Science, Empire, and Nationality: Ethnography in the Russian Geographical Society, 1845–1855." In *Imperial Russia: New Histories for the Empire*, ed. Jane Burbank and David L. Ransel. Bloomington: Indiana University Press, 1998.

Koenig, Samuel. "Geographic and Ethnic Characteristics of Galicia." *Journal of Central European Affairs* 1, no. 1 (April 1941): 55–65.

Konefał, Jan. "Parlamentarna działalność posłów chłopskich Jana i Stanisława Potoczków (1889–1922)." *Roczniki humanistyczne* 29, no. 2 (1981): 223–43.

Kowalczyk, Stanisław. "Ruch ludowy wobec wyborów do Sejmu w Galicji w 1895 r." *Roczniki Dziejów Ruchu Ludowego*, no. 7 (1965): 280–318.

Kowalczyk, Stanisław, et al. *Zarys historii polskiego ruchu ludowego*. Warsaw: Ludowa Spółdzielnia Wydawnicza, 1965.

Kulczycki, John J. *School Strikes in Prussian Poland, 1901–1907: The Struggle over Bilingual Education*. Boulder: East European Monographs, 1981.

Kutrzeba-Pojnarowa, Anna. "Kultura ludowa w dotychczasowych polskich pracach etnograficznych." In Kapeluś and Krzyżanowski, *Dzieje folklorystyki polskiej*.

Łato, Stanisław. "Galicyjska prasa 'dla ludu' 1848–1913." *Rocznik historii czasopiśmiennictwa polskiego* 2 (1963): 57–74.

Łato, Stanisław, and Witold Stankiewicz, eds. *Programy Stronnictwa Ludowego, zbiór dokumentów*. Warsaw, 1969.

Layton, Susan. "The Creation of an Imaginative Caucasian Geography." *Slavic Review* 45, no. 3 (fall 1986): 470–85.

——. *Russian Literature and Empire: Conquest of the Caucasus from Pushkin to Tolstoy*. Cambridge: Cambridge University Press, 1994.

Lerski, Jerzy J., ed. *Jewish-Polish Coexistence, 1772–1939: A Topical Bibliography*. New York: Greenwood Press, 1986.

Leskiewiczowa, Janina, ed. *Zarys historii gospodarstwa wiejskiego w Polsce*. Vol. 2. Warsaw: Państwowe Wydawnictwo Rolnicze i Leśne, 1964.

Lewis, Richard D. "The Revolution in the Countryside: Russian Poland, 1905–1906." *Carl Beck Papers in Russian and East European Studies*, no. 506. Pittsburgh: Center for Russian and East European Studies, University of Pittsburg, 1986.

Link, Edith Murr. *The Emancipation of the Austrian Peasant, 1740–1798*. New York, 1949.

Livezeanu, Irina. *Cultural Politics and Greater Romania*. Ithaca: Cornell University Press, 1995.

Lofgren, Orvar. "The Nationalization of Culture." *Ethnologia Europaea* 19 (1989): 5–23.

Łyś, Władysław. *Powstanie chochołowskie: w 110 rocznicę 1846–1956*. Warsaw, 1956.

Magocsi, Paul Robert. *Galicia: A Historical Survey and Bibliographic Guide.* Toronto: University of Toronto Press, 1983.

Majorek, Czesław. *System kształcenia nauczycieli szkół ludowych w Galicji doby autonomicznej (1871–1914).* Wrocław, 1871.

———. "Ustrój galicyjskiego szkolnictwa ludowego w czasie walki o autonomię i w okresie kampanii rewolucyjnej (1860–1873)." *Roczn. Nauk.-Dydakt. WSP w Krakowie 32: Prace Historyczne,* no. 4 (1968): 211–34.

Mallon, Florencia. *Peasant and Nation: The Making of Postcolonial Mexico and Peru.* Berkeley: University of California Press, 1995.

Markiewicz, Henryk. *Literatura pozytywizmu.* Warsaw: Państwowe Wydawnictwo Naukowe, 1989.

McCagg, William O., Jr., *A History of Habsburg Jews, 1670–1918.* Bloomington: Indiana University Press, 1989.

McPhee, Peter. "Popular Culture, Symbolism, and Rural Radicalism in Nineteenth-Century France." *Journal of Peasant Studies* 5, no. 2 (January 1978): 238–50.

Mężyk, Józef. Młodzież chłopska na Uniwersytecie Jagiellońskim i jej udział w ruchu ludowym (od Powstania Styczniowego do 1923 r.). *Roczniki Dziejów Ruchu Ludowego,* no. 7 (1965): 17–50.

Michalski, Stanisław, ed. *Dzieje szkolnictwa i oświaty na wsi polskiej,* vol. 1: *do 1918.* Warsaw: Ludowa Spółdzielnia Wydawnicza, 1982.

Miller, Saul. *Dobromil: Life in a Galician Shtetl, 1890–1907.* New York, 1980.

Miłosz, Czesław. *The History of Polish Literature.* Berkeley: University of California Press, 1983.

Moeller, Robert. "Peasants and Tariffs in the *Kaiserreich*: How Backward Were the *Bauern*?" *Agricultural History* 55, no. 4 (October 1981): 370–84.

Molenda, Jan. "The Formation of National Consciousness of the Polish Peasants and the Part They Played in the Regaining of Independence by Poland." *Acta Poloniae Historica,* nos. 63–64 (1991): 121–48.

Müller, Elżbieta, and Agata Skrukwa. "Oskar Kolberg (1814–1890)." In Kapeluś and Krzyżanowski, *Dzieje folklorystyki polskiej, 25–48.*

Myśliński, Jerzy. "Prasa polska w galicji w dobie autonomicznej (1867–1918)." In *Prasa polska w latach 1864–1918,* ed. Jerzy Łojek. Warsaw, 1976.

Narkiewicz, Olga. *The Green Flag: Polish Populist Politics, 1867–1970.* London : Croom Helm, 1976.

Obrebski, Joseph. *The Changing Peasantry of Eastern Europe.* Ed. Barbara Halpern and Joel Halpern. Cambridge, Mass.: Schenkman, 1976.

Opalski, Magdalena, and Israel Bartal. *The Jewish Tavern-Keeper and His Tavern in Nineteenth-Century Polish Literature.* Jerusalem: Zalman Shazar Center for the Furtherance of the Study of Jewish History, 1986.

———. *Poles and Jews: A Failed Brotherhood.* Hanover, N.H.: University Press of New England, 1992.

Orton, Lawrence D. "The *Stańczyk* Portfolio and the Politics of Galician Loyalism." *Polish Review* 27, nos. 1–2 (1982): 55–64.

Pajakowski, Philip. "History, the Peasantry, and the Polish Nation in the Thought of Michał Bobrzyński." *Nationalities Papers* 26, no. 2 (1998): 249–64.

——. "The Polish Club and Austrian Parliamentary Politics, 1873–1900." Ph.D. diss., Indiana University, 1989.

Pastuszka, Stefan. "Rola Karola Lewakowskiego w powstaniu i działalności ruchu ludowego." *Roczniki Dziejów Ruchu Ludowego,* no. 19 (1977/78): 3–26.

Perkowska, Urzula. *Kształtowanie się zespołu naukowego w Uniwersytecie Jagiellońskim (1860–1920).* Wrocław, 1975.

Pilat, Tadeusz. *Podręcznik statystyki Galicji.* Lwów, 1878.

——. *Pogląd historyczny na urządzenie gminne w Galicyi.* Lwów, 1878.

——. *Wiadomości statystyczne o stosunkach krajowych.* Lwów, 1881.

Piszczkowski, Mieczysław. *Obrońcy chłopów w literaturze polskiej.* Cracow, 1948.

Plechta, Józef. "Chłopscy posłowie z obwodu sądeckiego w sejmie wiedeńskim w 1848 roku." *Rocznik Dziejów Ruchu Ludowego* 8 (1966).

——. "Rada Narodowa obwodu sądeckiego i pierwsze wystąpienie posłów chłopskich." *Rocznik Sądecki* 8 (1967).

Podgórska, E. *Krajowy Związek Nauczycielstwa Ludowego w Galicji 1905–1918.* Warsaw: Nasza Księgarnia, 1973.

——. "Walka o szkołę ludową w sejmie galicyjskim w latach 1880–1900." *Studia Pedagogiczne* 1 (1954).

Podraza, Antoni. "Kształtowanie się elity wiejskiej na przykładzie Galicji na przełomie XIX i XX w." *Acta Universitatis Lodziensis. Zeszyty Naukowe Uniwersytutu Lódzkiego. Nauki Humanistyczno-społeczne* 1, no. 43 (1979).

——. "Ruch Ludowy w Polsce południowej na przełomie XIX i XX wieku." *Republika Tarnobrzeska w świetle faktów i dokumentów.* Tarnobrzeg, 1982.

Porter, Brian. *When Nationalism Began to Hate: Imagining Modern Politics in Nineteenth-Century Poland.* New York: Oxford, 2000.

Potoczek, Jerzy. "Chłopi sądeccy a reprezentacja powiatowa (1890–1914)." *Rocznik Sądecki* 10/11 (1969–70): 313–48.

——. "Kalendarium historii ruchu chłopskiego sądeczczyzy w latach 1848–1918." *Rocznik Sądecki* 12 (1971): 165–219.

Putek, Józef. *Pierwsze występy polityczne włościaństwa polskiego, 1848–1861.* Cracow, 1948.

Redfield, Robert. *Peasant Society and Culture: An Anthropological Approach to Civilization.* Chicago: University of Chicago Press, 1956.

Schipper, Naftali. *Dzieje Żydów w Polsce oraz przegląd ich kultury duchowej (z uwzględnieniem krajów ościennych).* 2 vols. Lwów, 1927.

Scott, James C. *Domination and the Art of Resistance: Hidden Transcripts.* New Haven: Yale University Press, 1990.

——. "Everyday Forms of Resistance." In *Everyday Forms of Peasant Resistance,* ed. Forrest Colburn. Armonk, N.Y.: M. E. Sharpe, 1989. 3–33.

——. *The Moral Economy of the Peasant: Rebellion and Subsistence in Southeast Asia.* New Haven: Yale University Press, 1976.

Shanin, Teodor. *The Roots of Otherness: Russia's Turn of Century.* 2 vols. New Haven: Yale University Press, 1986.

——. *Russia as a Developing Society.* New Haven: Yale University Press, 1985.

Siegelbaum, Lewis. "Exhibiting *Kustar'* Industry in Late Imperial Russia / Exhibiting Late Imperial Russia in *Kustar'* Industry." In *Transforming Peasants: Society, State and the Peasantry, 1861–1930*, ed. Judith Pallot. London: Macmillan, 1998.

Simons, Thomas W., Jr. "The Peasant Revolt of 1846 in Galicia: Recent Polish Historiography." *Slavic Review* 30, no. 4 (December 1971): 795–817.

Sirka, Ann. *The Nationality Question in Austrian Education. The Case of the Ukrainians in Galicia, 1867–1914*. Frankfurt: Peter D. Lang, 1980.

Śliwa, Franciszek. "Z dziejów ruchu ludowego w powiecie mieleckim: początki myśli klasowej i patriotycznej." *Roczniki Dziejów Ruchu Ludowego*, no. 12 (1970): 25–56.

Słomka, Jan. *From Serfdom to Self-Government: Memoirs of a Village Mayor*. Trans. William John Rose. London: Minerva, 1941.

Smith, Anthony D. *The Ethnic Origins of Nations*. Oxford: Blackwell, 1986.

Sommer, Doris. "Irresistible Romance: The Foundational Fictions of Latin America." In Bhabha, *Nation and Narration*, 71–98.

Staszyński, Edmund. *Polityka Oświatowa Caratu w Krolestwie Polskim od Powstania Styczniowego do I Wojny Światowej*. Warsaw: Państwowe Zakłady Wydawnictw Szkolnych, 1968.

Stauter-Halsted, Keely. "Peasant Patriotic Celebrations in Austrian Poland: The Centennial of the Kościuszko Uprising and the Rise of the Kościuszko Cult in Galician Villages." *Austrian History Yearbook* 25 (1994): 79–95.

Steinberg, Mark D. *Moral Communities: The Culture of Class Relations in the Russian Printing Industry, 1867–1907*. Berkeley: University of California Press, 1992.

——. "Vanguard Workers and the Morality of Class." In *Making Workers Soviet*, ed. Lewis Siegelbaum and Ronald G. Suny. Ithaca: Cornell University Press, 1994. 66–84.

Stępień, Stanisław. *Prasa ludowa w Polsce: Zarys historyczny*. Warsaw: Prasa ZSL, 1984.

Stomma, Ludwik. *Antropologia kultury wsi polskiej XIX w*. Warsaw: Instytut Wydawniczy Pax, 1986.

Struve, Kai. "Die Juden in der Sicht der polnischen Bauernparteien vom Ende des 19. Jahrhunderts bis 1939." *Zeitschrift für Ostmitteleuropaforschung* 48, no. 2 (1999).

Styś, Wincenty. *Drogi postępu gospodarczego wsi*. Wrocław, 1947.

——. *Rozdrabnianie gruntów chłopskich w byłym zaborze austrjackim od roku 1787 do 1931*. Lwów: Nakładem Towarzystwa Naukowego, 1934.

——. *Współzależność rozwoju rodziny chłopskiej i jej gospodarstwa*. Praca Wrocławskiego Towarzystwa Naukowego, ser. A, no. 62. Wrocław, 1959.

Suchonek, Stefan. "Działalność polityczna ks. St. Stojałowskiego w żywiecczyźnie." *Gronie* 2 (1939): 127–42.

——. "Poseł Jan Siwiec: Karta z dziejów ruchu ludowego w Galicji." In *Studia dziejów kultury*. Warsaw, 1949.

Sugar, Peter F. "The Nature of the Non-Germanic Societies ˘under Habsburg Rule." *Slavic Review* 22, no. 1 (March 1963): 1–30.

Syska, Henryk. *Od "Kmiotka" do "Zarania": z historii prasy ludowej.* Warsaw, 1949.

Szaflik, Józef Ryszard. "Czynniki kształtującę świadomość narodową chłopa polskiego w końcu XIX i w początkach XX wieku." *Przegląd humanistyczny 26*, no. 12 (1982): 1–15; 27, no. 4 (1983): 43–82.

———. "Geneza ruchu ludowego w Polsce." *Wieś współczesna 24*, no. 10 (1980): 88–97.

———. *O rząd chłopskich dusz.* Warsaw: Ludowa Spółdzielnia Wydawnicza, 1976.

Szczepanowski, Stanisław. *Nędza Galicyi w cyfrach i program energicznego rozwoju gospodarstwa.* Lwów, 1888.

Tabaka, Zbigniew. *Analiza zbiórowości studenckiej Uniwersytetu Jagiellońskiego w latach 1850–1918 (studium statystyczne).* Cracow, 1970.

Tarnowski, Stanisław. *Lud wiejski między ładem i rozkładem.* Cracow, 1896.

Terlecka, Małgorzata, ed. *Historia Etnografii Polski.* Wrocław. Zakład Narodowy im. Ossolińskich, 1973.

Thomas, William, and Florian Znaniecki. *The Polish Peasant in Europe and America.* 2 vols. Chicago: University of Chicago Press, 1919.

Thompson, E. P. *Customs in Common: Studies in Traditional Popular Culture.* New York: New Press, 1993.

Trzeciakowski, Lech. *Kulturkampf w zaborze pruskim.* Poznań: Wydawnictwo Poznańskie, 1970.

———. *Pod pruskim zaborem, 1850–1918.* Warsaw: Wiedza Powszechna, 1973.

Turowska-Bar, Irena. *Polskie czasopisma o wsi i dla wsi od XVII w. do r. 1960.* Warsaw, 1963.

Walczewska, Sławomira. *Damy, rycerze i feministki. Kobiecy dyskurs emancypacyjny w Polsce.* Cracow: Wydawnictwo eFKa, 1999.

Walicki, Andrzej. *The Enlightenment and the Birth of Modern Nationhood: Polish Political Thought from Noble Republicanism to Tadeusz Kościuszko.* Notre Dame, Ind., 1989.

———. *Philosophy and Romantic Nationalism: The Case of Poland.* Notre Dame, Ind., 1994.

Wandycz, Piotr. "The Poles in the Habsburg Monarchy." In *Nation-Building and the Politics of Nationalism: Essays on Austrian Galicia*, ed. Andrei S. Markovitz and Frank E. Sysyn. Cambridge, Mass.: Harvard Ukrainian Research Institute, 1982.

Wasiutyński, Bohdan. *Ludność żydowska w Polsce w wiekach XIX i XX: studjum statystyczne.* Warsaw: Instytut Popierania Nauki, 1930.

Webb, Stephen B. "Agricultural Protection in Wilhelmine Germany: Forging an Empire with Pork and Rye." *Journal of Economic History 42*, no. 2 (June 1982): 309–26.

Weber, Eugen. *Peasants into Frenchmen: The Modernization of Rural France, 1870–1914.* Stanford: Stanford University Press, 1976.

Weeks, Theodore R. *Nation and State in Late Imperial Russia: Nationalism and Russification on the Western Frontier, 1863–1914.* DeKalb: Northern Illinois University Press, 1996.

Wereszycki, Henryk. *Historia polityczna Polski, 1864–1918.* Wrocław: Zakład Narodowy im. Ossolińskich—Wydawnictwo, 1990.

Wierzbicki, Edward. "Poglądy Stanisława Szczepanowskiego na rozwój oświaty wychowania w Galicji." *Rocznik Przemyski* 21 (1979): 273–82.

——. "Wpływ 'Nędzy Galicji' Stanisława Szczepanowskiego na rozwój ekonomiczny Galicji." *Rocznik Przemyski* 22/23 (1983): 473–78.

Winiarski, Bohdan. *Ustrój polityczny ziem polskich w XIX wieku.* Poznań, 1923.

Wolf, Eric R. *Peasant Wars of the Twentieth Century.* New York: Harper and Row, 1969.

Woźniak, Andrzej. "Źródła zainteresowań ludoznawczych w ideologii polskiego Oświecenia." *Etnografia Polska* 15, no. 2, (1959): 37–51.

Wrobel, Piotr. "The Jews under Austrian-Polish Rule, 1869–1918." *Austrian History Yearbook* 25 (1994): 97–138.

Wroczyński, Ryszard. *Dzieje oświaty polskiej, 1795–1945.* Warsaw: Państwowe Wydawnictwo Naukowe, 1980.

Young, John. *Peasant Revolution in Ethiopia: The Tigray People's Liberation Front, 1975–1991.* Cambridge, 1997.

Zakrzewski, Andrzej. *Od Stojałowskiego do Witosa.* Vol. 3 in series *Dzieje narodu i państwa polskiego,* ed. Józef Burszka and Andrzej Garlicki. Warsaw, 1988.

Zaretsky, Eli, ed. *The Polish Peasant in Europe and America: A Classic Work in Immigration History.* Urbana: University of Illinois Press, 1996.

Żarnowska, Anna, and Andrzej Szwarc, eds. *Kobieta i społeczeństwo na ziemiach Polskich w XIX w.* Warsaw, 1990.

Zdrada, Jerzy. "Galicyjskie wybory sejmowie i parlamentarne w latach 1861–1889." *Rocznik Biblioteki PAN w Krakowie* 19 (1973): 229–56.

——. "Wybory do galicyjskiego Sejmu Krajowego w 1867 roku." *Rocznik Biblioteki PAN w Krakowie* 9 (1963): 39–96.

Index

Note: Page numbers with an *f* indicate figures.

263